The *FEDER* Guide to Where to Park Your Car in Manhattan (and Where Not to Park It!)

Downtown Edition

Erik Feder

Rhythmo Productions ✳ Long Beach, New York

The FEDER Guide to Where to Park Your Car in Manhattan
(and Where Not to Park It!!) - Downtown Edition

by Erik Feder

Published by:
Rhythmo Productions
525 East Olive Street
Long Beach, NY 11561 USA
www.federguide.com
info@federguide.com
or
rhythmo.productions@verizon.net

Cover design and layout -
Erik Feder and Manuela Sander-Feder
Marketing plan - Manuela Sander-Feder
Proofreading - Karen Putnam

ISBN, print ed. 0-9763401-8-6

Library of Congress Control Number Data
Feder, Erik
The FEDER Guide to Where to Park Your Car
in Manhattan (and Where Not to Park It!!)
Downtown Edition
Library of Congress Control Number: 2004099494
ISBN 0-9763401-8-6 Printed in Canada

Contents

Acknowledgements

Thanks to my e-friends at pub-forum.net and especially to Mayapriya Long for being so willing to share your ideas, advice and experience.

Special thanks to my mother Joan, my father Bud, my sisters Laurie and Karen, and my best friends Jason and John for being there, for listening and most of all for being supportive no matter what my crazy plans include (writing a rock opera, selling everything I own (almost) and moving away, creating this book, next???).

Extra special thanks to my wife Manuela who is my other (better) half, for putting up with me, building me up, believing in me, making me stronger and giving so much of yourself all the time. Ich habe viel Glueck, mit dir zusammen zu sein.

Chapter 1 -

Introduction

- The Purpose of this Book
- How to Use this Book

The Purpose of this Book

Parking in Manhattan can be very confusing and very difficult to find. The traffic can be an added pressure and finding a legal place to park in a specific area can be a harrowing affair. *The FEDER Guide to Where to Park Your Car in MANHATTAN (and Where Not to Park It!)* has been compiled in order to provide the reader with as much information pertaining to parking in Manhattan as possible. There are three main sections in this book: An *Introduction* with helpful hints, a section covering *street parking regulations* and a section covering *parking garages.* The *street parking regulations* section lays out street by street parking regulations from 30th street all the way down to the southern tip of Manhattan at Battery Park. Parking regulations pertaining to trucks and commercial vehicles are also included in this guide - specifically regulations which specify when and for how long a truck or commercial vehicle may park while loading and unloading. The *Parking garages* section provides the locations, hours of operation and contact information for parking garages and lots in these areas of Manhattan including the prices charged by these facilities. Maps for the different areas of the downtown part of Manhattan can be found at the beginning of each section. The *Introduction* section (which you are presently reading) provides information on what to do if your car:

- ❑ has been towed
- ❑ is missing from where you just left it (suspected stolen)
- ❑ has been given a parking ticket

The FEDER Guide to Where to Park Your Car in MANHATTAN (and Where Not to Park It!) also provides a list of the current parking violations and the accompanying fines that must be paid for each violation. By using this book to avoid just one of these violations, the reader will have paid for this book up to seven times over!!

Available Autumn 2005:

The

FEDER **Guide to Where to Park Your Car in Manhattan (and Where Not to Park It!)**

Midtown Edition

Covers 124th Street to 30th Street

How to Use this Book

This *Downtown* edition of *the FEDER Guide to Where to Park Your Car in MANHATTAN (and Where Not to Park It!)* defines the area of downtown Manhattan as 30th Street and below running south to the southern tip of Manhattan at Battery Park. This area has been broken down into three segments:

❑ Downtown West
✻ runs from West 30th Street to White Street✻

❑ Downtown East
✻ runs from East 30th Street to White Street✻

❑ Downtown South
✻ runs from White Street to Battery Park✻

The pages of this book have black strips running down the sides that help readers identify which chapter of the book they are reading. With a quick glance at these black strips, readers can easily locate the desired section of *Downtown* Manhattan.

❑ The *Street Parking Regulations* Section

When reading the *Street Parking Regulations* section of this book, you can find the actual parking regulations in any given segment of *Downtown* Manhattan listed as either the *East*, *West*, *North* or *South* side of a given street. When a street runs north to south or south to north, the parking regulations governing the *East* and *West* sides of that street are listed; when a street runs east to west or west to east, the parking regulations governing the *North* and *South* sides of that street are listed. It's important to note that some streets have many regulations on them and that some of these regulations may be for only part of that street. If a regulation is listed under a given street, at least *some* part of that street will be governed by that regulation. In this book, when a street has more than one regulation on it, all the regulations are listed and are separated by a slash - "/".

The streets in each segment of the *Street Parking Regulations* section of this book are listed numerically and alphabetically. This means that in each given segment, first the numbered streets are listed in descending order (e.g. 30th St., 29th St., 28th St., etc.). These are followed by the numbered avenues listed in ascending order (e.g. 1st Ave., 2nd Ave., 3rd Ave., etc.). Finally the streets with normal, lettered names are listed alphabetically (e.g. Bond, Broadway, Broome, etc.). All the occurrences of each street in a given segment are listed **in the order** they appear when driving that street. As an example, in the *Downtown East* segment of the *Street Parking Regulations* section of this book, **29th Street** is listed in the following order:

29th Street (1st-2nd)
29th Street (2nd-3rd)
29th Street (3rd-Lexington)
29th Street (Lexington-Park)
29th Street (Park-Madison)
29th Street (Madison-5th), etc.

This listing represents the way **29th Street** actually runs - the way you would drive it in reality and that you'd see it on a street map. This makes it easier to find legal places to park in a given area as opposed to listing the occurrences of each street alphabetically, which would be much less practical.

Many streets in Manhattan are one-way streets; there

are also some two-way streets and occasionally one part of a street will be one-way while another section of the same street is two-way. To make it more practical for the reader, the directions in which one-way streets are listed indicate the direction one is permitted to drive on that street. Since Lexington is one-way running north → south, this is listed as **Lexington (30th-29th)**, indicating that one can drive heading south on Lexington from 30th Street to 29th Street. As Spring Street is one-way running from west → east, this is listed as **Spring (Mercer-Broadway)** indicating that one can drive heading east on Spring Street from Mercer Street to Broadway. The direction that two-way streets are listed was chosen randomly. Regardless if a street is one-way or two-way, you can always drive in the direction that streets are listed in this book.

In the index at the back of this book, under the heading *Street Parking Regulations* you will find each street listed under the segment in which it is located. The numbers next to each street indicate on which pages in the given segment each street can be found. For example, in the index you will see under the segment heading **Downtown West** the listing:

Broadway... 97-101

This means that in the segment *Downtown West*, all the listings for Broadway can be found on pages 97-101. As stated earlier, all the occurrences of each street are listed as one would drive them and as one would find them on a street map. The same procedure holds true for all the different segments.

Dashes, ampersands ("&") and commas are used in specific ways in this guide; they're used to indicate on which days a given regulation is valid. So for example, if you read the regulation:

No parking 8am-6pm (M-F),

the dash between the "M" and the "F" means "through"; in other words, you can't park on the part of this street governed by this regulation from 8am until 6pm on Mondays *through* Fridays.If you see this similar regulation:

No parking 8am-6pm (M&F)

the ampersand ("&") between the "M" and the "F" means "and"; in other words, you can't park on the part of this street governed by this regulation from 8am until 6pm on Mondays *and* Fridays.Lastly, if you see this similar regulation:

No parking 8am-6pm (M,W,F)

the commas between the "M", the "W", and the "F" also mean "and", but are used in cases in which there are more than two days involved; in other words, you can't park on the part of this street governed by this regulation from 8am until 6pm on Mondays *and* Wednesdays *and* Fridays.

As you read through the different street listings, at various points you will see smiley faces☺ and frowney faces☹.

A smiley face next to a street listing indicates that at least some part of this street is a very good place to park your car because it is legal to park there at least 20 hours a day. Smiley faces most often are found on streets which have *alternate side of the street parking regulations*.

These are usually designated so that on the north or west sides of the street it is legal to park your car on all days except for a listed duration of time (2-3 hours) on Mondays and Thursdays. On the south and east sides of streets that have *alternate side of the street parking regulations* it is usually legal to park your car on all days except for a listed duration of time (2-3 hours) on Tuesdays and Fridays. If timed right, these spaces can be good for 2-3 days at a time.

A frowney face next to a street listing indicates that this street is a bad place to park. These usually are found when *both* sides of a given street are regulated by "No parking anytime" or "No standing anytime" signs. Therefore, a frowney face on a given street means you should never park on that street. Drivers of trucks and commercial vehicles should note that while frowneys indicate that cars shouldn't park in a given area, in some cases trucks and commercial vehicles may still be able to load and unload in these areas.

When a street has neither a smiley nor a frowney face, this means that at certain times it is legal to park on this street but that there are substantial amounts of time where it is not legal to park on this street, so caution must be used. These streets can be thought of as potential places to park, but probably not for very long periods of time, and rarely overnight.

Special attention should be called to streets with parking meters. Since late 2002, the borough of Manhattan has been in the process of changing regulations on streets that have parking meters. Before the changes, some streets with meters had a specific regulation followed by the words "except Sunday". This meant that no matter what the given regulations were, on Sundays it was free to park and legal for the whole day. Since that time period, the regulations have been changing so that many of the signs which formerly said "except Sunday" now say "including Sunday", meaning that the same rules which apply on these streets during the week and on Saturday now also apply on Sunday - including putting money in the meter. As it appears that the city is changing all the meter regulations to "including Sunday" in Manhattan, they have all been listed as "including Sunday" in this book. Should you be lucky enough to find a street with a sign that still says "except Sunday", then you can park there free on Sundays with no time limit - but - be careful that the regulations haven't changed next time you visit this street on a Sunday! Note that these regulation changes happened first in the *Downtown* areas of Manhattan (more so on the East side) so you are less likely to still find an "except Sunday" meter in the *Downtown* areas of Manhattan.

Manhattan uses standard parking meters, in which one puts in coins and also "Muni-Meters", which accept coins (quarters and dollar coins) and NYC Parking Cards (call **212-669-8246** for purchasing info). To use the Muni-Meter, purchase an amount of time, take a receipt and display it on the dashboard of your vehicle.

Downtown is a particularly confusing area of Manhattan. The separation between the east and west sides of Manhattan are easy in Midown/Uptown: above 5th Avenue is the west side of Manhattan and below 5th Avenue is the east side of Manhattan. Downtown Manhattan is not so easy. From 30th Street to 8th Street, east and west are still separated by 5th Avenue. 5th avenue, however, ends at 8th Street. For this reason, the east - west separator runs down 8th Street from 5th Avenue to Lafayette and then continues along Lafayette

from 8th Street until White Street.
As Broadway cuts diagonally across Manhattan, it can be hard to find - especially as it intersects the separator streets that divide the east and west segments of *Downtown*. You can find Broadway listed under *Downtown West* from 30th Street to 23rd Street, then under *Downtown East* from 23rd Street to 8th Street and back again under *Downtown West* from 8th Street all the way to White Street.

The devastating events of September 11, 2001 affected many aspects of Manhattan, including the street parking situation. Many of the streets in the area where the World Trade Center stood are still under temporary construction as of the writing of this book. In most cases, streets which are under construction have the parking regulation "**No standing anytime**", although you may find some which are marked as "Blue Zones". Streets undergoing construction with the "Blue Zone" designation generally have the parking regulation "**No parking 7am-7pm (M-F)**". Check the signs carefully to be sure.

If you find that a street parking regulation has changed and is different than is listed in this book or that there is a mistake listed in this book, or if you have a suggestion that you think would improve this book, please send it in to the address listed on the copyright page along with your name and address. Upon confirmation that such a correction, change, or improvement is needed, you will receive a free copy of the next updated edition of this book. Please be sure to include your name, address and date of submission with all correspondence. Please note that in the case of multiple submissions for the same change, suggestion or correction only the first received submission will receive the complimentary book.

It is the sole responsibility of the reader to exercise caution at all times and to read the parking signs on each street in Manhattan before parking. Although they don't change very often, parking regulations are subject to change and this book cannot guarantee that the regulations will not have changed by the time the reader parks on a given street. Any parking tickets and/or fines that may accrue are the sole responsibility of the reader and are in no way, shape, or form the liability of the publishers or creators of this book. Any information in this book regarding towing, parking tickets, parking regulations and parking garages and lots is included for information purposes only and does not relieve the reader of their responsibility to read and understand the laws. Readers are solely responsible for any actions they take, regardless of whether or not such actions are based on information provided in this book. This book is not intended to be used while driving a vehicle of any kind. Please do not use this book while driving.

❑ The *Parking Garages* Section

The *Parking garages* section of this book also breaks *Downtown* Manhattan into the three segments of:

❑ Downtown West
✳ runs from West 30th Street to White Street✳

❑ Downtown East
✳ runs from East 30th Street to White Street✳

❑ Downtown South
✳ runs from White Street to Battery Park✳

Parking garages are listed under each segment the same way street parking regulations are listed in the *Street Parking Regulations* section: numerically and alphabetically. In each given segment, first the numbered streets are listed in descending order (e.g. 30th St., 29th St., 28th St., etc.). These are followed by the numbered avenues listed in ascending order (e.g. 1st Ave, 2nd Ave, 3rd Ave, etc.). Finally, the streets with normal, lettered names are listed alphabetically (e.g. Bond, Broadway, Broome, etc.).

In the index at the back of this book, under the heading *Parking garage locations,* you will find each street on which there is a parking garage listed under the segment in which it is appears. The numbers next to these streets indicate on which pages in the given segment each street with a parking garage can be found. For example, in the index you will see under the segment heading **Parking garage locations: Downtown West** the listing:

28th St. ... 378-379

This means that in the segment *Downtown West*, all the listings for parking garages on 28th St. can be found on pages 378-379. The same procedure holds true for all the different segments.

A smiley face ☺ next to a garage listing indicates that this garage has chosen to advertise in this book and that more information on this garage can be found in the *advertising* section. The presence of a smiley face next to a garage listing does not indicate any endorsement by Rhythmo Productions or in any way imply that Rhythmo Productions is recommending these garages. Readers who choose to utilize the services of any parking facility listed in this book do so at their own discretion and at their own risk.

It should be noted that while parking facility firms aren't charged to be listed in this book, they are (for a fee) offered the opportunity to advertise. Listings are not included or excluded according to the willingness of any firm to pay for advertising. Furthermore, Rhythmo Productions doesn't endorse any company or its services and isn't liable for any problems caused by the services (or lack thereof) provided by any company mentioned in this book. All advertisements are marked as such. Advertisements are not indications that Rhythmo Productions is in any way recommending the firms who have chosen to advertise in this book. Readers should also be aware that the prices of the parking facilities listed in this book are subject to change as each parking facility sees fit and that Rhythmo Productions can in no way be held responsible if and when a parking facility changes its prices.

Not all parking facilities that exist in *Downtown* Manhattan are represented in this book. While every attempt to contact all the parking facilities in *Downtown* Manhattan was made, in some cases it was not possible to contact a facility and in other cases parking facilities may have declined to take part in this project. All parking facilities that agreed to take part in this project have been included free of charge. While the participating facilities have been offered the chance to advertise in this book (for a fee), they were not required to do so and their choice to advertise or not had no effect on their ability to list their garages free of charge. If a reader is in some way connected to a parking facility that is not currently listed in this book and would like to have that facility listed in future printings (including the soon-to-come *Midtown/Uptown* edition) of *The FEDER Guide to Where to Park Your Car in MANHATTAN (and Where Not to Park It!)*, please contact Rhythmo Productions at the address listed on the copyright page in the front of this book.

It is the sole responsibility of readers to exercise caution at all times and to read the signs in each parking facility in Manhattan that they wish to utilize. Fees charged by participating parking facilities are subject to change at the discretion of each facility. Any overtime charges and/or fines that may accrue are the sole responsibility of the reader and are in no way, shape, or form the liability of the publishers or creators of this book. Any information in this book regarding parking garages and lots is included for information purposes only and does not relieve readers of their responsibility to read and understand the laws. All information about parking facilities has been provided by those facilities and any errors are the responsibility of those facilities and in no way the responsibility of Rhythmo Productions. Readers are solely responsible for any actions they take, regardless of whether or not such actions are based on information provided in this book. This book is not intended to be used while driving a vehicle of any kind. Please do not use this book while driving.

Chapter 2 -

Parking Violations and their Accompanying Fines

NYC Parking Violations and their Accompanying Fines

The following is a list of the current parking violations in Manhattan as well as their accompanying fines:

Violation	Violation code #	Fine
No Stopping	10	$115
No Standing (except hotel loading)	11	$115
No Standing (snow emergency)	12	$ 95
No Standing (taxi stand)	13	$115
No Standing	14	$115
No Standing (except trucks loading and unloading)	16	$ 95
No Standing (except authorized vehicles)	17	$ 95
No Standing (bus lane)	18	$115
No Standing (bus stop)	19	$115
No Parking	20	$ 65
No Parking (street cleaning)	21	$ 65

Violation	Violation code #	Fine
No Parking (hotel loading)	22	$ 65
No Parking (taxi stand)	23	$ 65
No Parking (except authorized vehicles)	24	$ 65
No Standing (Commuter Van Stop)	25	$115
No Standing (For-Hire Vehicles)	26	$115
No Parking (except hand-icapped plates/permits)	27	$180
Overtime Standing – Diplomat	28	$ 95
No Standing – Commercial Vehicle Metered Zone	31	$115
Overtime Parking at Missing/Broken Meter	32	$ 35
Feeding the Meter	33	$ 65
Expired Meter	34	$ 65
Selling Merchandise in Metered Space	35	$ 65

Violation	Violation code #	Fine
Expired Muni Meter	37	$ 65
Failure to Display Muni Meter Receipt	38	$ 65
Overtime Parking – Time Limit Posted	39	$ 65
Fire Hydrant	40	$115
Expired Muni Meter - Commercial Metered Zone	42	$ 65
Parking In Excess of Posted Time Limit – Commercial Zone	44	$ 65
Traffic Lane	45	$115
Double Parking	46	$115
Midtown Double Parking - Angle Parking	47	$115
Bike Lane	48	$115
Excavation (vehicle obstructing traffic)	49	$ 95
Crosswalk	50	$115
Sidewalk	51	$115
Intersection	52	$115

Violation	Violation code #	Fine
Safety Zone	53	$115
Tunnel/Elevated Roadway	55	$115
Divided Highway	56	$115
Manhattan Blue Zone	57	$ 65
Marginal Street/Waterfront	58	$ 65
Angle Parking – Commercial Vehicle	59	$115
Angle Parking	60	$ 65
Wrong Way	61	$ 65
Beyond Marked Space	62	$ 65
Nighttime Standing or Parking in Park	63	$ 95
Registration Sticker Missing/Expired	70	$ 65
Inspection Sticker Missing/Expired	71	$ 65
Missing or Improperly Displayed Plates	74	$ 65
Nighttime Commercial Vehicle Parking on Residential Street	78	$ 65

Violation	Violation code #	Fine
No Standing Except Diplomat	81	$ 95
Improper Registration	83	$ 65
Midtown Standing/Parking – 3 Hour Limit	86	$115
No Standing Except Trucks/Vans with Commercial Plates	89	$115
Washing/Repairing Vehicle	92	$ 65
Removing/Replacing Flat Tire (major roadway)	93	$ 65
Obstructing Driveway	98	$ 95

Chapter 3 -

What to Do if:

- Your Car is Towed or Missing
- You Get a Parking Ticket

What to Do if Your Car is Towed or Missing

One of the most sickening feelings a driver can have is returning to the spot where you *know* you left your car, only to find it missing. Take a few deep breaths to calm down, then call:

- 212-504-4041 or # 311 in Manhattan

or search online at:

- nyc.gov/finance - under the *Parking in NYC* icon, click on *Find Towed Vehicles*

to verify if your car has been towed. If it has not been towed, report to the nearest police precinct that your car is missing. While the natural conclusion is that your car has been stolen, there are a few instances in which the local police will relocate your car due to a demonstration, parade or street fair. Whether stolen or relocated, the nearest police precinct can assist you.

Your car can be towed for one of two reasons. Either:

- Your car was parked illegally, or
- You have outstanding parking tickets which are overdue and the fines and penalties total more than $230

It's also possible that you were parked legally and your car was towed in error. Even if you believe this to be the case, the best thing to do is to get your car back now and worry about fighting it later. How to fight tickets (and towing) received in error will be covered later in this book in *What to do if you get a parking ticket.* Towed cars are taken to a tow pound. When a car is towed below 96th street in Manhattan it is almost always taken to the tow pound at:

❑ Pier 76 at West 38th Street & 12th Avenue
Monday: 7AM - 11PM Tuesday-Saturday: opens
Tuesday at 7AM and stays open 24 hours a day
through Sunday at 6PM
(212) 971-0771 or (212) 971-0772

It will cost you $185 to get your car back, plus an additional charge of $15 for each night that your car is stored at the tow pound. This does not include the fine for the parking violation for which you were towed, but at least this can be paid later. As a matter of fact, it must be paid later (unless you choose to fight it - and win); parking tickets cannot be paid at the tow pound. You can pay to retrieve your car at the tow pound by using:

❑ Cash
❑ Credit cards - Discover, American Express, MasterCard, Visa
❑ Certified Checks - payable to NYC Police Department
❑ ATM Bank Debit Cards that allow withdrawals from checking accounts only (e.g. NYC, MAC, etc.)
❑ Money Orders or Traveler's Checks (all parts are required to be presented)

Bring the following items with you when picking up your car from the tow pound:

❑ Valid driver's license
❑ Current vehicle registration
❑ Current insurance card

Vehicles will only be released to the registered owners, their spouses or authorized representatives. An authorized representative must have this authorization in written form, including the notarized signature of the registered owner. If your car has judgements (overdue, unpaid tickets) against it, these must first be paid to the Parking Violations Bureau before you can pick up your car. Don't forget - you cannot pay these at the tow pound. For more information on how to pay parking tickets, see the section *What to do if you get a parking ticket* later in this book.

If you don't claim your towed car within the first 96 hours after it is towed, the city will consider it abandoned. If you leave your car unclaimed for 30 days it will be sold off at an auction.

During midday, be prepared to wait. It's not an especially pleasant place; bring a book, magazine, or something to help pass the time.

What to Do if You Get a Parking Ticket

If you get a parking ticket you have two options: you can plead guilty and pay the ticket or if you believe you were given the parking ticket in error, you can fight it and plead not guilty. Either way, you must enter a claim within 30 days of receiving the parking ticket. If you decide to pay it, simply follow the instructions on the back of the ticket. You can pay by mail by sending the signed and filled out ticket (make yourself a copy first) and your payment (check, money order or certified check) to:

❑ NYC DOF Parking Violations
Peck Slip Station P.O. Box 2127
New York, NY 10272-2127

or by calling from a touch-tone phone and using a MasterCard, VISA, AmEX, or Discover card (a convenience fee applies):

❑ 212-504-4041

or online by using a MasterCard, VISA, AmEx, or Discover card (a convenience fee applies) at:

❑ nyc.gov/finance - click on *Pay NYC parking tickets*

or in person at the Manhattan Department of Finance business center (cash, personal checks, certified checks, money orders, MasterCard, VISA, AmEx, and Discover cards):

❑ 66 John Street, Second Floor
New York, NY 10038

You can also call the Manhattan Parking Violations Bureau at:

❑ (212) 477-4430

Always keep your cancelled check or receipt as proof that you paid your parking ticket on time. It's a good idea to use certified mail/return receipt when mailing payments so that you know your payments were received and to prove when they were received.

If you decide not to pay the parking ticket, you must plead not guilty. You can do this by phone or in person at the telephone number and address given above. You can do this online at the website given above and by clicking on *Parking ticket hearings*. You can plead not guilty by mail at:

❑ NYC Department of Finance
Hearings by mail unit
Cadman Plaza Station P.O. Box 29021
Brooklyn, NY 11202-9021

After you have pled not guilty, it will take some time for the powers that be to get back to you. Be patient - any late fees that you receive after you have pled not guilty should be ignored, as the city cannot impose late fees once you have entered your plea. If you are indeed found not guilty, you won't have to pay anything. If you are found guilty, you will either have to pay the original fine (and not any late fees provided that you entered your plea within the allotted time frame) or you can appeal this ruling. Appeals will be covered later in this section. If you are found guilty, wish to pay the fine and are charged a late fee in error, contact the Parking Violations Bureau using one of the methods listed above and you should be instructed to pay the original fine only.

There are two reasons you can legitimately plead not guilty. Either you feel that you were given the ticket in error or the ticket is "defective", meaning that it was filled out incorrectly by the issuing police officer.

If you feel that you were issued the parking ticket in error, submit as much evidence as possible that can help you make your case. This evidence can include photographs, sworn and notarized affidavits from eye-witnesses and other documents (for instance, a printout of the Department of Transportation's calendar of days indicating that alternate side of the street parking rules are suspended, if this shows that you were falsely given a parking ticket). Keep in mind that if submitting evidence that is signed, the original(s) must be submitted. *Always* keep copies for yourself.

If the issuing officer filled out the parking ticket you have received incorrectly, this is *reason enough by itself* to have your ticket dismissed. In this case, contact the Parking Violations Bureau using one of the methods listed above and request to have the ticket dismissed.

Under New York City law, a parking ticket will be dismissed when any of the following categories on the summons are missing, incomplete, illegible or incorrectly described:

❑ LICENSE PLATE INFORMATION

❑ MAKE

❑ ISSUANCE TIME (to the minute and must include "AM" or "PM")

❑ TIME FIRST OBSERVED (when multiple observations are required - for example when parking longer than allowed)

❑ DATE OF OFFENSE (must be complete)

❑ PLACE OF OCCURRENCE (must be specifically indicated)

❑ EXPIRATION DATE (the expiration date on the registration sticker must be listed except if covered, mutilated, faded, etc., which then must be indicated)

❑ PLATE TYPE (if covered, mutilated, faded, etc. this must be indicated)

❑ BODY TYPE

❑ PARKING METER (meter number must be given as well as days and hours in effect, including "AM" or "PM")

❑ SIGN VIOLATIONS (days and hours in effect must be given as well as "AM" or "PM," unless parking always prohibited)

❑ VIOLATION (the charged violation must be listed)

❑ FIRE HYDRANT ("feet from" box must be filled out. You must be 15 feet from either side of a fire hydrant)

❑ ISSUER'S SIGNATURE (must be signed by the issuing officer)

If you have pled not guilty to a parking ticket and have received notice that your plea has been denied, you can either pay the fine as described above or you can appeal the ruling. Even if you decide to appeal, you should pay the fine; it will be reimbursed to you if your appeal is upheld. If your appeal is denied, that is the final ruling and you must pay the ticket.

You can request an appeal by filing a Notice of Appeal form. You can obtain this form at this website:

❑ nyc.gov/finance - under the *Parking in NYC* icon click on *Parking Forms*

This form can also be requested by calling the following phone numbers:

❑ 212-504-4041 or
❑ 311(in Manhattan)

or by visiting the Manhattan Department of Finance business center at:

❑ 66 John Street
New York, NY 10038

Appeal hearings are by appointment only and are held at the above address on the third floor.

You will be notified in writing as to the time and date of your appeal hearing. Although you can request a date and time for your appeal hearing, keep in mind that you may not get the time or date that you requested. If you do not show up for your hearing you will automatically be found guilty.

Map of Downtown West

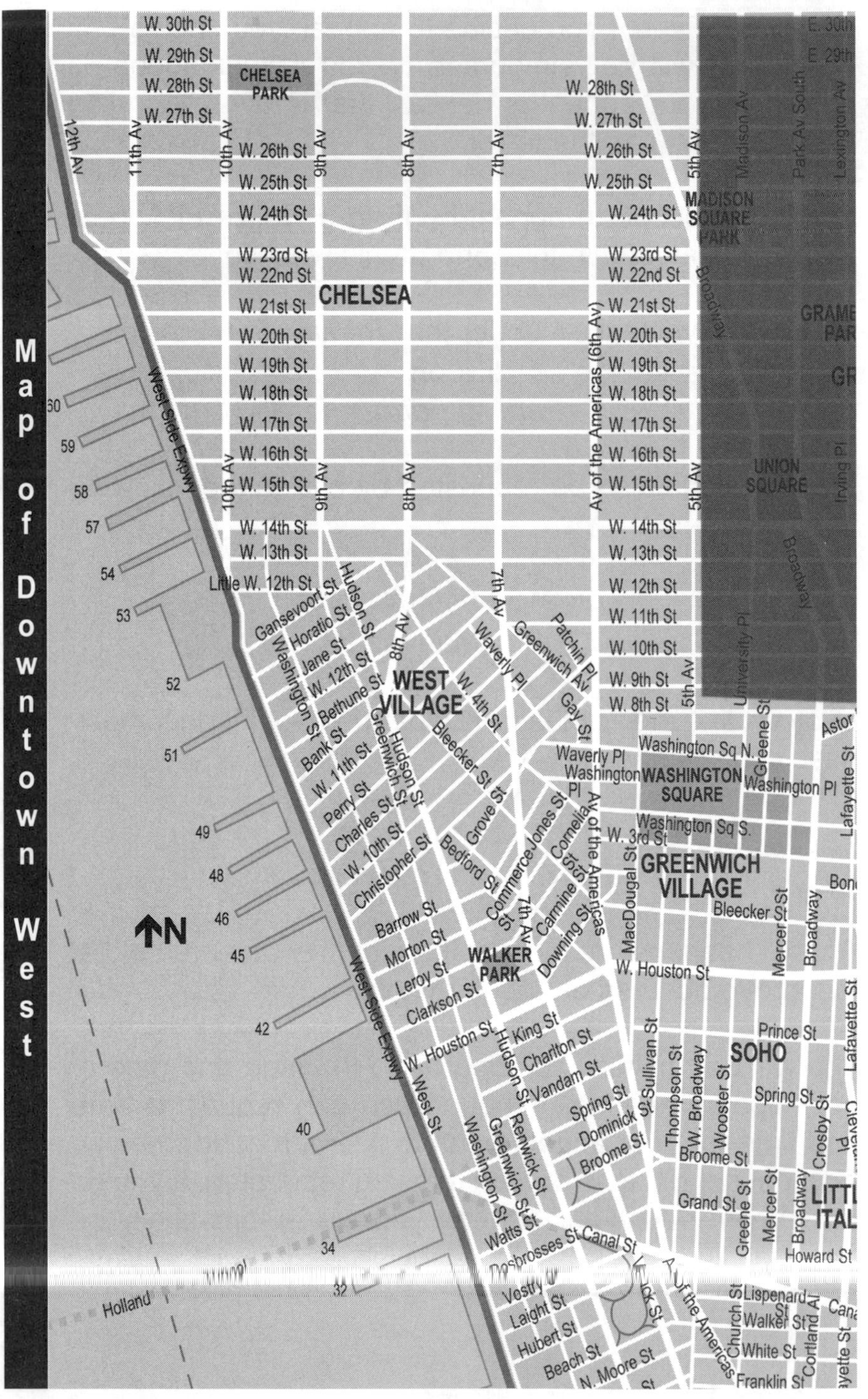

Chapter 4 -

DOWNTOWN WEST:

Street Parking Regulations

(West 30TH Street - White Street)

30TH ST (12TH-11TH) ☹

North

No parking anytime

South

No parking anytime

30TH ST (11TH-10TH)

North

No standing 8am-7pm (M-F)/No Standing 8am-10pm (including Sun)

South

No standing except trucks loading & unloading 8am-7pm (M-F)

30TH ST (10TH-9TH) ☹

North

No standing anytime

South

No standing anytime

30TH ST (9TH-8TH)

North

No standing except trucks loading & unloading 8am-6pm (except Sun)

South

No parking 8am-6pm (except Sun)

30TH ST (8TH-7TH)

North

No standing except trucks loading & unloading 7am-7pm (except Sun)

South

No standing except trucks loading & unloading 7am-7pm (except Sun)

30TH ST (7TH-6TH)

North

No standing except trucks loading & unloading 7am-7pm (except Sun)

South

No Standing anytime (except police vehicles)

30TH ST (6TH-BROADWAY)

North

No standing except trucks loading & unloading 8am-6pm (except Sun)

South

No standing 8am-6pm (except Sun)

30TH ST (BROADWAY-5TH)

North

No standing except trucks loading & unloading 8am-6pm (M-F)

South

No standing except trucks loading & unloading 8am-6pm (M-F)

29TH ST (5TH-BROADWAY)

North

No standing except trucks loading & unloading 8am-6pm (M-F)

South

No standing except trucks loading & unloading 8am-6pm (M-F)

29TH ST (BROADWAY-6TH)

North

No standing except trucks loading & unloading 8am-7pm (M-F)

South

No standing except trucks loading & unloading 8am-6pm (M-F)

29TH ST (6TH-7TH)

North

No standing except trucks loading & unloading 8am-6pm (M-F)

South

No standing except trucks loading & unloading 8am-7pm (M-F)

29TH ST (7TH-8TH)

North

No standing except trucks loading & unloading 8am-6pm (M-F)

South

No standing except trucks loading & unloading 8am-7pm (M-F)

29TH ST (8TH-9TH) ☺

North

No parking 11am-12:30pm (M & F)

South

No parking 11am-12:30pm (Tu & F)

29TH ST (9TH-10TH) ☹

North

No parking anytime

South

No parking anytime

29TH ST (10TH-11TH)

North

No parking 8am-6pm (M-F)

South

No parking 8am-6pm (M-F)

29TH ST (11TH-12TH)

North

No parking 7am-7pm (except Sun)

South

No standing anytime

28TH ST (12TH-11TH)

North

No standing 8am-7pm (M-F)/No standing 11pm-6am (including Sun)

South

No standing except trucks loading & unloading 8am-7pm (M-F)/No standing 11pm-6am (including Sun)

28TH ST (11TH-10TH)

North

No Parking 6am-6pm (M-F)

South

No standing except trucks loading & unloading 8am-7pm (M-F)/No standing 11pm-6am (including Sun)

28TH ST (10TH-9TH) ☺

North

No Parking 11am-7pm (M-F)

South

No parking 11am-12:30pm (Tu & F)

28TH ST (9TH-8TH) ☺

North

No parking 11am-12:30pm (M & F)/No parking 8am-6pm (M-F)

South

No parking 11am-12:30pm (Tu & F)

28TH ST (8TH-7TH)

North

No standing except trucks loading & unloading 8am-6pm (except Sun)

South

No standing except trucks loading & unloading 8am-6pm (except Sun)

28TH ST (7TH-6TH)

North

No standing except trucks loading & unloading 6am-7pm (M-F)

South

No standing except trucks loading & unloading 6am-7pm (M-F)

28TH ST (6TH-BROADWAY)

North

No standing except trucks loading & unloading 8am-7pm (M-F)

South

No standing except trucks loading & unloading 8am-7pm (M-F)

28TH ST (BROADWAY-5TH)

North

No standing except trucks loading & unloading 8am-7pm (M-F)

South

No standing except trucks loading & unloading 8am-7pm (M-F)

27TH ST (5TH-BROADWAY)

North

No standing except trucks loading & unloading 8am-7pm (M-F)

South

No standing except trucks loading & unloading 8am-7pm (M-F)

27TH ST (BROADWAY-6TH)

North

No standing except trucks loading & unloading 8am-6pm (M-F)

South

No standing except trucks loading & unloading 8am-6pm (M-F)

27TH ST (6TH-7TH)

North

No standing except trucks loading & unloading 8am-6pm (M-F)

South

No standing except trucks loading & unloading 8am-6pm (M-F)

27TH ST (7TH-8TH)

North

No parking 8am-6pm (M-F)

South

No parking 8am-6pm (M-F)

27TH ST (10TH-11TH)

North

No parking 8am-6pm (M-F)

South

No parking 8am-6pm (M-F)

27TH ST (11TH-12TH)

North

No parking 8am-6pm (M-F)/No standing 11pm-6am (including Sun)

South

No parking 8am-6pm (M-F)/No standing 11pm-6am (including Sun)

26TH ST (12TH-11TH)

North

No parking 8am-6pm (M-F)

South

No parking 8am-6pm (M-F)

26TH ST (11TH-10TH)

North

No standing except trucks loading & unloading 8am-6pm (M-F)

South

No standing except trucks loading & unloading 8am-6pm (M-F)

26TH ST (10TH-9TH) ☺

North

No parking 9:30am-11am (M & Th)/No parking 8am-6pm (M-F)

South

No parking 9:30am-11am (Tu & F)/No parking 8am-6pm (M-F)

26TH ST (9TH-8TH) ☺

North

No parking 9:30am-11am (M & Th)/No parking 8am-6pm (M-F)

South

No parking 9:30am-11am (Tu & F)/No parking 7am-4pm (school days)

26TH ST (8TH-7TH)

North

No standing except trucks loading & unloading 8am-6pm (M-F)

South

No standing except trucks loading & unloading 8am-6pm (M-F)

26TH ST (7TH-6TH)

North

No standing except trucks loading & unloading 8am-7pm (M-F)/No Standing 1am-7am including Sun

South

No standing except trucks loading & unloading 8am-7pm (M-F)/No Standing 1am-7am including Sun

26TH ST (6TH-BROADWAY)

North

No standing except trucks loading & unloading 8am-7pm (M-F)

South

No standing except trucks loading & unloading 8am-7pm (M-F)

26TH ST (BROADWAY-5TH)

North

No standing except trucks loading & unloading 8am-7pm (M-F)

South

No standing anytime

25TH ST (5TH-BROADWAY)

North

No standing anytime

South

No standing anytime

25TH ST (BROADWAY-6TH)

North

No standing except trucks loading & unloading 7am-7pm (M-F)

South

No standing except trucks loading & unloading 8am-6pm (M-F)

25TH ST (6TH-7TH)

North

No standing except trucks loading & unloading 8am-7pm (M-F)

South

No standing except trucks loading & unloading 8am-7pm (M-F)

25TH ST (7TH-8TH)

North

No standing 7am-7pm (except Sun)/No parking 8am-6pm (M-F)

South

No standing except trucks loading & unloading 7am-6pm (M-F)/No parking 8am-6pm (M-F)/No parking 7am-4pm (school days)

25TH ST (8TH-9TH) ☺

North

No parking 11am-12:30pm (M & F)

South

No parking 11am-12:30pm (Tu & F)

25TH ST (9TH-10TH) ☺

North

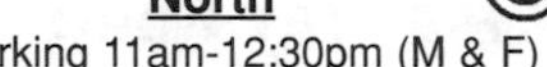
No parking 11am-12:30pm (M & F)

South

No parking 11am-12:30pm (Tu & F)/No parking 7am-7pm (M-F)

25TH ST (10TH-11TH)

North

No parking 8am-6pm (M-F)

South

No parking 8am-6pm (M-F)

24TH ST (12TH-11TH) ☺

North

No parking 8am-6pm (M-F)

South

No parking 8am-6pm (M-F)/No Parking 10am-1pm (Tu,Fri)

24TH ST (11TH-10TH)

North

No parking 8am-6pm (M-F)

South

No parking 8am-6pm (M-F)

24TH ST (10TH-9TH) ☺

North

No parking 11am-12:30pm (M & F)

South

No parking 11am-12:30pm (Tu & F)

24TH ST (9TH-8TH) ☺

North

No parking 11am-12:30pm (M & F)

South

No parking 11am-12:30pm (Tu & F)

24TH ST (8TH-7TH)

North

No parking 8am-6pm (M-F)/No parking 7am-4pm (school days)

South

No parking 8am-6pm (M-F)

24TH ST (7TH-6TH)

North

No standing except trucks loading & unloading 8am-7pm (M-F)

South

No standing except trucks loading & unloading 8am-7pm (M-F)

24TH ST (6TH-5TH)

North

No standing except trucks loading & unloading 8am-7pm (M-F)

South

No standing except trucks loading & unloading 8am-6pm (M-F)

23RD ST (5TH-6TH)

North

No standing 7am-10am & 4pm-7pm (except Sun)/No standing except trucks loading & unloading 10am-4pm (except Sun)

South

No standing 7am-10am & 4pm-7pm (except Sun)/No standing except trucks loading & unloading 10am-4pm (except Sun)

23RD ST (6TH-7TH)

North

No standing except trucks loading & unloading 8am-6pm (except Sun)

South

No standing except trucks loading & unloading 9am-4pm (except Sun.)/No Standing 7am-9am & 4pm-7pm (except Sun.)

23RD ST (7TH-8TH)

North

No standing except trucks loading & unloading 9am-4pm (except Sun.)/No Standing 8am-9am & 4pm-6pm (except Sun.)

South

No standing except trucks loading & unloading 9am-4pm (except Sun.)/No Standing 7am-9am & 4pm-7pm (except Sun.)

23RD ST (8TH-9TH)

North

1 hr. metered parking (8am-7pm) including Sun/No parking 7:30am-8am (except Sun)

South

1 hr. metered parking (8am-7pm) including Sun/No parking 7:30am-8am (except Sun)

23RD ST (9TH-10TH)

North

No parking 8am-6pm (M-F)

South

No parking 8am-6pm (M-F)

23RD ST (10TH-11TH)

North

No standing except trucks loading & unloading 7am-7pm (except Sun)/No standing 11pm-6am (including Sun)

South

No standing except trucks loading & unloading 7am-7pm (except Sun)/No standing 11pm-6am (including Sun)

22ND ST (11TH-10TH)

North

No standing except trucks loading & unloading 8am-6pm (M-F)

South

No standing except trucks loading & unloading 8am-6pm (M-F)

22ND ST (10TH-9TH) ☺

North

No parking 9am-10:30am (M & Th)

South

No parking 9am-10:30am (Tu & F)

22ND ST (9TH-8TH) ☺

North

No parking 9am-10:30am (M & Th)

South

No parking 9am-10:30am (Tu & F)

22ND ST (8TH-7TH) ☺

North

No parking 9am-10:30am (M & Th)

South

No parking 9am-10:30am (Tu & F)

22ND ST (7TH-6TH)

North

No standing except trucks loading & unloading 8am-7pm (M-F)

South

No standing except trucks loading & unloading 8am-7pm (M-F)

22ND ST (6TH-5TH)

North

No standing except trucks loading & unloading 8am-6pm (M-F)

South

No standing except trucks loading & unloading 8am-6pm (M-F)/No Standing 10pm-6am including Sun.

21ST ST (5TH-6TH)

North

No standing except trucks loading & unloading 8am-7pm (M-F)

South

No standing except trucks loading & unloading 8am-6pm (M-F)/No standing 11pm-6am (including Sun)

21ST ST (6TH-7TH)

North

No standing except trucks loading & unloading 8am-7pm (M-F)

South

No standing except trucks loading & unloading 8am-7pm (M-F)/No Standing 3pm-6pm ex authorized vehicles

21ST ST (7TH-8TH) ☺

North

No parking 9am-10:30am (M & Th)

South

No parking 9am-10:30am (Tu & F)

21ST ST (8TH-9TH)

North

No Parking 8am-4pm (M-F)/No parking 8am-6pm (M-F)

South

No Parking 8am-4pm (M-F)/No parking 8am-6pm (M-F)

21ST ST (9TH-10TH) ☺

North

No parking 9am-10:30am (M & Th)

South

No parking 9am-10:30am (Tu & F)

21ST ST (10TH-11TH)

North

No parking 8am-6pm (M-F)

South

No parking 8am-6pm (M-F)/No Standing 7am-3pm (M-F)/No Standing 3am-7am & 3pm-6pm except authorized vehicles

20TH ST (11TH-10TH)

North

No parking 8am-6pm (M-F)

South

No parking 8am-6pm (M-F)

20TH ST (10TH-9TH) ☺

North

No parking 9am-10:30am (M & Th)

South

No parking 9am-10:30am (Tu & F)

20TH ST (9TH-8TH) ☺

North

No parking 9am-10:30am (M & Th)/No parking 7am-4pm (school days)

South

No parking 9am-10:30am (Tu & F)/No parking 8am-6pm (M-F)

20TH ST (8TH-7TH)

North

No parking 8am-6pm (M-F)

South

No parking 8am-6pm (M-F)

20TH ST (7TH-6TH)

North

No standing except trucks loading & unloading 8am-7pm (M-F)/No Parking 10am-6pm (Th, F, Sat)

South

No standing except trucks loading & unloading 8am-7pm (M-F)/No Parking 10am-6pm (Th, F, Sat)

20TH ST (6TH-5TH)

North

No standing except trucks loading & unloading 8am-6pm (M-F)/No standing 11pm-6am (including Sun)

South

No standing except trucks loading & unloading 8am-6pm (M-F)/No standing 11pm-6am (including Sun)

19TH ST (5TH-6TH)

North

No standing except trucks loading & unloading 8am-7pm (M-F)/No standing 11pm-6am (including Sun)

South

No standing except trucks loading & unloading 8am-7pm (M-F)/No standing 11pm-6am (including Sun)

19TH ST (6TH-7TH)

North

No standing except trucks loading & unloading 8am-6pm (M-F)/No standing 11pm-6am (including Sun)

South

No standing except trucks loading & unloading 8am-7pm (M-F)

19TH ST (7TH-8TH)

North

No parking 8am-6pm (M-F)

South

No parking 8am-6pm (M-F)

19TH ST (8TH-9TH) ☺

North

No parking 8am-6pm (M-F)

South

No parking 8am-6pm (M-F)/No parking 8:30am-10am (Sat)

19TH ST (9TH-10TH) ☺

North

No parking 9am-10:30am (M & Th)

South

No parking 9am-10:30am (Tu & F)/No parking 8am-6pm (M-F)

19TH ST (10TH-11TH)

North

No parking 8am-6pm (M-F)/No standing 11pm-6am (including Sun)

South

No parking 8am-6pm (except Sun)/No standing 11pm-6am (including Sun)

18TH ST (11TH-10TH)

North

No parking 8am-6pm (M-F)/No standing 11pm-6am (including Sun)

South

No standing 7am-7pm (except Sun)/No standing 11pm-6am (including Sun)

18TH ST (10TH-9TH) ☺

North

No parking 8:30am-10am (M & Th)

South

No parking 8:30am-10am (Tu & F)/No parking 8am-6pm (M-F)

18TH ST (9TH-8TH)

North

No parking 8am-6pm (M-F)/No parking 7am-6pm (school days)/No parking 8:30am-10am (Sat)

South

No parking 8am-6pm (M-F)

18TH ST (8TH-7TH)

North

No parking 8am-6pm (M-F)

South

No parking 8am-6pm (M-F)/No parking 7am-4pm (school days)

18TH ST (7TH-6TH)

North

No standing except trucks loading & unloading 8am-7pm (M-F)

South

No standing except trucks loading & unloading 8am-6pm (M-F)

18TH ST (6TH-5TH)

North

No standing except trucks loading & unloading 7am-6pm (M-F)

South

No standing except trucks loading & unloading [illegible] (M-F)

17TH ST (5TH-6TH)

North

No standing except trucks loading & unloading 8am-7pm (M-F)

South

No standing except trucks loading & unloading 7am-6pm (M-F)

17TH ST (6TH-7TH)

North

No standing except trucks loading & unloading 8am-6pm (M-F)/No Standing 10am-6pm (M-F)

South

No standing except trucks loading & unloading 8am-6pm (M-F)

17TH ST (7TH-8TH)

North

No parking 8am-6pm (M-F)

South

No parking 8am-6pm (M-F)

17TH ST (8TH-9TH)

North

No parking 8am-6pm (M-F)/No Parking 8am-6pm school days

South

No parking 8am-6pm (M-F)

17TH ST (9TH-10TH) ☺

North

No parking 8:30am-10am (M & Th)

South

No parking 8:30am-10am (Tu & F)/No parking 8am-6pm (M-F)

17TH ST (10TH-11TH) ☹

North

No standing anytime

South

No standing anytime

16TH ST (11TH-10TH)

North

No parking anytime

South

No parking 7am-4pm (school days)/No parking 7am-7pm (except Sun)

16TH ST (10TH-9TH)

North

No standing except trucks loading & unloading 7am-7pm (except Sun)

South

No parking 8am-6pm (M-F)

16TH ST (9TH-8TH)

North

No parking 8am-6pm (M-F)

South

No parking 8am-6pm (M-F)

16TH ST (8TH-7TH) ☺

North

No parking 8:30am-10am (M & Th)

South

No parking 8:30am-10am (Tu & F)

16TH ST (7TH-6TH) ☺

North

No parking 8:30am-10am (M & Th)

South

No parking 8:30am-10am (Tu & F)/No parking 7am-6pm (M-F)

16TH ST (6TH-5TH)

North

No parking 8am-6pm (M-F)

South

No parking 8am-6pm (M-F)

15TH ST (5TH-6TH)

North

No parking 8am-6pm (M-F)

South

No parking 8am-6pm (M-F)

15TH ST (6TH-7TH) ☺

North

No parking 8:30am-10am (M & Th)/No standing except trucks loading & unloading 8am-6pm (M-F)

South

No parking 8:30am-10am (Tu & F)

15TH ST (7TH-8TH) ☺

North

No parking 8:30am-10am (M & Th)

South

No parking 8:30am-10am (Tu & F)

15TH ST (8TH-9TH)

North

No standing anytime

South

No standing 7am-7pm (M-F)/No parking 8am-6pm (M-F)

15TH ST (9TH-10TH)

North

No standing except trucks loading & unloading 7am-7pm (M-F)

South

No parking 8am-6pm (M-F)

15TH ST (10TH-11TH)

North

No parking 8am-6pm (M-F)

South

No standing anytime

14TH ST (11TH-10TH)

North

No parking 8am-6pm (M-F)

South

No standing anytime

14TH ST (10TH-WASHINGTON)

North

No standing except trucks loading & unloading 2am-4pm (M-F)

South

No standing except trucks loading & unloading 2am-4pm (M-F)/No Standing 6pm-8pm (M,Th)

14TH ST (WASHINGTON-9TH)

North

No standing except trucks loading & unloading 2am-4pm (M-F)/No Standing 6pm-8pm (Tu,F)

South

No standing except trucks loading & unloading 2am-4pm (M-F)/No Standing 6pm-8pm (M,Th)

14TH ST (9TH-8TH)

North

No parking 8am-6pm (M-F)

South

1 hr. metered parking (9am-7pm) including Sun/No parking 8:30am-9am (except Sun)

14TH ST (8TH-7TH)

North

1 hr. metered parking (8:30am-7pm) including Sun/No parking 8am-8:30am (except Sun)/No standing except trucks loading & unloading 7pm-8am (including Sun)/No standing 7am-7pm (except Sun)

South

1 hr. metered parking (8:30am-7pm) including Sun/No parking 8am-8:30am (except Sun)/No standing except trucks loading & unloading 7pm-8am (including Sun)/No parking 8am-6pm (M-F)

14TH ST (7TH-6TH)

North

1 hr. metered parking (8:30am-10pm) including Sun/No parking 8am-8:30am (except Sun)

South

1 hr. metered parking (8:30am-10pm) including Sun/No parking 8am-8:30am (except Sun)

14TH ST (6TH-5TH)

North

1 hr. metered parking (9am-10pm) including Sun/No parking 8am-9am (except Sun)/No parking 7am-4pm (school days)

South

1 hr. metered parking (9am-10pm) including Sun/No parking 8am-9am (except Sun)

13TH ST (5TH - 6TH)

North

No parking 8am-6pm (M-F)/No parking 8am-midnite (except Sun)

South

No parking 8am-6pm (M-F)

13TH ST (6TH - 7TH)

North

No parking 8am - 6pm (M, W, F)

South

No parking 8am - 6pm (Tu, Th, Sat)/No parking 7am-4pm (school days)

13TH ST (7TH - GREENWICH AVE/8TH AVE)

North

No parking 8am-11am (M & Th)

South

No parking 8am-11am (Tu & F)

13TH ST (GREENWICH AVE/8TH AVE - W. 4TH ST)

North

No parking 8am-6pm (M-F)

South

No parking 8am-6pm (except Sun)

13TH ST (W. 4TH ST - HUDSON)

North

No parking 8am-6pm (M-F)

South

No parking 8am-6pm (except Sun)

13TH ST (HUDSON - 9TH)

North

No parking 2am-4pm (M-F) except trucks loading & unloading “Ganesvoort market”

South

No parking 2am-4pm (M-F) except trucks loading & unloading “Ganesvoort market”

13TH ST (9TH - WASHINGTON)

North

No parking 2am-4pm (M-F) except trucks loading & unloading “Ganesvoort market”/No standing 6pm-8pm (M, Th)

South

No parking 2am-4pm (M-F) except trucks loading & unloading “Ganesvoort market”/No standing 6pm-8pm (Tu, F)

13TH ST (WASHINGTON - 10TH AVE)

North

No parking 2am-4pm (M-F) except trucks loading & unloading “Ganesvoort market”

South

No parking 2am-4pm (M-F) except trucks loading & unloading “Ganesvoort market”

12TH ST (WEST - WASHINGTON)

North

No parking 8am-6pm (M-F)

South

No parking 11am-2pm (Tu & F)

12TH ST (WASHINGTON - GREENWICH ST) ☺

North

No parking 11am-2pm (M & Th)/No parking 8am-6pm (M-F)

South

No parking 8am-6pm (M-F)

12TH ST (GREENWICH ST - HUDSON) ☺

North

No parking 11am-2pm (M & Th)

South

No parking 8am-6pm (M-F)

12TH ST (HUDSON - 8TH AVE) ☺

North

No parking 11am-2pm (M & Th)

South

No parking 11am-2pm (Tu & F)

12TH ST (8TH AVE - W. 4TH ST) ☺

North

No parking 11am-2pm (M & Th)

South

No parking 11am-2pm (Tu & F)

12TH ST (W. 4TH ST - GREENWICH AVE) ☺

North

No parking 11am-2pm (M & Th)

South

No parking 11am-2pm (Tu & F)

12TH ST (GREENWICH AVE - 7TH AVE)

North

No standing 7am - 4pm (M-F)

South

No standing anytime

12TH ST (7TH - 6TH) ☺

North

No parking 8am-11am (M & Th)

South

No parking 8am-11am (Tu & F)

12TH ST (6TH - 5TH)

North

No parking 8am-11am (M & Th)

South

No parking 8am-11am (Tu & F)/No parking 8am-6pm (M-F)

11TH ST (5TH - 6TH)

North

No parking 8am-11am (M & Th)

South

No parking 8am-11am (Tu & F)

11TH ST (6TH - GREENWICH AVE/7TH AVE S.)

North

No parking 8am-11am (M & Th)

South

No parking 8am-11am (Tu & F)/No parking 7am-4pm (school days)

11TH ST (7TH AVE - WAVERLY PL.)

North

No parking 8am-6pm (M, W, Fri)

South

1 hr. metered parking (9am-7pm) including Sun/No parking 8am-9am (except Sun)

11TH ST (WAVERLY PL. - W. 4TH ST)

North

No parking 8am-11am (M & Th)

South

No parking 8am-11am (Tu & F)

11TH ST (W. 4TH ST - BLEECKER)

North

No parking 8am-11am (M & Th)

South

No parking 8am-11am (Tu & F)

11TH ST (BLEECKER - HUDSON)

North

No parking 8am-11am (M & Th)

South

No parking 8am-11am (Tu & F)

11TH ST (HUDSON - GREENWICH ST)

North

No parking 11am-2pm (M & Th)

South

No parking 11am-2pm (Tu & F)

11TH ST (GREENWICH ST - WASHINGTON)

North

No parking 11am-2pm (M & Th)

South

No parking 11am-2pm (Tu & F)

11TH ST (WASHINGTON - WEST)

North

No parking 11am-2pm (M & Th)

South

No parking 8am-6pm (M-F)

10TH ST (WEST - WASHINGTON)

North

No parking 8am-6pm (M-F)

South

No standing anytime

10TH ST (WASHINGTON - GREENWICH)

North

No parking 11am-2pm (M & Th)

South

No parking anytime

10TH ST (GREENWICH ST - HUDSON)

North

No standing anytime (except authorized vehicles)

South

No standing anytime (except authorized vehicles)

10TH ST (HUDSON - BLEECKER)

North

No standing anytime (except authorized vehicles)

South

No parking 8am-11am (Tu & F)

10TH ST (BLEECKER - W. 4TH)

North

No parking anytime

South

No parking 8am-11am (Tu & F)

10TH ST (W. 4TH - 7TH AV SOUTH)

North

No parking anytime

South

No parking anytime

10TH ST (7TH AV SOUTH - WAVERLY PL)

North

No parking anytime

South

1 hr. metered parking (9am-7pm) including Sun/No parking 8am-9am (except Sun)

10TH ST (WAVERLY PL - GREENWICH AVE)

North

No parking anytime

South

No parking 8am-11am (Tu & F)

10TH ST (GREENWICH AVE - 6TH AVE)

North

No parking anytime

South

No parking anytime

10TH ST (6TH - 5TH)

North

No parking 8am - 6pm (M, W, F)

South

No parking 8am - 6pm (Tu, Th, Sat)/No parking 8am-7pm (M-F) except authorized vehicles (post office)

9TH ST (5TH - 6TH)

North

No standing anytime

South

No parking 8am-6pm (except Sun)

8TH ST (6TH - 5TH)

North

No standing 11pm-6am (including Sun)/1 hr. metered parking (9am-10pm) including Sun/No parking 8am-9am (except Sun)

South

No standing 11pm-6am (including Sun)/1 hr. metered parking (9am-10pm) including Sun/No parking 8am-9am (except Sun)

4TH ST (7TH AVE SOUTH - W. 10TH)

East

No standing anytime

West

No parking 8am-6pm (M-F)

4TH ST (W. 10TH - CHARLES)

East

No standing anytime

West

No parking 8am-11am (M & Th)

4TH ST (CHARLES - PERRY)

East

No standing anytime

West

No parking 8am-11am (M & Th)/No standing except trucks loading & unloading 8am-6pm (except Sun)

4TH ST (PERRY - W. 11TH)

East

No standing anytime

West

No parking 8am-11am (M & Th)/No standing except trucks loading & unloading 8am-6pm (except Sun)

4TH ST (W. 11TH - BANK)

East

No standing anytime

West

No parking 8am-11am (M & Th)/No standing except trucks loading & unloading 8am-6pm (except Sun)

4TH ST (BANK - W. 12TH)

East

No standing anytime

West

No parking 8am-11am (M & Th)/No standing except trucks loading & unloading 8am-6pm (except Sun)

4TH ST (W. 12TH - 8TH AVE)

East

No standing anytime

West

2 hr. metered parking (9am-7pm) including Sun/No parking 8am-9am (except Sun)

4TH ST (8TH AVE - HORATIO)

East

No parking anytime

West

No parking anytime

4TH ST (HORATIO - W. 13TH)

East

No parking 8am-11am (Tu & F)

West

2 hr. metered parking (9am-7pm) including Sun/No parking 8am-9am (except Sun)

4TH ST (7TH AVE SOUTH - GROVE)

North

No standing anytime

South

No parking 8am-6pm (except Sun)

4TH ST (GROVE - BARROW)

North

No standing anytime

South

No parking 8am-6pm (except Sun)

4TH ST (BARROW - JONES)

North

1 hr. metered parking (9am-10pm) including Sun/No parking 8am-9am (except Sun)

South

No parking 8am-6pm (except Sun)

4TH ST (JONES - CORNELIA)

North

1 hr. metered parking (9am-10pm) including Sun/No parking 8am-9am (except Sun)

South

No parking 8am-6pm (except Sun)

4TH ST (CORNELIA - 6TH)

North

1 hr. metered parking (9am-10pm) including Sun/No parking 8am-9am (except Sun)

South

No parking 8am-6pm (except Sun)

4TH ST (6TH - MACDOUGAL)

North

1 hr. metered parking (9am-10pm) including Sun/No parking 8am-9am (except Sun)

South

No parking 8am-6pm (except Sun)

4TH ST (MACDOUGAL - SULLIVAN)

North

No standing anytime

South

No parking 8am-6pm (M-F)

4TH ST (SULLIVAN - THOMPSON)

North

No standing anytime

South

No parking 8am-6pm (M-F)

4TH ST (THOMPSON - LAGUARDIA) ☹

North

No standing anytime

South

No standing anytime

4TH ST (LAGUARDIA - WASHINGTON SQ. E.) ☹

North

No standing anytime

South

No standing anytime

4TH ST (WASHINGTON SQ. E. - GREENE)

North

No standing anytime

South

No parking 8am-6pm (M-F)

4TH ST (GREENE - MERCER)

North

No standing anytime

South

No parking 8am-6pm (M-F)

4TH ST (MERCER - BROADWAY)

North

No parking 8am-6pm (M-F)

South

No parking 8am-6pm (M-F)

4TH ST (BROADWAY - LAFAYETTE)

North

No standing except trucks loading & unloading 7am-7pm (except Sun)

South

No standing except trucks loading & unloading 7am-7pm (except Sun)

3RD ST (BROADWAY - MERCER)

North

No parking 8am-6pm (except Sun)

South

No parking 8am-6pm (M-F)

3RD ST (MERCER - LAGUARDIA)

North

No parking 8am-11am (M & Th)

South

No parking 8am-11am (Tu & F)

3RD ST (LAGUARDIA - THOMPSON)

North

No standing anytime

South

No parking 8am-11am (Tu & F)

3RD ST (THOMPSON - SULLIVAN) ☺

North

No standing anytime

South

No parking 8am-11am (Tu & F)

3RD ST (SULLIVAN - MACDOUGAL) ☺

North

No Standing 7am-6pm except trucks loading and unloading (all days)

South

No parking 8am-11am (Tu & F)

3RD ST (MACDOUGAL - 6TH)

North

No parking anytime

South

1 hr. metered parking (9am-10pm) including Sun/No parking 8am-9am (except Sun)

5TH AVE (30TH-29TH)

East

No parking 8am-6pm (M-F)

West

No standing anytime

5TH AVE (29TH-28TH)

East

No parking 8am-6pm (M-F)

West

No standing 7am-10am & 4pm-7pm (except Sun)/No standing except trucks loading & unloading 10am-4pm (except Sun)

5TH AVE (28TH-27TH)

East

No parking 8am-6pm (M-F)

West

No standing anytime

5TH AVE (27TH-26TH)

East

No parking 8am-6pm (M-F)/1 hr. metered parking (8am-7pm) including Sun/No parking 7:30am-8am (except Sun)

West

No standing anytime

5TH AVE (26TH-25TH) ☹

East

No standing anytime

West

No standing anytime

5TH AVE (25TH-24TH)

East

No standing 8am-6pm (except Sun) except authorized vehicles

West

No standing anytime

5TH AVE (24TH-23RD) ☹

East

No standing anytime

West

No standing anytime

5TH AVE (23RD-22ND)

East

1 hr. metered parking (9am-7pm) including Sun/No parking 8:30am-9am (except Sun)

West

No standing except trucks loading & unloading 7am-7pm (except Sun)

5TH AVE (22ND-21ST)

East

1 hr. metered parking (9am-7pm) including Sun/No parking 8:30am-9am (except Sun)

West

No standing except trucks loading & unloading 7am-7pm (except Sun)

5TH AVE (21ST-20TH)

East

1 hr. metered parking (9am-7pm) including Sun/No parking 8:30am-9am (except Sun)

West

No standing except trucks loading & unloading 7am-7pm (except Sun)

5TH AVE (20TH-19TH)

East

1 hr. metered parking (9am-7pm) including Sun/No parking 8:30am-9am (except Sun)/No standing except trucks loading & unloading 8am-7pm (except Sun)

West

No standing except trucks loading & unloading 7am-7pm (except Sun)

5TH AVE (19TH-18TH)

East

1 hr. metered parking (9am-7pm) including Sun/No parking 8:30am-9am (except Sun)

West

No standing except trucks loading & unloading 7am-7pm (except Sun)

5TH AVE (18TH-17TH)

East

1 hr. metered parking (9am-7pm) including Sun/No parking 8:30am-9am (except Sun)/No standing except trucks loading & unloading 8am-7pm (except Sun)

West

No standing except trucks loading & unloading 7am-7pm (except Sun)

5TH AVE (17TH-16TH)

East

1 hr. metered parking (9am-7pm) including Sun/No parking 8:30am-9am (except Sun)

West

No standing except trucks loading & unloading 7am-7pm (except Sun)

5TH AVE (16TH-15TH)

East

1 hr. metered parking (9am-7pm) including Sun/No parking 8:30am-9am (except Sun)

West

No standing except trucks loading & unloading 8am-7pm (except Sun)

5TH AVE (15TH-14TH)

East

1 hr. metered parking (9am-7pm) including Sun/No parking 8:30am-9am (except Sun)

West

No standing except trucks loading & unloading 8am-7pm (except Sun)

5TH AVE (14TH - 13TH)

East

1 hr. metered parking (9am-10pm) including Sun/No parking 8am-9am (except Sun)

West

1 hr. metered parking (9am-10pm) including Sun/No parking 8am-9am (except Sun)

5TH AVE (13TH - 12TH)

East

1 hr. metered parking (9am-10pm) including Sun/No parking 8am-9am (except Sun)

West

1 hr. metered parking (9am-10pm) including Sun/No parking 8am-9am (except Sun)

5TH AVE (12TH - 11TH)

East

1 hr. metered parking (9am-10pm) including Sun/No parking 8am-9am (except Sun)

West

No parking 8am-11am (M & Th)

5TH AVE (11TH - 10TH)

East

No parking 8am-11am (Tu & F)

West

No parking 8am-11am (M & Th)

5TH AVE (10TH - 9TH)

East

No parking 8am-11am (Tu & F)

West

No parking 8am-11am (M & Th)

5TH AVE (9TH - 8TH)

East

No parking 8am-11am (Tu & F)

West

No parking 8am-6pm (M-F)

5TH AVE (8TH - WASHINGTON MEWS)

East

No standing anytime

West

No parking 8am-11am (M & Th)

5TH AVE (WASHINGTON MEWS - WASH. SQ. N.)

East

No parking 8am-11am (Tu & F)

West

No parking 8am-11am (M & Th)

6TH AVE (WHITE - WALKER)

East

No parking 8am-6pm (M-F)

West

1 hr. metered parking (9am-4pm) including Sun/No parking 2am-6am (M, Th)

6TH AVE (WALKER - ERICCSON PL)

East

No parking 8am-6pm (M-F)

West

No standing anytime

6TH AVE (ERICCSON PL - LISPENARD)

East

No parking 8am-6pm (M-F)

West

No standing anytime

6TH AVE (LISPENARD - YORK)

East

No standing anytime

West

No standing 3pm-7pm (M-F) other times - No standing anytime (except authorized vehicles) (Police vehicles only)

6TH AVE (YORK - LAIGHT)

East

No parking 8am-6pm (M-F)

West

No parking 8am - 4pm (M-F)/No standing 4pm-7pm (M-F)

6TH AVE (LAIGHT - CANAL)

East

No parking 8am-6pm (M-F)

West

No parking 8am - 4pm (M-F)/No standing 4pm-7pm (M-F)

6TH AVE (CANAL - GRAND)

East

No standing 4pm-7pm (M-F)/No standing except trucks loading & unloading 7am-4pm (except Sun)

West

No standing 3pm-7pm (M-F) other times - No standing anytime (except authorized vehicles)

6TH AVE (GRAND - WATTS)

East

No standing 4pm-7pm (M-F)/No parking 8am-7pm (except Sun)

West

No standing 3pm-7pm (M-F)/No parking 8am-7pm (except Sun)

6TH AVE (WATTS - BROOME)

East

No parking 8am-6pm (except Sun)

West

No standing 4pm-7pm (except Sun)/No standing except trucks loading & unloading 8am-4pm (except Sun)

6TH AVE (BROOME - DOMINICK)

East

No parking anytime

West

2 hr. metered parking (9am-7pm) including Sun/No parking 8am-9am (M, Th)

6TH AVE (DOMINICK - SPRING)

East

No parking 8am-11am (Tu & F)

West

2 hr. metered parking (9am-7pm) including Sun/No parking 8am-9am (M, Th)

6TH AVE (SPRING - VANDAM)

East

No parking 8am-11am (Tu & F)

West

1 hr. metered parking (9am-7pm) including Sun/No parking 8am-9am (M, Th)

6TH AVE (VANDAM - CHARLTON/PRINCE)

East

No parking 8am-11am (Tu & F)

West

1 hr. metered parking (9am-7pm) including Sun/No parking 8am-9am (M, Th)

6TH AVE (CHARLTON/PRINCE - KING)

East

No parking 8am-11am (Tu & F)

West

1 hr. metered parking (9am-7pm) including Sun/No parking 8am-9am (M, Th)

6TH AVE (KING - HOUSTON)

East

No parking 8am-11am (Tu & F)

West

No standing anytime (except authorized vehicles) (fire dept. only)

6TH AVE (HOUSTON - BLEECKER/DOWNING) ☺

East

No parking 11am-2pm (Tu & F)

West

2 hr. metered parking (9am-7pm) including Sun/No parking 8am-9am (M, Th)

6TH AVE (BLEECKER/DOWNING - MINETTA/CARMINE)

East

2 hr. metered parking (9am-7pm) including Sun/No parking 8am-9am (M, Th)

West

No parking anytime

6TH AVE (MINETTA/CARMINE - W. 3RD)

East

No standing anytime

West

1 hr. metered parking (9am-10pm) including Sun/No parking 8am-9am (except Sun)

6TH AVE (W. 3RD - W. 4TH)

East

1 hr. metered parking (9am-10pm) including Sun/No parking 8am-9am (except Sun)

West

1 hr. metered parking (9am-10pm) including Sun/No parking 8am-9am (except Sun)

6TH AVE (W. 4TH - W. WASHINGTON PL)

East

1 hr. metered parking (9am-10pm) including Sun/No parking 8am-9am (except Sun)

West

1 hr. metered parking (9am-10pm) including Sun/No parking 8am-9am (except Sun)

6TH AVE (W. WASHINGTON PL - WAVERLY)

East

No standing except trucks loading & unloading

West

1 hr. metered parking (9am-10pm) including Sun/No parking 8am-9am (except Sun)

6TH AVE (WAVERLY - 8TH)

East

No standing anytime

West

1 hr. metered parking (9am-10pm) including Sun/No parking 8am-9am (except Sun)/1 hr. metered parking (9am-4pm) including Sun/No standing 4pm - midnite including Sun

6TH AVE (8TH - GREENWICH)

East

No standing anytime

West

1 hr. metered parking (9am-10pm) including Sun/No parking 8am-9am (except Sun)/1 hr. metered parking (9am-4pm) including Sun/No standing 4pm - midnite including Sun

6TH AVE (GREENWICH - 9TH)

East

No standing anytime

West

No parking anytime

6TH AVE (9TH - 10TH)

East

No parking 7am-10am (except Sun)/1 hr. metered parking (10am-7pm) including Sun

West

1 hr. metered parking (9am-7pm) including Sun/No parking 8am-9am (except Sun)

6TH AVE (10TH -11TH)

East

1 hr. metered parking (9am-7pm) including Sun/No parking 8am-9am (except Sun)

West

1 hr. metered parking (9am-7pm) including Sun/No parking 8am-9am (except Sun)

6TH AVE (11TH - 12TH)

East

1 hr. metered parking (9am-7pm) including Sun/No parking 8am-9am (except Sun)

West

1 hr. metered parking (9am-7pm) including Sun/No parking 8am-9am (except Sun)

6TH AVE (12TH - 13TH)

East

1 hr. metered parking (9am-7pm) including Sun/No parking 8am-9am (except Sun)

West

1 hr. metered parking (9am-7pm) including Sun/No parking 8am-9am (except Sun)/No parking 8am-6pm (except Sun)

6TH AVE (13TH - 14TH)

East

1 hr. metered parking (9am-7pm) including Sun/No parking 8am-9am (except Sun)

West

1 hr. metered parking (9am-7pm) including Sun/No parking 8am-9am (except Sun)

6TH AVE (14TH-15TH)

East

No standing anytime

West

No standing except trucks loading & unloading 7am-7pm (M-F)

6TH AVE (15TH-16TH)

East

No standing except trucks loading & unloading 7am-7pm (M-F)

West

No standing except trucks loading & unloading 7am-7pm (M-F)

6TH AVE (16TH-17TH)

East

No standing except trucks loading & unloading 7am-7pm (M-F)

West

No standing except trucks loading & unloading 7am-7pm (M-F)

6TH AVE (17TH-18TH)

East

No standing except trucks loading & unloading 7am-7pm (M-F)

West

No standing except trucks loading & unloading 7am-7pm (M-F)

6TH AVE (18TH-19TH)

East

No standing except trucks loading & unloading 7am-7pm (M-F)/No Standing 7am-7pm (including Sun)

West

No standing except trucks loading & unloading 7am-7pm (M-F)

6TH AVE (19TH-20TH)

East

No standing except trucks loading & unloading 7am-7pm (M-F)

West

No standing except trucks loading & unloading 7am-7pm (M-F)

6TH AVE (20TH-21ST)

East

No standing except trucks loading & unloading 7am-7pm (M-F)

West

No standing except trucks loading & unloading 7am-7pm (M-F)

6TH AVE (21ST-22ND)

East

No standing except trucks loading & unloading 7am-7pm (M-F)

West

No standing except trucks loading & unloading 7am-7pm (M-F)

6TH AVE (22ND-23RD)

East

No standing except trucks loading & unloading 7am-7pm (M-F)

West

No standing except trucks loading & unloading 7am-7pm (M-F)

6TH AVE (23RD-24TH)

East

No standing except trucks loading & unloading 7am-7pm (M-F)

West

No standing except trucks loading & unloading 7am-7pm (M-F)

6TH AVE (24TH-25TH)

East

No standing except trucks loading & unloading 7am-7pm (M-F)

West

No standing except trucks loading & unloading 7am-7pm (M-F)

6TH AVE (25TH-26TH)

East

No standing except trucks loading & unloading 7am-7pm (M-F)

West

No standing except trucks loading & unloading 7am-7pm (M-F)

6TH AVE (26TH-27TH)

East

No standing except trucks loading & unloading 7am-7pm (M-F)

West

No standing except trucks loading & unloading 7am-7pm (M-F)

6TH AVE (27TH-28TH)

East

No standing except trucks loading & unloading 7am-7pm (M-F)

West

No standing except trucks loading & unloading 7am-7pm (M-F)

6TH AVE (28TH-29TH)

East

No standing except trucks loading & unloading 7am-7pm (M-F)

West

No standing except trucks loading & unloading 7am-7pm (M-F)

6TH AVE (29TH-30TH)

East

No standing except trucks loading & unloading 7am-7pm (M-F)

West

No standing except trucks loading & unloading 7am-7pm (M-F)

7TH AVE (30TH-29TH)

East

No standing except trucks loading & unloading 7am-7pm (except Sun)

West

No standing except trucks loading & unloading 7am-7pm (except Sun)

7TH AVE (29TH-28TH)

East

No standing except trucks loading & unloading 7am-7pm (except Sun)

West

No standing except trucks loading & unloading 7am-7pm (except Sun)

7TH AVE (28TH-27TH)

East

No standing except trucks loading & unloading 7am-7pm (except Sun)

West

No parking 8am-6pm (M-F)

7TH AVE (27TH-26TH)

East

No standing except trucks loading & unloading 8am-7pm (M-F)

West

No standing 7am-7pm (M-F)

7TH AVE (26TH-25TH)

East

1 hr. metered parking (9am-7pm) including Sun/No parking 8:30am-9am (except Sun)

West

No standing anytime

7TH AVE (25TH-24TH)

East

1 hr. metered parking (9am-7pm) including Sun/No parking 8:30am-9am (except Sun)

West

1 hr. metered parking (9am-7pm) including Sun

7TH AVE (24TH-23RD)

East

1 hr. metered parking (9am-7pm) including Sun/No parking 8:30am-9am (except Sun)

West

No parking 8am-6pm (M-F)

7TH AVE (23RD-22ND)

East

1 hr. metered parking (9am-7pm) including Sun/No parking 8:30am-9am (except Sun)

West

No standing anytime

7TH AVE (22ND-21ST)

East

No Parking 7am-10am (M-F)/1 hour metered parking 10am-7pm (M-F) & 9am-7pm (Sat & Sun)

West

No Parking 7am-10am (M-F)/1 hour metered parking 10am-7pm (M-F) & 9am-7pm (Sat & Sun)

7TH AVE (21ST-20TH)

East

No Parking 7am-10am (M-F)/1 hour metered parking 10am-7pm (M-F) & 9am-7pm (Sat & Sun)

West

No Parking 7am-10am (M-F)/1 hour metered parking 10am-7pm (M-F) & 9am-7pm (Sat & Sun)

7TH AVE (20TH-19TH)

East

No Parking 7am-10am (M-F)/1 hour metered parking 10am-7pm (M-F) & 9am-7pm (Sat & Sun)

West

No Parking 7am-10am (M-F)/1 hour metered parking 10am-7pm (M-F) & 9am-7pm (Sat & Sun)

7TH AVE (19TH-18TH)

East

No Parking 7am-10am (M-F)/1 hour metered parking 10am-7pm (M-F) & 9am-7pm (Sat & Sun)

West

No Parking 7am-10am (M-F)/1 hour metered parking 10am-7pm (M-F) & 9am-7pm (Sat & Sun)

7TH AVE (18TH-17TH)

East

No Parking 7am-10am (M-F)/1 hour metered parking 10am-7pm (M-F) & 9am-7pm (Sat & Sun)

West

No Parking 7am-10am (M-F)/1 hour metered parking 10am-7pm (M-F) & 9am-7pm (Sat & Sun)

7TH AVE (17TH-16TH)

East

No Parking 7am-10am (M-F)/1 hour metered parking 10am-7pm (M-F) & 9am-7pm (Sat & Sun)/No standing 7am-7pm (except Sun)

West

No Parking 7am-10am (M-F)/1 hour metered parking 10am-7pm (M-F) & 9am-7pm (Sat & Sun)/No parking 7am-7pm (M-F)

7TH AVE (16TH-15TH)

East

No Parking 7am-10am (M-F)/1 hour metered parking 10am-7pm (M-F) & 9am-7pm (Sat & Sun)

West

No Parking 7am-10am (M-F)/1 hour metered parking 10am-7pm (M-F) & 9am-7pm (Sat & Sun)

7TH AVE (15TH-14TH)

East

No Parking 7am-10am (M-F)/1 hour metered parking 10am-7pm (M-F) & 9am-7pm (Sat & Sun)

West

No Parking 7am-10am (M-F)/1 hour metered parking 10am-7pm (M-F) & 9am-7pm (Sat & Sun)

7TH AVE SOUTH (14TH - 13TH)

East

No Parking 7am-10am (M-F)/1 hour metered parking 10am-7pm (M-F) & 9am-7pm (Sat & Sun)

West

No parking 8am-6pm (M-F)

7TH AVE SOUTH (13TH - 12TH)

East

No Parking 7am-10am (M-F)/1 hour metered parking 10am-7pm (M-F) & 9am-7pm (Sat & Sun)

West

No standing 7am-7pm (all days) except authorized vehicles

7TH AVE SOUTH (12TH - 11TH)

East

No standing anytime except authorized vehicles

West

No parking 8am-6pm (M-F)

7TH AVE SOUTH (11TH - GREENWICH AVE)

East

1 hr. metered parking (8am-7pm) including Sun/No parking 7:30am-8am (except Sun)

West

1 hr. metered parking (7:30am-7pm) including Sun/No parking 7am-7:30am (except Sun)

7TH AVE SOUTH (GREENWICH AVE - PERRY)

East

1 hr. metered parking (8am-7pm) including Sun/No parking 7:30am-8am (except Sun)

West

1 hr. metered parking (7:30am-7pm) including Sun/No parking 7am-7:30am (except Sun)

7TH AVE SOUTH (PERRY-WAVERLY PL)

East

1 hr. metered parking (8am-7pm) including Sun/No parking 7:30am-8am (except Sun)

West

1 hr. metered parking (7:30am-7pm) including Sun/No parking 7am-7:30am (except Sun)

7TH AVE SOUTH (WAVERLY PL - CHARLES)

East

1 hr. metered parking (8am-7pm) including Sun/No parking 7:30am-8am (except Sun)

West

1 hr. metered parking (7:30am-7pm) including Sun/No parking 7am-7:30am (except Sun)

7TH AVE SOUTH (CHARLES - 10TH)

East

1 hr. metered parking (8am-7pm) including Sun/No parking 7:30am-8am (except Sun)

West

1 hr. metered parking (7:30am-10pm) including Sun/No parking 7am-7:30am (except Sun)

7TH AVE SOUTH (10TH - CHRISTOPHER)

East

1 hr. metered parking (8am-10pm) including Sun/No parking 7:30am-8am (except Sun)

West

1 hr. metered parking (7:30am-10pm) including Sun/No parking 7am-7:30am (except Sun)

7TH AVE SOUTH (CHRISTOPHER - W. 4TH)

East

1 hr. metered parking (8am-10pm) including Sun/No parking 7:30am-8am (except Sun)

West

1 hr. metered parking (7:30am-10pm) including Sun/No parking 7am-7:30am (except Sun)

7TH AVE SOUTH (W. 4TH - GROVE)

East

No parking anytime

West

1 hr. metered parking (7:30am-10pm) including Sun/No parking 7am-7:30am (except Sun)

7TH AVE SOUTH (GROVE - BARROW)

East

1 hr. metered parking (8am-10pm) including Sun/No parking 7:30am-8am (except Sun)

West

1 hr. metered parking (7:30am-10pm) including Sun/No parking 7am-7:30am (except Sun)

7TH AVE SOUTH (BARROW - BLEECKER)

East

1 hr. metered parking (8am-7pm) including Sun/No parking 7:30am-8am (except Sun)

West

1 hr. metered parking (7:30am-10pm) including Sun/No parking 7am-7:30am (except Sun)

7TH AVE SOUTH (BLEECKER - COMMERCE)

East

1 hr. metered parking (8am-7pm) including Sun/No parking 7:30am-8am (except Sun)

West

1 hr. metered parking (7:30am-10pm) including Sun/No parking 7am-7:30am (except Sun)

7TH AVE SOUTH (COMMERCE - MORTON)

East

1 hr. metered parking (8am-7pm) including Sun/No parking 7:30am-8am (except Sun)

West

1 hr. metered parking (7:30am-7pm) including Sun/No parking 7am-7:30am (except Sun)

7TH AVE SOUTH (MORTON - BEDFORD)

East

1 hr. metered parking (8am-7pm) including Sun/No parking 7:30am-8am (except Sun)

West

No standing anytime

7TH AVE SOUTH (BEDFORD - LEROY)

East

1 hr. metered parking (9am-7pm) including Sun/No parking 8am-9am (except Sun)

West

1 hr. metered parking (9am-7pm) including Sun/No parking 8am-9am (except Sun)

7TH AVE SOUTH (LEROY - CLARKSON/CARMINE)

East

1 hr. metered parking (9am-7pm) including Sun/No parking 8am-9am (except Sun)

West

1 hr. metered parking (9am-7pm) including Sun/No parking 8am-9am (except Sun)

7TH AVE SOUTH (CLARKSON/CARMINE - DOWNING)

East

1 hr. metered parking (9am-7pm) including Sun/No parking 8am-9am (except Sun)

West

1 hr. metered parking (9am-7pm) including Sun/No parking 8am-9am (except Sun)

7TH AVE SOUTH (DOWNING - W. HOUSTON)

East

1 hr. metered parking (9am-7pm) including Sun/No parking 4am-6am (Tu, Th, Sat)

West

1 hr. metered parking (9am-7pm) including Sun/No parking 4am-6am (M, W, F)

7TH AVE SOUTH/VARICK (W. HOUSTON - KING)

East

1 hr. metered parking (9am-7pm) including Sun/No parking 4am-6am (Tu, Th, Sat)

West

No standing 7am-7pm (M-F) except authorized vehicles

8TH AVE (HUDSON - ABINGDON SQ./W. 12TH)

East

No standing anytime

West

No parking 8am-11am (M & Th)

8TH AVE (ABINGDON SQ./W. 12TH - JANE)

East

2 hr. metered parking (9am-7pm) including Sun/No parking 8am-9am (except Sun)

West

2 hr. metered parking (9am-7pm) including Sun/No parking 8am-9am (except Sun)

8TH AVE (JANE - W. 4TH)

East

No standing anytime

West

No parking 8am-11am (M & Th)

8TH AVE (W. 4TH - HORATIO)

East

2 hr. metered parking (9am-7pm) including Sun/No parking 8am-9am (except Sun)

West

2 hr. metered parking (9am-7pm) including Sun/No parking 8am-9am (except Sun)

8TH AVE (HORATIO - 13TH)

East

No standing anytime

West

2 hr. metered parking (9am-7pm) including Sun/No parking 8am-9am (except Sun)

8TH AVE (13TH - GREENWICH AVE)

East

No standing anytime

West

1 hr. metered parking (9am-7pm) including Sun/No parking 8am-9am (except Sun)

8TH AVE (GREENWICH AVE - 14TH)

East

No standing anytime

West

1 hr. metered parking (9am-7pm) including Sun/No parking 8am-9am (except Sun)

8TH AVE (14TH-15TH)

East

No Parking 7am-10am (M-F)/1 hr. metered parking 10am-7pm (M-F) & 9am-7pm (Sa & Sun)

West

No Parking 4pm-7pm (M-F)/1 metered parking 9am-4pm (M-F) & 9am-7pm (Sa & Sun)

8TH AVE (15TH-16TH)

East

No Parking 7am-10am (M-F)/1 hr. metered parking 10am-7pm (M-F) & 9am-7pm (Sa & Sun)

West

No Parking 4pm-7pm (M-F)/1 metered parking 9am-4pm (M-F) & 9am-7pm (Sa & Sun)

8TH AVE (16TH-17TH)

East

No Parking 7am-10am (M-F)/1 hr. metered parking 10am-7pm (M-F) & 9am-7pm (Sa & Sun)

West

No Parking 4pm-7pm (M-F)/1 metered parking 9am-4pm (M-F) & 9am-7pm (Sa & Sun)

8TH AVE (17TH-18TH)

East

No Parking 7am-10am (M-F)/1 hr. metered parking 10am-7pm (M-F) & 9am-7pm (Sa & Sun)

West

No Parking 4pm-7pm (M-F)/1 metered parking 9am-4pm (M-F) & 9am-7pm (Sa & Sun)

8TH AVE (18TH-19TH)

East

No Parking 7am-10am (M-F)/1 hr. metered parking 10am-7pm (M-F) & 9am-7pm (Sa & Sun)

West

No Parking 4pm-7pm (M-F)/1 metered parking 9am-4pm (M-F) & 9am-7pm (Sa & Sun)

8TH AVE (19TH-20TH)

East

No Parking 7am-10am (M-F)/1 hr. metered parking 10am-7pm (M-F) & 9am-7pm (Sa & Sun)

West

No Parking 4pm-7pm (M-F)/1 metered parking 9am-4pm (M-F) & 9am-7pm (Sa & Sun)

8TH AVE (20TH-21ST)

East

No Parking 7am-10am (M-F)/1 hr. metered parking 10am-7pm (M-F) & 9am-7pm (Sa & Sun)

West

No Parking 4pm-7pm (M-F)/1 metered parking 9am-4pm (M-F) & 9am-7pm (Sa & Sun)

8TH AVE (21ST-22ND)

East

No Parking 7am-10am (M-F)/1 hr. metered parking 10am-7pm (M-F) & 9am-7pm (Sa & Sun)

West

No Parking 4pm-7pm (M-F)/1 metered parking 9am-4pm (M-F) & 9am-7pm (Sa & Sun)

8TH AVE (22ND-23RD)

East

No Parking 7am-10am (M-F)/1 hr. metered parking 10am-7pm (M-F) & 9am-7pm (Sa & Sun)

West

No Parking 4pm-7pm (M-F)/1 metered parking 9am-4pm (M-F) & 9am-7pm (Sa & Sun)

8TH AVE (23RD-24TH)

East

No Parking 7am-10am (M-F)/1 hr. metered parking 10am-7pm (M-F) & 9am-7pm (Sa & Sun)

West

No Parking 4pm-7pm (M-F)/1 metered parking 9am-4pm (M-F) & 9am-7pm (Sa & Sun)

8TH AVE (24TH-25TH)

East

No Parking 7am-10am (M-F)/1 hr. metered parking 10am-7pm (M-F) & 9am-7pm (Sa & Sun)

West

1 hr. metered parking (8am-7pm) including Sun/No parking 7:30am-8am (except Sun)

8TH AVE (25TH-26TH)

East

No standing except trucks loading & unloading 7am-7pm (M-F)

West

1 hr. metered parking (8am-7pm) including Sun/No parking 7:30am-8am (except Sun)

8TH AVE (26TH-27TH)

East

No standing except trucks loading & unloading 7am-7pm (M-F)

West

1 hr. metered parking (8am-7pm) including Sun/No parking 7:30am-8am (except Sun)

8TH AVE (27TH-28TH)

East

No standing except trucks loading & unloading 7am-7pm (M-F)

West

1 hr. metered parking (8am-7pm) including Sun/No parking 7:30am-8am (except Sun)

8TH AVE (28TH-29TH)

East

No standing except trucks loading & unloading 7am-7pm (M-F)

West

1 hr. metered parking (8am-7pm) including Sun/No parking 7:30am-8am (except Sun)

8TH AVE (29TH-30TH)

East

No standing except trucks loading & unloading 7am-7pm (M-F)

West

1 hr. metered parking (8am-7pm) including Sun/No parking 7:30am-8am (except Sun)

9TH AVE (30TH-29TH)

East

No Standing 7am-10am (except Sun)/No parking 7am-7pm (except Sun)

West

No Standing 4pm-7pm (M-F)/No parking 7am-7pm (M-F)

9TH AVE (29TH-28TH)

East

2 hour metered parking 10am-7pm (M-F) & 9am-7pm (Sa & Sun)/No parking 8am-9am (except Sun)

West

No Standing 4pm-7pm (M-F)/No parking 7am-7pm (M-F)

9TH AVE (28TH-27TH)

East

2 hour metered parking 10am-7pm (M-F) & 9am-7pm (Sa & Sun)/No parking 8am-9am (except Sun)

West

No Standing 4pm-7pm (M-F)/No Parking 7am-4pm (M-F)

9TH AVE (27TH-26TH)

East

2 hour metered parking 10am-7pm (M-F) & 9am-7pm (Sa & Sun)/No parking 8am-9am (except Sun)

West

No Standing 4pm-7pm (M-F)/No Parking 7am-4pm (M-F)

9TH AVE (26TH-25TH)

East

2 hour metered parking 10am-7pm (M-F) & 9am-7pm (Sa & Sun)/No parking 8am-9am (except Sun)

West

No Standing 4pm-7pm (M-F)/No parking 7am-7pm (M-F)

9TH AVE (25TH-24TH)

East

No Standing 7am-10am (M-F)/1 hour metered parking 10am-7pm (M-F) & 9am-7pm (Sa & Sun)

West

No Standing 4pm-7pm (except Sun)/
1 hr. metered parking 9am-4pm (M-Sat) & 9am-7pm (Sun)

9TH AVE (24TH-23RD)

East

No Standing 7am-10am (M-F)/1 hour metered parking 10am-7pm (M-F) & 9am-7pm (Sa & Sun)

West

No Standing 4pm-7pm (except Sun)/
1 hr. metered parking 9am-4pm (M-Sat) & 9am-7pm (Sun)

9TH AVE (23RD-22ND)

East

No Parking 7:30am-8am (M-F)/1 hour metered parking 8am-7pm (including Sun)

West

No Parking 8am-8:30am (M-F)/1 hour metered parking 8:30am-7pm (including Sun)

9TH AVE (22ND-21ST)

East

No Parking 7:30am-8am (M-F)/1 hour metered parking 8am-7pm (including Sun)

West

No Parking 8am-8:30am (M-F)/1 hour metered parking 8:30am-7pm (including Sun)

9TH AVE (21ST-20TH)

East

No Parking 7:30am-8am (M-F)/1 hour metered parking 8am-10pm (including Sun)

West

No Parking 8am-8:30am (M-F)/1 hour metered parking 8:30am-7pm (including Sun)

9TH AVE (20TH-19TH)

East

No Parking 7:30am-8am (M-F)/1 hour metered parking 8am-7pm (including Sun)

West

No Parking 8am-8:30am (M-F)/1 hour metered parking 8:30am-7pm (including Sun)

9TH AVE (19TH-18TH)

East

No Parking 7:30am-8am (M-F)/1 hour metered parking 8am-7pm (including Sun)

West

No Parking 8am-8:30am (M-F)/1 hour metered parking 8:30am-7pm (including Sun)

9TH AVE (18TH-17TH)

East

No Parking 7:30am-8am (M-F)/1 hour metered parking 8am-7pm (including Sun)

West

No Parking 8am-8:30am (M-F)/1 hour metered parking 8:30am-7pm (including Sun)

9TH AVE (17TH-16TH)

East

No Parking 7:30am-8am (M-F)/1 hour metered parking 8am-7pm (including Sun)

West

No Parking 8am-8:30am (M-F)/1 hour metered parking 8:30am-7pm (including Sun)

9TH AVE (16TH-15TH)

East

No Standing 7am-10am (except Sun)

West

No standing 7am-10am & 4pm-7pm (except Sun)/No standing except trucks loading & unloading 10am-4pm (except Sun)

9TH AVE (15TH-14TH)

East

No Parking 7am-4pm (M-F)

West

No standing 7am-10am & 4pm-7pm (except Sun)/No standing except trucks loading & unloading 10zm-4pm (except Sun)

9TH AVE (14TH - 13TH)

East

No standing anytime

WEST

No parking 2am-4pm (M-F) except trucks loading & unloading "Ganesvoort market"

9TH AVE (13TH - LITTLE W. 12TH)

East

No parking 2am-4pm (M-F) except trucks loading & unloading "Ganesvoort market"

West

No parking 2am-4pm (M-F) except trucks loading & unloading "Ganesvoort market"

10TH AVE (GANESVOORT - LITTLE W.12TH)

East

No parking 2am-4pm (M-F) except trucks loading & unloading "Ganesvoort market"

West

No standing anytime

10TH AVE (LITTLE W.12TH - 13TH)

No parking 2am-4pm (M-F) except trucks loading & unloading "Ganesvoort market"

West

No standing anytime

10TH AVE(13TH - 14TH)

East

No parking 2am-4pm (M-F) except trucks loading & unloading "Ganesvoort market"

West

No standing anytime

10TH AVE (14TH-15TH)

East

No Standing 7am-10am (except Sun)

West

No Stopping any time

10TH AVE (15TH-16TH)

East

No Standing 7am-10am (except Sun)/No Parking 7am-10pm (except Sun)

West

No Standing 4pm-7pm (except Sun)/No parking 7am-7pm (except Sun)

10TH AVE (16TH-17TH) ☹

East

No standing anytime

West

No standing anytime

10TH AVE (17TH-18TH)

East

No Standing 7am-10am (except Sun)/No parking 7am-7pm (except Sun)

West

No standing anytime

10TH AVE (18TH-19TH)

East

No Standing 7am-10am (except Sun)/No parking 7am-7pm (except Sun)

West

No Standing 7am-10am (except Sun)/No parking 7am-7pm (except Sun)

10TH AVE (19TH-20TH)

East

No Standing 7am-10am (except Sun)/No parking 7am-7pm (except Sun)

West

No Standing 7am-10am (except Sun)/No parking 7am-7pm (except Sun)

10TH AVE (20TH-21ST)

East

No Standing 7am-10am (except Sun)/No parking 7am-7pm (except Sun)

West

No standing anytime

10TH AVE (21ST-22ND)

East

No Standing 7am-10am (except Sun)/No Parking 7am-4pm (except Sun)

West

No Standing 4pm-7pm (except Sun)/No Parking 7am-4pm (except Sun)

10TH AVE (22ND-23RD)

East

No Standing 7am-10am (except Sun)/
1 hour metered parking 10am-7pm (M-F) & 9am-7pm (Sa & Sun)

West

No Standing 4pm-7pm (except Sun)/No parking 7am-7pm (except Sun)

10TH AVE (23RD-24TH)

East

No Standing 7am-10am & 4pm-7pm (except Sun)/1 hour metered parking 10am-4pm (M-F) & 9am-7pm (Sa & Sun)

West

No Standing 4pm-7pm (except Sun)

10TH AVE (24TH-25TH)

East

No standing 7am-10am & 4pm-7pm (M-F)/No parking except trucks loading and unloading 10am-4pm (M-F)

West

No Standing 4pm-7pm (except Sun)/No Parking 7am-4pm (except Sun)

10TH AVE (25TH-26TH)

East

No Standing 7am-10am & 4pm-7pm (except Sun)/1 hour metered parking 10am-4pm (M-F) & 9am-7pm (Sa & Sun)

West

No Standing 4pm-7pm (except Sun)/No Parking 7am-4pm (except Sun)

10TH AVE (26TH-27TH)

East

No Standing 7am-10am & 4pm-7pm (except Sun)/1 hour metered parking 10am-4pm (M-F) & 9am-7pm (Sa & Sun)

West

No Standing 4pm-7pm (except Sun)/No Parking 7am-4pm (except Sun)

10TH AVE (27TH-28TH)

East

No standing anytime

West

No Standing 7am-10am (except Sun)/No parking 7am-7pm (except Sun)

10TH AVE (28TH-29TH)

East

No Standing 7am-10am & 4pm-7pm (except Sun)/1 hour metered parking 10am-4pm (M-F) & 9am-7pm (Sa & Sun)

West

No Standing 4pm-7pm (M-F)/No Parking other times

10TH AVE (29TH-30TH) ☹

East

No standing anytime

West

No Standing 4pm-7pm (M-F)/No Parking other times

11TH AVE (30TH-29TH)

East

No parking 8am-6pm (M-F)

West

No parking 8am-6pm (M-F)

11TH AVE (29TH-28TH)

East

No parking 8am-6pm (M-F)

West

No parking 8am-6pm (M-F)

11TH AVE (28TH-27TH)

East

No parking 8am-6pm (M-F)/No standing 11pm-6am (including Sun)

West

No parking 8am-6pm (M-F)/No standing 11pm-6am (including Sun)

11TH AVE (27TH-26TH)

East

No parking 8am-6pm (M-F)

West

No parking 8am-6pm (M-F)

11TH AVE (26TH-25TH)

East

No parking 8am-6pm (M-F)

West

No parking anytime

11TH AVE (25TH-24TH)

East

No parking anytime

West

No parking anytime

11TH AVE (24TH-23RD)

East

No parking anytime

West

No parking anytime

11TH AVE (23RD-22ND)

East

No parking anytime

West

No parking anytime

11TH AVE (22ND-21ST)

East

No Parking 10am-1pm (Tu,F)

West

No standing anytime

11TH AVE (21ST-20TH)

East

No Parking 10am-1pm (Tu,F)

West

No standing anytime

11TH AVE (20TH-19TH)

East

No Parking 10am-1pm (Tu,F)

West

No standing anytime

11TH AVE (19TH-18TH) ☺

East

No Parking 10am-1pm (Tu,F)

West

No standing anytime

11TH AVE (18TH-17TH) ☹

East

No standing anytime

West

No standing anytime

11TH AVE (17TH-16TH) ☹

East

No standing anytime

West

No standing anytime

11TH AVE (16TH-15TH) ☹

East

No standing anytime

West

No standing anytime

11TH AVE (15TH-14TH) ☹

East

No standing anytime

West

No standing anytime

ASTOR (4TH AVE-BROADWAY) ☹

North

No parking anytime

South

No parking anytime

BANK (WEST - WASHINGTON) ☺

North

No parking 11am-2pm (M & Th)

South

No parking 11am-2pm (Tu & F)

BANK (WASHINGTON - GREENWICH ST)

North

No parking 8am-6pm (M-F)

South

No parking 11am-2pm (Tu & F)

BANK (GREENWICH ST - HUDSON)

North

No parking 8am-6pm (M-F)

South

No parking 11am-2pm (Tu & F)

BANK (HUDSON - BLEECKER)

North

No parking 8am-6pm (M-F)

South

No parking 11am-2pm (Tu & F)

BANK (BLEECKER - W. 4TH) 

North

No parking 8am-11am (M & Th)

South

No parking 8am-11am (Tu & F)

BANK (W. 4TH - WAVERLY) 

North

No parking 8am-11am (M & Th)

South

No parking 8am-11am (Tu & F)

BANK (WAVERLY - GREENWICH AVE) 

North

No parking 8am-11am (M & Th)

South

No parking 8am-11am (Tu & F)

BARROW (WASHINGTON PL - W. 4TH ST) 

North

No parking anytime

South

No parking anytime

BARROW (W. 4TH ST - 7TH AVE SOUTH) ☹

North
No parking anytime

South
No parking anytime

BARROW (7TH AV SOUTH - BEDFORD) ☺

North
No parking anytime

South
No parking 8am-11am (Tu & F)

BARROW (BEDFORD - COMMERCE) ☺

North
No parking anytime

South
No parking 8am-11am (Tu & F)

BARROW (COMMERCE - HUDSON) ☺

North
No parking 8am-11am (M & Th)

South
No parking 8am-11am (Tu & F)

BARROW (HUDSON - GREENWICH ST) ☺

North
No parking 8am-6pm (M-F)

South
No parking 8am-11am (Tu & F)

BARROW (GREENWICH ST - WASHINGTON) ☺

North
No parking 11am-2pm (M & Th)/No parking 8am-6pm (M-F)

South
No standing anytime

BARROW (WASHINGTON - WEST) ☺

North
No parking 11am-2pm (M & Th)/No parking 8am-6pm (M-F)

South
No parking 11am-2pm (Tu & F)

BAXTER (GRAND - HESTER)

East

1 hr. metered parking (9am-7pm) including Sun/No parking 8am-9am (except Sun)/No parking 7am-4pm (school days)/No parking 8am-11am (Tu & F)

West

No parking 8am-6pm (M-F)

BAXTER (HESTER - CANAL)

East

No parking 8am-6pm (M-F)

West

No parking 8am-6pm (except Sun)

BAXTER (CANAL - WHITE)

East

No standing except trucks loading & unloading 7am-7pm (M-F)

West

No standing 7am-7pm (M-F) exceopt authorized vehicles

BEACH (HUDSON - VARICK)

North

No parking anytime

South

No parking anytime

BEACH (VARICK - W. BROADWAY)

North

No standing anytime (except authorized vehicles)

South

No parking 8am-6pm (M-F)

BEDFORD (HOUSTON - DOWNING)

East

No parking 8am-6pm (Tu, Th, Sat)

West

No parking 8am-11am (M & Th)

BEDFORD (DOWNING - CARMINE)

East

No parking 8am-6pm (Tu, Th, Sat)

West

No parking 8am-6pm (M, W, F)

BEDFORD (CARMINE - LEROY)

East

No parking 8am-6pm (Tu, Th, Sat)

West

No parking 8am-6pm (M, W, F)

BEDFORD (LEROY - 7TH AVE SOUTH)

East

No standing anytime

West

No standing anytime

BEDFORD (7TH AVE SOUTH - MORTON)

East

No standing anytime

West

No standing anytime

BEDFORD (MORTON - COMMERCE)

East

No standing anytime

West

No parking 8am-11am (M & Th)

BEDFORD (COMMERCE - BARROW)

East

No standing anytime

West

No parking 8am-11am (M & Th)

BEDFORD (BARROW - GROVE)

East

No standing anytime

West

No parking 8am-11am (M & Th)

BEDFORD (GROVE - CHRISTOPHER)

East

No standing anytime

West

No parking 11am-2pm (M & Th)/No parking 7am-4pm (school days) except BoE

BETHUNE (HUDSON - GREENWICH)

North

No standing anytime

South

No standing anytime

BETHUNE (GREENWICH - WASHINGTON)

North

No parking 11am-2pm (M & Th)

South

No parking 8am-6pm (M-F)

BETHUNE (WASHINGTON - WEST)

North

No parking 11am-2pm (M & Th)/No parking 8am-6pm (M-F)

South

No parking 11am-2pm (Tu & F)/No parking 8am-6pm (M-F)

BLEECKER (8TH AVE - BANK)

North

No parking anytime

South

No parking anytime

BLEECKER (BANK - W. 11TH)

North

No parking anytime

South

No parking anytime

BLEECKER (W. 11TH - PERRY)

North

No parking 8am-6pm (except Sun)

South

No standing 7am -10am & 4pm - 7pm including Sun/No parking anytime

BLEECKER (PERRY - CHARLES)

North

No parking 8am-6pm (except Sun)

South

No standing 7am -10am & 4pm - 7pm including Sun/No parking anytime

BLEECKER (CHARLES - W. 10TH)

North

No standing anytime

South

No standing 7am -10am & 4pm - 7pm including Sun/No parking anytime

BLEECKER (W. 10TH - CHRISTOPHER)

East

No standing 7am-10am & 4pm-7pm (except Sun)/No parking except trucks loading and unloading 10am-4pm (except Sun)

West

1 hr. metered parking (9am-10pm) including Sun/No parking 8am-9am (except Sun)

BLEECKER (CHRISTOPHER - GROVE)

East

No standing 7am-10am & 4pm-7pm including Sun/No parking anytime

West

1 hr. metered parking (9am-7pm) including Sun/No parking 8am-9am (except Sun)

BLEECKER (GROVE - 7TH AVE SOUTH)

East

No standing 7am-10am & 4pm-7pm including Sun/No parking anytime

West

No parking 8am-6pm (except Sun)

BLEECKER (7TH AVE SOUTH - JONES)

East

No parking anytime

West

No parking 8am-6pm (M-F)

BLEECKER (JONES - MORTON)

East

No parking anytime

West

No parking 8am-6pm (M-F)

BLEECKER (MORTON - CORNELIA)

East

No parking anytime

West

No parking 8am-6pm (M-F)

BLEECKER (CORNELIA - LEROY)

East

No parking anytime

West

No parking 8am-6pm (M-F)

BLEECKER (LEROY - CARMINE)

East

No parking anytime

West

No parking 8am-6pm (M-F)

BLEECKER (CARMINE - 6TH)

East

No parking anytime

West

No parking 8am-6pm (M-F)

BLEECKER (6TH - MACDOUGAL)

North

No parking 6am-6pm (M-F)/No standing 6am-6pm including Sun

South

No parking 6am-6pm including Sun/No standing 6am-6pm including Sun

BLEECKER (MACDOUGAL - SULLIVAN)

North

No parking 6am-6pm (M-F)/No standing 6am-6pm including Sun

South

No parking 6am-6pm including Sun/No standing 6am-6pm including Sun

BLEECKER (SULLIVAN - THOMPSON)

North

No parking 6am-6pm including Sun/No standing 6am-6pm including Sun

South

No parking 6am-6pm including Sun/No standing 6am-6pm including Sun

BLEECKER (THOMPSON - LAGUARDIA)

North

No parking 6am-6pm (M-F)/No standing 6am-6pm including Sun

South

No parking 6am-6pm including Sun/No standing 6am-6pm including Sun

BLEECKER (LAGUARDIA - MERCER)

North

No parking 8am-11am (M & Th)

South

No parking 8am-11am (Tu & F)

BLEECKER (MERCER - BROADWAY)

North

No parking 8am-11am (M & Th)

South

No parking 8am-6pm (Tu, F)

BLEECKER (BROADWAY - CROSBY)

North

No parking 8am-6pm (M-F)

South

No parking 8am-6pm (M-F)

BLEECKER (CROSBY - LAFAYETTE)

North

No parking 8am-6pm (M-F)

South

No parking 7am-6pm (except Sun)

BOND (BROADWAY - SHINBONE ALLEY)

North

No parking 8am-6pm (M-F)

South

No parking 8am-6pm (M-F)

BOND (SHINBONE ALLEY - LAFAYETTE)

North

No parking 8am-6pm (M-F)

South

No parking 8am-6pm (M-F)

BROADWAY (30TH-29TH)

East

No standing except trucks loading & unloading 8am-6pm (except Sun)

West

No standing except trucks loading & unloading 8am-6pm (except Sun)

BROADWAY (29TH-28TH)

East

No standing except trucks loading & unloading 8am-6pm (except Sun)

West

No standing except trucks loading & unloading 8am-6pm (except Sun)

BROADWAY (28TH-27TH)

East

No standing except trucks loading & unloading 8am-6pm (except Sun)

West

No standing except trucks loading & unloading 8am-6pm (except Sun)

BROADWAY (27TH-26TH)

East

No standing except trucks loading & unloading 8am-6pm (except Sun)

West

No standing except trucks loading & unloading 8am-6pm (except Sun)

BROADWAY (26TH-25TH)

East

No parking 8am-6pm (M-F)

West

No parking 8am-6pm (M-F)

BROADWAY (25TH-24TH) ☹

East

No standing anytime

West

No standing anytime

BROADWAY (24TH-23RD) ☹

East

No standing anytime

West

No standing anytime

BROADWAY (8TH - ASTOR) ☹

North

No standing except trucks loading & unloading/No standing 4pm-7pm including Sun

South

No standing except trucks loading & unloading

BROADWAY (ASTOR - WAVERLY PL) ☹

North

No standing except trucks loading & unloading/No standing 4pm-7pm including Sun

South

No standing except trucks loading & unloading

BROADWAY (WAVERLY PL - WASHINGTON PL) ☹

North

No standing except trucks loading & unloading/No standing 4pm-7pm including Sun

South

No standing except trucks loading & unloading

BROADWAY (WASHINGTON PL - 4TH ST) ☹

North

No standing except trucks loading & unloading/No standing 4pm-7pm including Sun

South

No standing except trucks loading & unloading

BROADWAY (4TH ST - 3RD ST) ☹

North

No standing except trucks loading & unloading/No standing 4pm-7pm including Sun

South

No standing except trucks loading & unloading

BROADWAY (3RD ST - BOND) ☹

North

No standing except trucks loading & unloading/No standing 4pm-7pm including Sun

South

No standing except trucks loading & unloading

BROADWAY (BOND - BLEECKER) ☹

North

No standing except trucks loading & unloading/No standing 4pm-7pm including Sun

South

No standing except trucks loading & unloading

BROADWAY (BLEECKER - HOUSTON) ☹

North

No standing except trucks loading & unloading/No standing 4pm-7pm including Sun

South

No standing except trucks loading & unloading

BROADWAY (HOUSTON - PRINCE)

North

No standing except trucks loading & unloading 7am-4pm (M-F)/No standing 4pm-7pm (M-F)

South

No standing except trucks loading & unloading 7am-7pm (M-F)

BROADWAY (PRINCE - SPRING)

North

No standing except trucks loading & unloading 7am-4pm (M-F)/No standing 4pm-7pm (M-F)

South

No standing except trucks loading & unloading 7am-7pm (M-F)

BROADWAY (SPRING - BROOME)

North

No standing except trucks loading & unloading 7am-4pm (M-F)/No standing 4pm-7pm (M-F)

South

No standing except trucks loading & unloading 7am-7pm (M-F)

BROADWAY (BROOME - GRAND)

North

No standing except trucks loading & unloading 7am-4pm (M-F)/No standing 4pm-7pm (M-F)

South

No standing except trucks loading & unloading 7am-7pm (M-F)

BROADWAY (GRAND - HOWARD)

East

No standing except trucks loading & unloading 7am-4pm (M-F)/No standing 4pm-7pm (M-F)

West

No standing except trucks loading & unloading 7am-4pm (M-F)/No standing 4pm-7pm (M-F)

BROADWAY (HOWARD - CANAL)

East

No standing except trucks loading & unloading 7am-4pm (M-F)/No standing 4pm-7pm (M-F)

West

No standing anytime

BROADWAY (CANAL - WALKER)

East

No standing except trucks loading & unloading 7am-7pm (except Sun)/No parking 2am-6am (Tu, F)

West

No parking anytime

BROADWAY (WALKER - WHITE)

East

No standing except trucks loading & unloading 7am-7pm (except Sun)/No parking 2am-6am (Tu, F)

West

No standing except trucks loading & unloading 7am-4pm (M-F)/No standing 4pm-7pm (M-F)/No parking 2am-6am (M, Th)

BROOME (CENTRE - LAFAYETTE)

North

1 hr. metered parking (9am-7pm) including Sun/No parking 8am-9am (except Sun)

South

No parking 8am-6pm (except Sun)

BROOME (LAFAYETTE - CROSBY)

North

No parking 7am-7pm (except Sun)

South

No parking 8am-6pm (M-F)

BROOME (CROSBY - BROADWAY)

North

No parking 8am-6pm (M-F)

South

No parking 8am-6pm (M-F)

BROOME (BROADWAY - MERCER)

North

No parking 8am-6pm (M-F)

South

No parking 8am-6pm (M-F)

BROOME (MERCER - GREENE)

North

No parking 8am-6pm (M-F)

South

No parking 8am-6pm (M-F)

BROOME (GREENE - WOOSTER)

North

No parking 8am-6pm (M-F)

South

No parking 8am-6pm (M-F)

BROOME (WOOSTER - W. BROADWAY)

North

No parking 8am-6pm (M-F)

South

No parking 8am-6pm (M-F)

BROOME (W. BROADWAY - THOMPSON)

North

No parking 8am-7pm (M-F)/No standing 4pm-7pm (M-F)

South

No parking anytime

BROOME (THOMPSON - SULLIVAN)

North

No parking 8am-7pm (M-F)/No standing 4pm-7pm (M-F)

South

No parking 7am - 4pm (M-F)/No standing 4pm-7pm (M-F)/No standing 10pm-7am including Sun

BROOME (SULLIVAN - 6TH)

North

No parking 8am-7pm (M-F)/No standing 4pm-7pm (M-F)

South

No parking 7am - 4pm (M-F)/No standing 4pm-7pm (M-F)/No standing 10pm-7am including Sun

BROOME (6TH - VARICK)

North

No parking 8am-6pm (M-F)

South

No parking 7am - 4pm (M-F)/No standing 4pm-7pm (M-F)

BROOME (VARICK - HUDSON) ☹

North

No parking anytime

South

No parking anytime

CANAL (BAXTER - CENTRE)

North

No standing 7am-10am & 4pm-7pm including Sun - other times - No standing except trucks loading & unloading

South

No standing 7am-10am & 4pm-7pm including Sun - other times - No standing except trucks loading & unloading

CANAL (CENTRE - LAFAYETTE)

North

No standing 7am-10am & 4pm-7pm including Sun - other times - No standing except trucks loading & unloading

South

No standing 7am-10am & 4pm-7pm including Sun - other times - No standing except trucks loading & unloading

CANAL (LAFAYETTE - BROADWAY)

North

No standing 7am-10am & 4pm-7pm (including Sun) - other times - No standing except trucks loading & unloading

South

No standing 7am-10am & 4pm-7pm (including Sun) - other times - No standing except trucks loading & unloading

CANAL (BROADWAY - MERCER)

North

No standing 7am-10am & 4pm-7pm (including Sun) - other times - No standing except trucks loading & unloading

South

No standing 7am-3pm (except Sun) except trucks loading and unloading/No standing 3pm-7pm (except Sun)

CANAL (MERCER - GREENE)

North

No standing 7am-1pm (except Sun) except trucks loading and unloading/No standing 1pm-7pm including Sun

South

No standing 7am-3pm (except Sun) except trucks loading and unloading/No standing 3pm-7pm (except Sun)

CANAL (GREENE - CHURCH)

North

No standing 7am-1pm (except Sun) except trucks loading and unloading/No standing 1pm-7pm including Sun

South

No standing 7am-3pm (except Sun) except trucks loading and unloading/No standing 3pm-7pm (except Sun)

CANAL (CHURCH - WOOSTER)

North

No standing 7am-1pm (except Sun) except trucks loading and unloading/No standing 1pm-7pm including Sun

South

No standing 7am-3pm (except Sun) except trucks loading and unloading/No standing 3pm-7pm (except Sun)

CANAL (WOOSTER - W. BROADWAY)

North

No standing 7am-1pm (except Sun) except trucks loading and unloading/No standing 1pm-7pm including Sun

South

No standing 7am-3pm (except Sun) except trucks loading and unloading/No standing 3pm-7pm (except Sun)

CANAL (W. BROADWAY - THOMPSON)

North

No standing 7am-1pm (except Sun) except trucks loading and unloading/No standing 1pm-7pm including Sun

South

No standing 7am-3pm (except Sun) except trucks loading and unloading/No standing 3pm-7pm (except Sun)

CANAL (THOMPSON - 6TH)

North

No standing 7am-1pm (except Sun) except trucks loading and unloading/No standing 1pm-7pm including Sun

South

No standing 7am-3pm (except Sun) except trucks loading and unloading/No standing 3pm-7pm (except Sun)

CANAL (6TH - VARICK)

North

No standing 7am-1pm (except Sun) except trucks loading and unloading/No standing 1pm-7pm including Sun

South

No standing anytime

CANAL (VARICK - GRAND) ☹

North

No standing anytime

South

No standing anytime

CANAL (GRAND - HOLLAND TUNNEL PLAZA)

North

No standing anytime

South

No standing anytime

CANAL (HOLLAND TUNNEL PLAZA - HUDSON)

North

No standing anytime

South

No standing anytime

CANAL (HUDSON - RENWICK)

North

No standing anytime

South

No standing anytime

CANAL (RENWICK - GREENWICH)

North

No standing anytime

South

No standing anytime

CANAL (GREENWICH - WASHINGTON)

North

No standing anytime

South

No standing anytime

CANAL (WASHINGTON - WEST)

North

No standing anytime

South

No standing anytime

CARMINE (VARICK - BEDFORD)

North

No parking 8am-11am (M & Th)

South

1 hr. metered parking (9am-7pm) including Sun/No parking 8am-9am (except Sun)

CARMINE (BEDFORD - BLEECKER)

North

No parking 8am-11am (M & Th)

South

1 hr. metered parking (9am-7pm) including Sun/No parking 8am-9am (except Sun)

CARMINE (BLEECKER - 6TH)

North

1 hr. metered parking (9am-7pm) including Sun/No parking 8am-9am (except Sun)

South

No parking anytime

CENTRE (CANAL - HOWARD)

East

No standing anytime

West

1 hr. metered parking (9am-7pm) including Sun/No parking 8am-9am (except Sun)

CENTRE (WALKER - CANAL)

East

No standing anytime

West

No standing except trucks loading & unloading 7am-7pm (M-F)/No parking 2am-6am (M, Th)

CENTRE (CANAL - HESTER)

East

No parking 7am-4pm (except Sun)/No standing 4pm-7pm (except Sun)

West

1 hr. metered parking (9am-7pm) including Sun/No parking 8am-9am (except Sun)

CENTRE (HESTER - HOWARD)

East

No parking 7am-4pm (except Sun)/No standing 4pm-7pm (except Sun)

West

1 hr. metered parking (9am-7pm) including Sun/No parking 8am-9am (except Sun)

CENTRE (HOWARD - GRAND)

East

No parking 7am-4pm (except Sun)/No standing 4pm-7pm (except Sun)

West

No parking 7am-6pm (M-F)

CENTRE (GRAND - BROOME)

East

No standing except trucks loading & unloading 7am-4pm (except Sun)/No standing 4pm-7pm (except Sun)

West

No standing except trucks loading & unloading 8am-6pm (M-F)

CHARLES LANE (WASHINGTON - WEST)

North

No parking anytime

South

No parking anytime

CHARLES ST (WAVERLY - 7TH AVE S.)

North

No parking anytime

South

No parking 8am-11am (Tu & F)

CHARLES ST (7TH AVE S. - W. 4TH ST)

North

No parking anytime

South

No parking 8am-11am (Tu & F)

CHARLES ST (W. 4TH ST - BLEECKER)

North

No parking anytime

South

No parking 8am-11am (Tu & F)

CHARLES ST (BLEECKER - HUDSON)

North

No parking anytime

South

No parking 8am-6pm (M-F)

CHARLES ST (HUDSON - GREENWICH ST)

North

No parking 11am-2pm (M & Th)

South

No parking 11am-2pm (Tu & F)

CHARLES ST (GREENWICH ST - WASHINGTON)

North

No parking anytime

South

No parking 11am-2pm (Tu & F)

CHARLES ST (WASHINGTON - WEST)

North

No parking 8am-6pm (M-F)/No parking 11am-2pm (M & Th)

South

No parking 8am-6pm (M-F)

CHARLTON (6TH - VARICK)

North

No parking 8am-11am (M & Th)

South

No parking 8am-6pm (M-F)/No parking 8am-6pm (M-F) except authorized vehicles

CHARLTON (VARICK - HUDSON)

North

No parking 8am-5pm (M-F)

South

No parking 8am-5pm (M-F)

CHARLTON (HUDSON - GREENWICH ST)

North

No parking 8am-5pm (M-F)

South

No parking 8am-5pm (M-F)

CHRISTOPHER (WAVERLY - W. 4TH)

East

1 hr. metered parking (9am-10pm) including Sun/No parking 8am-9am (except Sun)

West

No parking anytime

CHRISTOPHER (W. 4TH - 7TH AV SOUTH)

East

No parking anytime

West

No parking anytime

CHRISTOPHER (GREENWICH AVE - GAY)

North

No parking anytime

South

No parking 8am-11am (Tu & F)

CHRISTOPHER (GAY - WAVERLY PL.)

North

No parking anytime

South

No parking 8am-11am (Tu & F)

CHRISTOPHER (WAVERLY PL. - 7TH AVE SOUTH)

North

No parking anytime

South

No parking 8am-11am (Tu & F)

CHRISTOPHER (7TH AVE SOUTH - BLEECKER)

North

No parking anytime

South

1 hr. metered parking (9am-10pm) including Sun/No parking 8am-9am (except Sun)

CHRISTOPHER (BLEECKER - BEDFORD)

North

No parking anytime

South

No parking 8am-11am (except Sun)

CHRISTOPHER (BEDFORD - HUDSON)

North

No parking anytime

South

No parking anytime

CHRISTOPHER (HUDSON - GREENWICH ST)

North

No parking anytime

South

No parking 11am-2pm (Tu & F)

CHRISTOPHER (GREENWICH ST - WASHINGTON) ☺

East

No parking 11am-2pm (Tu & F)

West

No parking anytime

CHRISTOPHER (WASHINGTON - WEST) ☺

East

No parking 11am-2pm (Tu & F)

West

No parking 8am-6pm (M-F)

CHURCH (FRANKLIN - WHITE)

East

1 hr. metered parking (8am-7pm) including Sun/No parking 2am-6am (Tu, F)

West

No parking 2am-6am (M, Th)

CHURCH (WHITE - WALKER)

East

1 hr. metered parking (8am-7pm) including Sun/No parking 2am-6am (Tu, F)

West

1 hr. metered parking (8am-7pm) including Sun/No parking 2am-6am (Tu, Th)

CHURCH (WALKER - LISPENARD)

East

1 hr. metered parking (8am-7pm) including Sun/No parking 2am-6am (Tu, F)/No parking 8am-6pm (M-F)

West

1 hr. metered parking (8am-7pm) including Sun/No parking 2am-6am (Tu, Th)

CHURCH (LISPENARD - CANAL)

East

1 hr. metered parking (8am-7pm) including Sun/No parking 2am-6am (Tu, F)

West

No standing except trucks loading & unloading 7am-7pm (M-F)/No parking 2am-6am (M, Th)

CLARKSON (WEST - WASHINGTON)

North

No parking 8am-6pm (M-F)

South

No parking 8am-6pm (M-F)

CLARKSON (WASHINGTON - GREENWICH ST)

North

No parking 8am-6pm (M-F)

South

No parking 8am-6pm (M-F)

CLARKSON (GREENWICH ST - HUDSON)

North

No standing except trucks loading & unloading 8am-4pm (M-F)

South

No standing except trucks loading & unloading 8am-4pm (M-F)

CLARKSON (HUDSON - VARICK)

North

No parking 8am-11am (M & Th)/No standing except trucks loading & unloading 8am-6pm (except Sun)

South

No parking 8am-6pm (M-F)/No parking 7am 4pm (school days)

CLEVELAND PL (BROOME - KENMARE)

East

No standing anytime

West

No standing except trucks loading & unloading 7am-4pm (except Sun)/No standing 4pm-7pm (except Sun)

CLEVELAND PL (KENMARE - SPRING)

East

No parking anytime

West

No standing anytime

COLLISTER (BEACH - HUBERT)

East

No standing anytime

West

No standing anytime

COLLISTER (HUBERT - LAIGHT)

East

No standing anytime

West

No standing anytime

CORNELIA (BLEECKER - W. 4TH)

North

No parking anytime

South

1 hr. metered parking (9am-10pm) including Sun/No parking 8am-9am (except Sun)

CORTLAND ALLEY (WHITE - WALKER) ☹

East

No parking anytime

West

No parking anytime

CORTLAND ALLEY (WALKER - CANAL) ☹

East

No parking anytime

West

No parking anytime

CROSBY (HOWARD - GRAND)

East

No parking 8am-6pm (M-F)

West

No parking 8am-6pm (M-F)

CROSBY (GRAND - BROOME)

East

No parking 8am-6pm (M-F)

West

No parking 8am-6pm (M-F)

CROSBY (BROOME - SPRING)

East

No parking 8am-6pm (M-F)

West

No parking 8am-6pm (M-F)

CROSBY (SPRING - PRINCE)

East

No standing except trucks loading & unloading 8am-6pm (M-F)

West

No standing except trucks loading & unloading 8am-6pm (M-F)

CROSBY (PRINCE - HOUSTON)

East

No parking 8am-6pm (M-F)

West

No parking 8am-6pm (M-F)

CROSBY (HOUSTON - BLEECKER)

East

No parking 8am-6pm (M-F)

West

No parking 8am-6pm (M-F)

DEBROSSES (HUDSON - GREENWICH)

North

No standing except trucks loading & unloading 8am-6pm (M-F)

South

No standing except trucks loading & unloading 8am-6pm (M-F)

DEBROSSES (GREENWICH - WASHINGTON)

North

No parking 8am-6pm (M-F)

South

No parking 8am-6pm (M-F)

DEBROSSES (WASHINGTON - WEST)

North

No parking 7am-6pm (M-F)

South

No parking 7am-6pm (M-F)

DOMINICK (6TH - VARICK)

North

No parking 8am-6pm (M-F)

South

No parking 7am-4pm (school days) except Board of Ed

DOMINICK (VARICK - HUDSON)

North

No standing except trucks loading & unloading 7am-7pm (including Sun)

South

No standing except trucks loading & unloading 7am-7pm (M-F)

DOWNING (6TH - BEDFORD)

North

No standing anytime

South

No parking 8am-6pm (M-F)

DOWNING (BEDFORD - VARICK) ☺

North

No standing anytime

South

No parking 8am-11am (Tu & F)

ERICCSON PL (6TH - VARICK) ☹

North

No parking anytime

South

No parking anytime

ERICCSON PL (VARICK - HUDSON)

North

No standing anytime

South

No standing except trucks loading & unloading 7am-7pm (M-F)

GANESVOORT (4TH ST - HUDSON)

North

No parking 8am-6pm (M-F)

South

No parking 8am-6pm (except Sun)

GANESVOORT (HUDSON - GREENWICH ST)

North

No parking 2am-4pm (M-F) except trucks loading & unloading “Ganesvoort market”

South

No parking 2am-4pm (M-F) except trucks loading & unloading “Ganesvoort market”

GANESVOORT (GREENWICH ST - WASHINGTON)

North

No parking 2am-4pm (M-F) except trucks loading & unloading “Ganesvoort market”

South

No parking 2am-4pm (M-F) except trucks loading & unloading “Ganesvoort market”

GANESVOORT (WASHINGTON - 10TH AVE/WEST)

North

No parking 2am-4pm (M-F) except trucks loading & unloading "Ganesvoort market"

South

No parking 2am-4pm (M-F) except trucks loading & unloading "Ganesvoort market"

GAY (WAVERLY - CHRISTOPHER) ☹

East

No parking anytime

West

No parking anytime

GRAND (VARICK - 6TH)

North

No parking 8am-6pm (except Sun)

South

No parking 8am-6pm (M-F)

GRAND (6TH - THOMPSON)

North

1 hr. metered parking (9am-7pm) including Sun/No parking 8am-9am (except Sun)

South

No parking 8am-6pm (M-F)

GRAND (THOMPSON - W. BROADWAY)

North

1 hr. metered parking (9am-7pm) including Sun/No parking 8am-9am (except Sun)/No standing 11pm-7am including Sun

South

No parking 8am-6pm (M-F)/No standing 11pm-7am including Sun

GRAND (W. BROADWAY - WOOSTER)

North

No parking 8am-6pm (M-F)/No standing 11pm-7am including Sun

South

No parking 8am-6pm (M-F)/No standing 11pm-7am including Sun

GRAND (WOOSTER - GREENE)

North

No parking 8am-6pm (M-F)

South

No parking 8am-6pm (M-F)

GRAND (GREENE - MERCER)

North

No standing except trucks loading & unloading 7am-7pm (M-F)

South

No parking 8am-6pm (M-F)

GRAND (MERCER - BROADWAY)

North

No standing anytime

South

No parking 8am-6pm (M-F)

GRAND (BROADWAY - CROSBY)

North

1 hr. metered parking (9am-7pm) including Sun/No parking 8am-9am (except Sun)

South

No parking 8am-6pm (M-F)

GRAND (CROSBY - LAFAYETTE)

North

No standing except trucks loading & unloading 8am-6pm (M-F)

South

No standing except trucks loading & unloading 8am-6pm (M-F)

GRAND (LAFAYETTE - CENTRE)

North

1 hr. metered parking (9am-7pm) including Sun/No parking 8am-9am (except Sun)

South

No parking 8am-6pm (M-F)

GRAND (CENTRE - BAXTER)

North

No parking anytime

South

No parking 8am-6pm (M-F)

GREAT JONES (LAFAYETTE - BROADWAY) ☺

North

No parking 8am-6pm (except Sun)

South

No parking 8am-11am (Tu, Th)

GREENE (CANAL - GRAND)

East

No parking 8am-6pm (M-F)/No standing 11am - midnite (Sat, Sun)

West

No parking 8am-6pm (M-F)

GREENE (GRAND - BROOME)

East

No parking 8am-6pm (M-F)/No standing 11am - midnite (Sat, Sun)

West

No parking 8am-6pm (M-F)

GREENE (BROOME - SPRING)

East

No parking 8am-6pm (M-F)/No standing 11am - midnite (Sat, Sun)

West

No parking 8am-6pm (M-F)

GREENE (SPRING - PRINCE)

East

No parking 8am-6pm (M-F)/No standing 11am - midnite (Sat, Sun)

West

No parking 8am-6pm (M-F)/No standing 11pm-7am including Sun

GREENE (PRINCE - HOUSTON)

East

No parking 8am-6pm (M-F)/No standing 11am - midnite (Sat, Sun)/No standing 7am-7pm (M-F) except authorized vehicles

West

No parking 8am-6pm (M-F)

GREENE (4TH ST - WASHINGTON PL)

East

No parking 8am-6pm (M-F)

West

No parking 8am-6pm (M-F)

GREENE (WASHINGTON PL - WAVERLY PL)

East

No parking 8am-6pm (M-F)

West

No parking 8am-6pm (M-F)

GREENE (WASHINGTON PL - 8TH ST)

East

No parking 8am-6pm (except Sun)

West

No parking 8am-6pm (M-F)/1 hr. metered parking (9am-10pm) including Sun/No parking 8am-9am (except Sun)

GREENWICH AVE (6TH - CHRISTOPHER)

North

No standing anytime

South

1 hr. metered parking (9am-7pm) including Sun/No parking 8am-9am (except Sun)

GREENWICH AVE (CHRISTOPHER - 10TH)

North

No parking 8am-6pm (M-F)

South

1 hr. metered parking (9am-7pm) including Sun/No parking 8am-9am (except Sun)

GREENWICH AVE (10TH - CHARLES)

North

No parking 8am-6pm (except Sun)

South

1 hr. metered parking (9am-7pm) including Sun/No parking 8am-9am (except Sun)

GREENWICH AVE (CHARLES - PERRY)

North

No parking 8am-6pm (M-F)

South

1 hr. metered parking (9am-7pm) including Sun/No parking 8am-9am (except Sun)

GREENWICH AVE (PERRY - 7TH AVE SOUTH)

North

No parking 8am-6pm (M-F)

South

1 hr. metered parking (9am-7pm) including Sun/No parking 8am-9am (except Sun)

GREENWICH AVE (7TH AVE SOUTH - BANK)

North

No parking 8am-6pm (M-F)

South

1 hr. metered parking (9am-7pm) including Sun/No parking 8am-9am (except Sun)

GREENWICH AVE (BANK - W. 12TH)

North

No parking 8am-6pm (M-F)

South

1 hr. metered parking (9am-7pm) including Sun/No parking 8am-9am (except Sun)

GREENWICH AVE (W. 12TH - JANE)

North

No parking 8am-6pm (M-F)

South

1 hr. metered parking (9am-7pm) including Sun/No parking 8am-9am (except Sun)

GREENWICH AVE (JANE - HORATIO)

North

No parking 8am-6pm (except Sun)

South

1 hr. metered parking (9am-7pm) including Sun/No parking 8am-9am (except Sun)

GREENWICH AVE (HORATIO - 8TH AVE)

North

1 hr. metered parking (9am-7pm) including Sun/No parking 8am-9am (except Sun)

South

No parking anytime

GREENWICH ST (CANAL - SPRING)

East

No standing except trucks loading & unloading 7am-7pm (M-F)

West

No standing except trucks loading & unloading 7am-7pm (M-F)

GREENWICH ST (SPRING - VANDAM)

East

No parking 8am-6pm (M-F)

West

No standing except trucks loading & unloading 7am-7pm (except Sun)

GREENWICH ST (VANDAM - CHARLTON)

East

No parking anytime

West

No standing except trucks loading & unloading 7am-7pm (except Sun)

GREENWICH ST (CHARLTON - KING)

East

No standing except trucks loading & unloading 7am-7pm (except Sun)

West

No standing except trucks loading & unloading 7am-7pm (except Sun)

GREENWICH ST (KING - HOUSTON)

East

No standing except trucks loading & unloading 7am-7pm (except Sun)

West

No standing except trucks loading & unloading 7am-7pm (except Sun)

GREENWICH ST (HOUSTON - CLARKSON)

East

No parking 11am-12:30pm (Tu & F)

West

No parking anytime

GREENWICH ST (CLARKSON - LEROY)

East

No parking 8am-6pm (M-F)

West

No parking 11am-12:30pm (M & Th)

GREENWICH ST (LEROY - MORTON)

East

No parking 8am-6pm (M-F)

West

No parking 8am-5pm (except Sun)

GREENWICH ST (MORTON - BARROW)

East

No parking 8am-6pm (M-F)

West

No parking 8am-6pm (M-F)

GREENWICH ST (BARROW - CHRISTOPHER)

East

No standing anytime

West

No parking 11am-2pm (M & Th)

GREENWICH ST (CHRISTOPHER - 10TH ST) ☺

East

No parking 11am-2pm (Tu & F)

West

No parking 11am-2pm (M & Th)

GREENWICH ST (10TH ST - CHARLES) ☺

East

No parking 11am-2pm (Tu & F)/No parking 8am-6pm (M-F)

West

No parking 11am-2pm (M & Th)

GREENWICH ST (CHARLES - PERRY) ☺

East

No parking 11am-2pm (Tu & F)

West

No parking 11am-2pm (M & Th)

GREENWICH ST (PERRY - W. 11TH ST) ☺

East

No parking 11am-2pm (Tu & F)

West

No parking 11am-2pm (M & Th)

GREENWICH ST (W. 11TH ST - BANK) ☺

East

No parking 11am-2pm (Tu & F)

West

No parking 11am-2pm (M & Th)

GREENWICH ST (BANK - BETHUNE) ☺

East

No parking 11am-2pm (Tu & F)

West

No parking 11am-2pm (M & Th)

GREENWICH ST (BETHUNE - W. 12TH ST) ☺

East

No parking 11am-2pm (Tu & F)

West

No parking 8am-6pm (M-F)

GREENWICH ST (W. 12TH ST - JANE)

East

No parking 8am-6pm (M-F)

West

No parking 8am-6pm (M-F)

GREENWICH ST (JANE - HORATIO)

East

No parking 5am-4pm (M-F)

West

No parking 5am-4pm (M-F)

GREENWICH ST (HORATIO - GANESVOORT)

East

No parking 5am-4pm (M-F)

West

No parking 5am-4pm (M-F)

GREENWICH ST (CANAL - WATTS)

East

No parking 8am-6pm (M-F)

West

No parking 8am-6pm (M-F)

GREENWICH ST (WATTS - DEBROSSES)

East

No parking 8am-6pm (M-F)

West

No parking 8am-6pm (M-F)

GREENWICH ST (DEBROSSES - VESTRY)

East

No parking 8am-6pm (M-F)

West

No parking 8am-6pm (M-F)

GREENWICH ST (VESTRY - LAIGHT)

East

No parking 8am-6pm (M-F)

West

No parking 8am-6pm (M-F)

GREENWICH ST (LAIGHT - HUBERT)

East

No parking anytime

West

No parking anytime

GREENWICH ST (HUBERT - BEACH)

East

No standing except trucks loading & unloading 7am-7pm (except Sun)

West

No standing anytime

GREENWICH ST (BEACH - N. MOORE)

East

No parking 8:30am-10am (Tu & F)

West

No standing anytime

GREENWICH ST (N. MOORE - FRANKLIN)

East

No parking 8am-6pm (M-F)

West

No standing anytime

GROVE (HUDSON - BEDFORD)

North

No standing anytime

South

No parking 8am-6pm (M-F)

GROVE (BEDFORD - BLEECKER)

North

No parking 8am-11am (M & Th)

South

No parking 8am-11am (Tu & F)

GROVE (BLEECKER - 7TH AVE SOUTH)

North

1 hr. metered parking (9am-10pm) including Sun/No parking 8am-9am (except Sun)

South

No parking 8am-6pm (except Sun)

HORATIO (WEST - WASHINGTON)

North

No parking 11am-2pm (M & Th)

South

No parking anytime

HORATIO (WASHINGTON - GREENWICH ST)

North

No parking 8am-6pm (M-F)

South

No parking 8am-6pm (except Sun)/No parking anytime

HORATIO (GREENWICH ST - HUDSON)

North

No parking 8am-6pm (M-F)

South

No parking 11am-2pm (Tu & F)

HORATIO (HUDSON - W. 4TH/8TH AVE)

North

No parking 11am-2pm (M & Th)

South

No parking 11am-2pm (Tu & F)

HORATIO (W. 4TH/8TH AVE - GREENWICH AVE)

North

No parking anytime

South

No parking 8am-6pm (except Sun)

HOUSTON (MULBERRY - LAFAYETTE)

North

No standing anytime

South

No standing anytime

HOUSTON (LAFAYETTE - CROSBY)

North

No standing anytime

South

No standing anytime

HOUSTON (CROSBY - BROADWAY)

North

No standing anytime

South

No standing anytime

HOUSTON (BROADWAY - MERCER)

North

No standing anytime

South

No standing anytime

HOUSTON (MERCER -GREENE)

North

No parking 8am-6pm (M-F)

South

No parking 8am-6pm (M-F)

HOUSTON (GREENE - WOOSTER)

North

No parking 8am-6pm (M-F)

South

No parking 8am-6pm (M-F)

HOUSTON (WOOSTER - LAGUARDIA)

North

No standing anytime

South

No standing anytime

HOUSTON (LAGUARDIA - THOMPSON)

North

No parking 8am-6pm (M-F)

South

No parking 8am-6pm (M-F)

HOUSTON (THOMPSON - SULLIVAN)

North

No parking 8am-6pm (M-F)

South

No parking 8am-6pm (M-F)

HOUSTON (SULLIVAN - MACDOUGAL)

North

No parking 8am-6pm (M-F)

South

No parking 8am-6pm (M-F)

HOUSTON (MACDOUGAL - 6TH)

North

No parking 8am-6pm (M-F)

South

No parking 8am-6pm (M-F)

HOUSTON (6TH - VARICK)

North

No parking 8am-6pm (M-F)

South

No parking 8am-6pm (except Sun)

HOUSTON (VARICK - HUDSON)

North

No parking 8am-6pm (M-F) except authorized vehicles/No parking 7am-4pm (school days)/No standing 7am-4pm (school days)

South

No standing anytime (except authorized vehicles)

HOUSTON (HUDSON - GREENWICH ST)

North

No parking 8am-6pm (M-F)

South

No parking 8am-6pm (M-F)

HOUSTON (GREENWICH ST - WASHINGTON)

North

No standing anytime

South

No parking 8am-6pm (M-F)

HOUSTON (WASHINGTON - WEST) ☹

North

No standing anytime

South

No standing anytime

HOWARD (CENTRE - LAFAYETTE)

North

No parking 8am-6pm (M-F)

South

No parking 8am-6pm (except Sun)

HOWARD (LAFAYETTE - CROSBY)

North

No standing except trucks loading & unloading 8am-6pm (M-F)

South

No parking 8am-6pm (M-F)

HOWARD (CROSBY - BROADWAY)

North

No standing except trucks loading & unloading 7am-4pm (M-F)

South

No parking 8am-6pm (M-F)

HOWARD (BROADWAY - MERCER)

North

No parking 8am-6pm (M-F)

South

No parking 8am-6pm (M-F)

HUBERT (WEST - WASHINGTON)

North

No parking 8am-6pm (M-F)

South

No parking 8am-6pm (M-F)

HUBERT (WASHINGTON - GREENWICH)

North

No parking 8am-6pm (M-F)

South

No parking 8am-6pm (M-F)

HUBERT (GREENWICH - COLLISTER)

North

No standing except trucks loading & unloading 8am-7pm (M-F)

South

No standing except trucks loading & unloading 8am-7pm (M-F)

HUBERT (COLLISTER - HUDSON)

North

No standing except trucks loading & unloading 8am-7pm (M-F)

South

No standing except trucks loading & unloading 8am-7pm (M-F)

HUDSON (14TH - 13TH)

East

No parking 2am-4pm (M-F) except trucks loading & unloading "Ganesvoort market"

West

No parking 8am-6pm (M-F)

HUDSON (13TH - GANESVOORT)

East

No parking 8am-6pm (M-F)

West

No parking anytime

HUDSON (GANESVOORT - HORATIO)

East

No parking 8am-6pm (M-F)

West

No parking 11am-2pm (M & Th)/No standing except trucks loading & unloading 7am-7pm (M-F)

HUDSON (HORATIO - JANE)

East

No parking 9am-10:30am (Tu & F)

West

No parking 9am-10:30am (M & Th)

HUDSON (JANE - W.12TH)

East

No parking 9am-10:30am (Tu & F)

West

No parking 8am-6pm (M-F)

HUDSON (W.12TH - ABINGDON SQ.)

East

No parking 8am-11am (Tu & F)/No parking 7am - 5pm (Saturdays - May - December) **Farmer's market**

West

No standing anytime

HUDSON (ABINGDON SQ. - BETHUNE) ☹

East

No standing anytime

West

No standing anytime

HUDSON (HARRISON - FRANKLIN)

East

No parking 8am-6pm (M-F)

West

1 hr. metered parking (9am-7pm) including Sun/No parking 2am-6am (Tu, F)

HUDSON (FRANKLIN - N. MOORE)

East

No parking 8am-6pm (M-F)/1 hr. metered parking (9am-7pm) including Sun/No parking 2am-6am (Tu, F)

West

No parking 2am-6am (W, Sat)

HUDSON (N. MOORE - ERICCSON PL)

East

No standing except trucks loading & unloading 7am-4pm (M-F)

West

No standing except trucks loading & unloading 7am-4pm (M-F)/No standing 4pm-7pm (M-F)

HUDSON (ERICCSON PL - HUBERT)

East

No standing anytime

West

No standing 7am-3pm (M-F) except trucks loading and unloading/No standing 3pm-7pm (M-F)

HUDSON (HUBERT - LAIGHT)

East

No standing anytime

West

No standing 7am-3pm (M-F) except trucks loading and unloading/No standing 3pm-7pm (M-F)

HUDSON (LAIGHT - VESTRY)

East

No standing anytime

West

No standing anytime

HUDSON (VESTRY - DESBROSSES)

East

No standing anytime

West

No standing 10am-3pm (M-F) except trucks loading and unloading/No standing 3pm-7pm (M-F)

HUDSON (DESBROSSES - CANAL)

East

No standing anytime

West

No standing 7am-3pm (M-F) except trucks loading and unloading/No standing 3pm-7pm (M-F)

HUDSON (CANAL - BROOME)

East

No standing except trucks loading & unloading

West

No parking 8am-6pm (M-F)

HUDSON (BROOME - DOMINICK)

East

No parking 7am-6pm (M-F)/No standing except trucks loading & unloading 7am-6pm (M-F)

West

No parking 8am-6pm (M-F)

HUDSON (DOMINICK - SPRING)

East

No parking 8am-6pm (M-F)

West

No parking 8am-6pm (M-F)

HUDSON (SPRING - VANDAM)

East

1 hr. metered parking (9am-7pm) including Sun/No parking 8am-9am (except Sun)

West

No standing anytime (except authorized vehicles)

HUDSON (VANDAM - CHARLTON)

East

No standing anytime (except authorized vehicles)

West

1 hr. metered parking (9am-7pm) including Sun/No parking 8am-9am (except Sun)

HUDSON (CHARLTON - KING)

East

1 hr. metered parking (9am-7pm) including Sun/No parking 8am-9am (except Sun)

West

1 hr. metered parking (9am-7pm) including Sun/No parking 8am-9am (except Sun)

HUDSON (KING - HOUSTON)

East

No standing 7am-7pm (M-F) except authorized vehicles (US Congress)

West

1 hr. metered parking (9am-7pm) including Sun/No parking 8am-9am (except Sun)

HUDSON (HOUSTON - CLARKSON)

East

1 hr. metered parking (9am-7pm) including Sun/No parking 8am-9am (except Sun)

West

1 hr. metered parking (9am-7pm) including Sun/No parking 8am-9am (except Sun)

HUDSON (CLARKSON - LEROY)

East

2 hr. metered parking (9am-7pm) including Sun/No parking 8am-9am (except Sun)

West

2 hr. metered parking (9am-7pm) including Sun/No parking 8am-9am (except Sun)

HUDSON (LEROY - MORTON)

East

No parking 8am-6pm (M-F)

West

2 hr. metered parking (9am-7pm) including Sun/No parking 8am-9am (except Sun)

HUDSON (MORTON - BARROW)

East

2 hr. metered parking (9am-7pm) including Sun/No parking 8am-9am (except Sun)

West

No parking 8am-6pm (M-F)

HUDSON (BARROW - GROVE)

East

2 hr. metered parking (9am-7pm) including Sun/No parking 8am-9am (except Sun)

West

No parking 8am-6pm (M-F)

HUDSON (GROVE - CHRISTOPHER)

East

2 hr. metered parking (9am-7pm) including Sun/No parking 8am-9am (except Sun)/No parking 7am-4pm (school days)

West

No parking 8am-6pm (M-F)

HUDSON (CHRISTOPHER - W. 10TH)

East

No parking 8am-6pm (M-F)

West

2 hr. metered parking (9am-7pm) including Sun/No parking 8am-9am (except Sun)

HUDSON (W. 10TH - CHARLES)

East

No parking 8am-6pm (except Sun)

West

2 hr. metered parking (9am-7pm) including Sun/No parking 8am-9am (except Sun)

HUDSON (CHARLES - PERRY)

East

2 hr. metered parking (9am-7pm) including Sun/No parking 8am-9am (except Sun)

West

No parking 8am-6pm (M-F)

HUDSON (PERRY - 11TH)

East

2 hr. metered parking (9am-7pm) including Sun/No parking 8am-9am (except Sun)

West

2 hr. metered parking (9am-7pm) including Sun/No parking 8am-9am (except Sun)

HUDSON (11TH - BANK)

East

No parking 8am-6pm (M-F)

West

2 hr. metered parking (9am-7pm) including Sun/No parking 8am-9am (except Sun)

HUDSON (BANK - BETHUNE) ☹

East

No standing anytime

West

No standing anytime

JANE (GREENWICH AVE - W. 4TH ST/8TH AVE)

North

No parking anytime

South

No parking 8am-11am (Tu & F)

JANE (W. 4TH ST/8TH AVE - HUDSON)

North

No parking anytime

South

No parking 11am-2pm (Tu & F)

JANE (HUDSON - GREENWICH ST)

North

No parking anytime

South

No parking 11am-2pm (Tu & F)

JANE (GREENWICH ST - WASHINGTON)

North

No parking anytime

South

No parking 11am-2pm (Tu & F)

JANE (WASHINGTON - WEST)

North

No parking anytime

South

No parking 11am-2pm (Tu & F)

JERSEY (CROSBY - LAFAYETTE)

North

No parking anytime

South

No parking anytime

JERSEY (LAFAYETTE - MULBERRY)

North

No parking anytime

South

No parking anytime

JONES (4TH ST - BLEECKER)

East

No parking 8am-6pm (M-F)

West

1 hr. metered parking (9am-10pm) including Sun/No parking 8am-9am (except Sun)

KING (GREENWICH - HUDSON)

North

No parking 8am-6pm (M-F)

South

No standing except trucks loading & unloading 7am-7pm (except Sun)

KING (HUDSON - VARICK)

North

No parking 8am-5pm (M-F)

South

No standing anytime (except authorized vehicles)

KING (VARICK - 6TH)

North

2 hr. metered parking (9am-7pm) including Sun/No parking 8am-9am (except Sun)/No parking 8am-6pm (M-F)/No parking 8am-6pm (M-F) except authorized vehicles

South

No parking 8am-11am (Tu & F)

KING (6TH - MACDOUGAL)

North

No parking 11am-2pm (M & Th)

South

No parking 11am-2pm (Tu & F)

LAFAYETTE (SPRING - PRINCE)

East

No standing except trucks loading & unloading 8am-6pm (M-F) except authorized vehicles (fire dept.)/No parking 8am-6pm (M-F)

West

No standing except trucks loading & unloading 7am-6pm (M-F)

LAFAYETTE (PRINCE - JERSEY)

East

No standing except trucks loading & unloading 7am-6pm (M-F)

West

No parking 7am-6pm (M-F)/No standing except trucks loading & unloading 8am-6pm (M-F) except authorized vehicles

LAFAYETTE (JERSEY - HOUSTON)

East

No parking 8am-6pm (M-F)/No parking 8am-midnite including Sun

West

No standing except trucks loading & unloading 7am-6pm (M-F)

LAFAYETTE (HOUSTON - BLEECKER)

East

No parking 7am-6pm (M-F)

West

No parking 8am-6pm (M-F)

LAFAYETTE (BLEECKER - BOND)

East

No parking 7am-7pm (M-F)

West

No parking 8am-6pm (M-F)

LAFAYETTE (BOND - GREAT JONES)

East

No parking 7am-7pm (M-F)

West

No parking 7am-7pm (M-F)

LAFAYETTE (GREAT JONES - 4TH ST)

East

No parking 7am-7pm (M-F)

West

No parking 7am-7pm (M-F)

LAFAYETTE (4TH ST - ASTOR)

East

No standing except trucks loading & unloading 7am-6pm (M-F)

West

No standing except trucks loading & unloading 7am-6pm (M-F)

LAFAYETTE (ASTOR - 8TH ST) ☹

East

No standing anytime

West

No standing anytime

LAFAYETTE (WHITE - WALKER)

East

No standing 7am-7pm (M-F) except authorized vehicles (Dept. Of Sanitation)/No parking 2am-6am (Tu, F)

West

1 hr. metered parking (9am-7pm) including Sun/No parking 2am-6am (M, Th)

LAFAYETTE (WALKER - CANAL) ☺

East

1 hr. metered parking (9am-7pm) including Sun/No parking 8am-9am (except Sun)

West

No parking 2am-6am (M, Th)

LAFAYETTE (CANAL - HOWARD)

East

No standing except trucks loading & unloading 7am-7pm (M-F)

West

No parking 8am-6pm (M-F)

LAFAYETTE (HOWARD - GRAND)

East

1 hr. metered parking (9am-7pm) including Sun/No parking 8am-9am (except Sun)

West

No standing except trucks loading & unloading 8am-6pm (M-F)

LAFAYETTE (GRAND - BROOME)

East

No parking 8am-6pm (except Sun)

West

1 hr. metered parking (9am-7pm) including Sun/No parking 8am-9am (except Sun)/No standing except trucks loading & unloading 8am-7pm (M-F)

LAFAYETTE (BROOME - KENMARE)

East

No parking 8am-6pm (except Sun)

West

No parking 8am-6pm (M-F)

LAFAYETTE (KENMARE - SPRING)

East

No standing anytime

West

No parking 8am-6pm (M-F)

LAGUARDIA (WASHINGTON SQ. S. - W. 3RD)

East

2 hr. metered parking (9am-7pm) including Sun/No parking 8am-9am (except Sun)

West

No parking 8am-6pm (M-F)

LAGUARDIA (W. 3RD - BLEECKER)

East

2 hr. metered parking (9am-7pm) including Sun/No parking 8am-9am (except Sun)

West

No parking 8am-6pm (M-F)

LAGUARDIA (BLEECKER - HOUSTON)

East

1 hr. metered parking (9am-7pm) including Sun/No parking 8am-9am (except Sun)

West

No parking 8am-6pm (M-F)

LAGUARDIA (HOUSTON - PRINCE)

East

No parking 8am-6pm (M-F)

West

No parking 8am-6pm (M-F)

LAIGHT (6TH - VARICK)

North

No parking anytime

South

No parking anytime

LAIGHT (VARICK - HUDSON)

North

No parking anytime

South

No parking anytime

LAIGHT (HUDSON - COLLISTER)

North

No standing 7am-10am including Sun/No standing 10am-3pm except trucks loading and unloading (except Sun)/No standing 3pm-7pm (except Sun)

South

No standing except trucks loading & unloading 8am-6pm (M-F)

LAIGHT (COLLISTER - GREENWICH)

North

No standing 7am-10am including Sun/No standing 10am-3pm except trucks loading and unloading (except Sun)/No standing 3pm-7pm (except Sun)

South

No standing except trucks loading & unloading 8am-6pm (M-F)

LAIGHT (GREENWICH - WASHINGTON)

North

No standing 7am-10am including Sun/No standing 10am-3pm except trucks loading and unloading (except Sun)/No standing 3pm-7pm (except Sun)

South

No standing except trucks loading & unloading 8am-6pm (M-F)

LAIGHT (WASHINGTON - WEST)

North

No standing 7am-10am including Sun/No standing 10am-3pm except trucks loading and unloading (except Sun)/No standing 3pm-7pm (except Sun)

South

No standing except trucks loading & unloading 8am-6pm (M-F)

LEONARD (W. BROADWAY - HUDSON)

North

No standing except trucks loading & unloading 7am-7pm (M-F)

South

No standing except trucks loading & unloading 7am-7pm (M-F)

LEROY (BLEECKER - BEDFORD)

North

No parking anytime

South

No parking 7am - 4pm (M-F)/No parking 7am - 6pm (M-F) except faculty vehicles

LEROY (BEDFORD - 7TH AVE SOUTH)

North

No parking anytime

South

No parking anytime

LEROY (7TH AVE SOUTH - HUDSON)

North

No parking 8am-11am (M & Th)

South

No parking 8am-6pm (Tu, Th, Sat)

LEROY (HUDSON - GREENWICH ST)

North

No parking 8am-6pm (M-F)

South

No parking 8am-6pm (M-F)

LEROY (GREENWICH ST - WASHINGTON)

North

No parking 8am-6pm (M-F)

South

No parking 8am-6pm (M-F)

LEROY (WASHINGTON - WEST)

North

No parking 8am-6pm (M-F)

South

No parking 8am-6pm (M-F)

LISPENARD (6TH - CHURCH)

North

No parking 8am-6pm (M-F)

South

No parking anytime

LISPENARD (CHURCH - BROADWAY)

North

No parking 8am-6pm (M-F)

South

No parking 8am-6pm (M-F)

LITTLE W. 12TH ST (10TH - WASHINGTON)

North

No parking 2am-4pm (M-F) except trucks loading & unloading "Ganesvoort market"

South

No parking 2am-4pm (M-F) except trucks loading & unloading "Ganesvoort market"

LITTLE W. 12TH ST (WASHINGTON - 9TH)

North

No parking 2am-4pm (M-F) except trucks loading & unloading "Ganesvoort market"

South

No parking 2am-4pm (M-F) except trucks loading & unloading "Ganesvoort market"

MACDOUGAL ALLEY (MACDOUGAL - 5TH AVE) ☹

North

No parking anytime

South

No parking anytime

MACDOUGAL (8TH ST - MACDOUGAL ALLEY)

East

1 hr. metered parking (9am-10pm) including Sun/No parking 8am-9am (except Sun)/No standing 11pm-6am (including Sun)

West

No parking 8am-6pm (M-F)/No standing 11pm-7am including Sun

MACDOUGAL (MACDOUGAL ALLEY - WASHINGTON SQ. N.)

East

1 hr. metered parking (9am-10pm) including Sun/No parking 8am-9am (except Sun)/No standing 11pm-6am (including Sun)

West

No parking 8am-6pm (M-F)/No standing 11pm-7am including Sun

MACDOUGAL (WASHINGTON SQ. N. - WASHINGTON PL)

East

No standing anytime

West

No parking 8am-6pm (M-F)

MACDOUGAL (WASHINGTON PL - 4TH ST)

East

No standing anytime

West

No parking 8am-6pm (M-F)

MACDOUGAL (4TH ST - 3RD ST)

East

No standing 6pm - 7am (all days)/No standing except trucks loading & unloading 7am-6pm (except Sun)

West

No standing 6pm - 7am (all days)/No standing except trucks loading & unloading 7am-6pm (except Sun)

MACDOUGAL (3RD ST - MINETTA LANE)

East

No parking anytime

West

No parking anytime

MACDOUGAL (MINETTA LANE - BLEECKER)

East

No parking anytime

West

No parking anytime

MACDOUGAL (BLEECKER - HOUSTON)

East

No parking 8am-6pm (Tu, Th, Sat)

West

No parking 8am-6pm (M, W, F)

MACDOUGAL (HOUSTON - KING)

East

No parking 7am-4pm (school days) except authorized vehicles/No parking 11am-2pm (Tu & F)

West

No parking 8am-6pm (M-F)

MACDOUGAL (KING - PRINCE)

East

No parking 11am-2pm (Tu & F)

West

No parking 11am-2pm (M & Th)

MERCER (8TH ST - WAVERLY PL)

North

1 hr. metered parking (9am-7pm) including Sun/No parking 8am-9am (except Sun)

South

No parking 8am-6pm (M-F)

MERCER (WAVERLY PL - WASHINGTON PL)

North

No parking 8am-6pm (M-F)

South

No parking 8am-6pm (M-F)

MERCER (WASHINGTON PL. - 4TH ST)

North

No parking 8am-6pm (M-F)

South

No parking 8am-6pm (M-F)

MERCER (4TH ST - 3RD ST)

North

No parking 8am-6pm (M-F)

South

No parking 8am-6pm (M-F)

MERCER (3RD ST - BLEECKER)

North

No parking 8am-6pm (M-F)

South

No parking 8am-6pm (M-F)

MERCER (BLEECKER - HOUSTON)

North

No standing anytime (except authorized vehicles) (Buses with permits)

South

No parking 8am-6pm (M-F)

MERCER (HOUSTON - PRINCE)

North

No parking 8am-6pm (M-F)

South

No parking 8am-6pm (M-F)

MERCER (PRINCE - SPRING)

North

No parking 8am-6pm (M-F)

South

No parking 8am-6pm (M-F)

MERCER (SPRING - BROOME)

North

No parking 8am-6pm (M-F)

South

No parking 8am-6pm (M-F)

MERCER (BROOME - GRAND)

North

No parking 8am-6pm (M-F)

South

No parking 8am-6pm (M-F)

MERCER (GRAND - HOWARD)

North

No parking 8am-6pm (M-F)

South

No parking 8am-6pm (M-F)

MERCER (HOWARD - CANAL)

North

No parking 8am-6pm (M-F)

South

No parking 8am-6pm (M-F)

MINETTA LANE (6TH - MACDOUGAL)

East

No parking anytime

West

No parking anytime

MINETTA ST (BLEECKER - MINETTA LANE)

East

No parking anytime

West

No parking anytime

MORTON (WEST - WASHINGTON)

North

No parking 11am-2pm (M & Th)

South

No parking 11am-2pm (Tu & F)

MORTON (WASHINGTON - GREENWICH ST)

North

No parking 8am-6pm (M-F)

South

No parking 11am-2pm (Tu & F)

MORTON (GREENWICH ST - HUDSON)

North

No parking 8am-6pm (M-F)

South

No parking 8am-6pm (M-F)

MORTON (HUDSON - BEDFORD)

North

No parking 8am-11am (M & Th)

South

No parking 8am-11am (Tu & F)

MORTON (BEDFORD - 7TH AVE SOUTH)

North

No parking anytime

South

No parking anytime

MORTON (7TH AVE SOUTH - BLEECKER)

North

No parking anytime

South

1 hr. metered parking (9am-7pm) including Sun/No parking 8am-9am (except Sun)

N. MOORE (VARICK - W. BROADWAY)

North

No parking 8am-6pm (M-F)

South

No parking 8am-6pm (M-F)

PERRY (WEST - WASHINGTON)

North

No parking 11am-2pm (M & Th)

South

No parking anytime

PERRY (WASHINGTON - GREENWICH ST)

North

No parking 8am-6pm (M-F)

South

No parking anytime

PERRY (GREENWICH ST - HUDSON)

North

No parking 11am-2pm (M & Th)

South

No parking anytime

PERRY (HUDSON - BLEECKER)

North

No parking 8am-11am (M & Th)

South

No parking anytime

PERRY (BLEECKER - W. 4TH)

North

No parking 8am-11am (M & Th)

South

No parking anytime

PERRY (BLEECKER - 7TH AVE SOUTH)

North

No parking 8am-11am (M & Th)

South

No parking anytime

PERRY (7TH AVE SOUTH - GREENWICH AVE)

North

No parking 8am-11am (M & Th)

South

No parking anytime

PRINCE (LAFAYETTE - CROSBY)

North

No parking 8am-6pm (M-F)

South

No parking 8am-6pm (M-F)

PRINCE (CROSBY - BROADWAY)

North

No parking 8am-6pm (M-F)

South

No standing anytime

PRINCE (BROADWAY - MERCER)

North

No parking 8am-6pm (M-F)/No standing 11am-midnite (Sat, Sun)

South

No standing anytime

PRINCE (MERCER - GREENE)

North

No parking 8am-6pm (M-F)/No standing 11am-midnite (Sat, Sun)

South

No parking 8am-6pm (M-F)

PRINCE (GREENE - WOOSTER)

North

No parking 8am-6pm (M-F)/No standing 11am-midnite (Sat, Sun)

South

No parking 8am-6pm (M-F)

PRINCE (WOOSTER - W. BROADWAY)

North

No parking 8am-6pm (M-F)/No standing 11am-midnite (Sat, Sun)

South

No parking 8am-6pm (M-F)

PRINCE (W. BROADWAY - THOMPSON)

North

No parking 8am-6pm (M-F)

South

No parking 8am-6pm (M-F)

PRINCE (THOMPSON - SULLIVAN)

North

No parking 8am-6pm (M-F)

South

No parking 8am-6pm (except Sun)

PRINCE (SULLIVAN - MACDOUGAL) ☺

North

No parking 11am-2pm (M & Th)

South

No parking 11am-2pm (Tu & F)

PRINCE (MACDOUGAL - 6TH)

North

No parking 11am-2pm (M & Th)

South

No parking 11am-2pm (Tu & F)

RENWICK (SPRING - CANAL)

East

No parking 8am-6pm (M-F)

West

No parking 8am-6pm (M-F)

SHERIDAN SQ (W. 4TH - WASHINGTON PL)

North

No parking 8am-6pm (M-F)

South

No standing anytime

SPRING (WEST - WASHINGTON)

North

No parking 8am-6pm (except Sun)

South

No parking 8am-6pm (except Sun)

SPRING (WASHINGTON - GREENWICH ST)

North

No parking anytime

South

No standing except trucks loading & unloading 8am-6pm (except Sun)

SPRING (GREENWICH ST - RENWICK)

North

No parking 8am-6pm (M-F)

South

No parking 8am-6pm (M-F)

SPRING (RENWICK - HUDSON)

North

No parking 8am-6pm (M-F)

South

No parking 8am-6pm (M-F)

SPRING (HUDSON - VARICK)

North

1 hr. metered parking (9am-7pm) including Sun/No parking 8am-9am (except Sun)/No parking 8am-6pm (M-F)

South

No standing anytime/No standing 7am-7pm (M-F)

SPRING (VARICK - 6TH)

North

No parking 8am-6pm (M-F)

South

No standing anytime

SPRING (6TH - SULLIVAN)

North

No parking 8am-6pm (M-F)

South

No parking 8am-6pm (M-F)

SPRING (SULLIVAN - THOMPSON)

North

No parking 8am-6pm (M-F)

South

No parking 8am-6pm (M-F)

SPRING (THOMPSON - W. BROADWAY)

North

No parking 8am-6pm (M-F)

South

No parking 8am-6pm (M-F)

SPRING (W. BROADWAY - WOOSTER)

North

No parking 8am-6pm (M-F)

South

No parking 8am-6pm (M-F)

SPRING (WOOSTER - GREENE)

North

No parking 8am-6pm (M-F)

South

No parking 8am-6pm (M-F)

SPRING (GREENE - MERCER)

North

No parking 8am-6pm (M-F)

South

No parking 8am-6pm (M-F)

SPRING (MERCER - BROADWAY)

North

No parking 8am-6pm (M-F)

South

No parking 8am-6pm (M-F)

SPRING (BROADWAY - CROSBY) ☹

North

No standing except trucks loading & unloading

South

No standing anytime

SPRING (CROSBY - LAFAYETTE) ☹

North

No standing except trucks loading & unloading

South

No standing anytime

SULLIVAN (WATTS - BROOME)

East

No parking 8am-6pm (except Sun)

West

No parking anytime

SULLIVAN (BROOME - SPRING)

East

No parking 8am-6pm (M-F)

West

No parking 8am-6pm (except Sun)

SULLIVAN (SPRING - PRINCE)

East

No parking 8am-6pm (M-F)

West

No parking 11am-2pm (M & Th)

SULLIVAN (PRINCE - HOUSTON)

East

No parking 8am-6pm (M-F)

West

No parking 11am-2pm (M & Th)

SULLIVAN (HOUSTON - BLEECKER)

East

No parking 8am-6pm (Tu, Th, Sat)

West

No parking 8am-6pm (M, W, F)

SULLIVAN (BLEECKER - 3RD ST)

East

No parking 8am-6pm (except Sun)

West

No parking 11am-2pm (M & Th)/No parking 8am-6pm (M-F)

SULLIVAN (3RD ST - WASINGTON SQ. S.)

East

No parking 8am-6pm (Tu, Th, Sat)

West

No parking 8am-6pm (M, W, F)

THOMPSON (WASHINGTON SQ. S. - 3RD ST)

East

No parking 11am-2pm (Tu & F)

West

No parking 11am-2pm (M & Th)

THOMPSON (3RD ST - BLEECKER)

East

No parking 8am-6pm (Tu, Th, Sat)

West

No parking 8am-6pm (M, W, F)

THOMPSON (BLEECKER - HOUSTON)

East

No parking 8am-6pm (Tu, Th, Sat)

West

No parking 8am-6pm (M, W, F)

THOMPSON (HOUSTON - PRINCE)

East

No parking 11am-2pm (Tu & F)

West

No parking 8am-6pm (M, W, F)

THOMPSON (PRINCE - SPRING)

East

No parking 11am-2pm (Tu & F)

West

No parking 11am-2pm (M & Th)/No parking 8am-5pm (M-F)

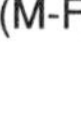

THOMPSON (SPRING - BROOME)

East

No parking 11am-2pm (Tu & F)

West

No parking 11am-2pm (M & Th)/No parking 8am-5pm (M-F)/No parking 7am-7pm (M-F)

THOMPSON (BROOME - WATTS)

East

No parking anytime

West

No parking anytime

THOMPSON (WATTS - GRAND)

East

No parking 8am-6pm (M-F)

West

No parking 8am-6pm (M-F)

THOMPSON (GRAND - CANAL)

East

No parking anytime

West

No parking 8am-6pm (M-F)

UNIVERSITY PL (WASH SQ. S. - WASHSQ. N.)

North

No standing anytime

South

No standing anytime

UNIVERSITY PL (WASHINGTON SQ. N. - WAVERLY) ☹

North

No standing anytime

South

No standing anytime

UNIVERSITY PL (WAVERLY - WASHINGTON MEWS)

North

1 hr. metered parking (9am-10pm) including Sun/No parking 8am-9am (except Sun)

South

No parking 8am-6pm (M-F)

UNIVERSITY PL (WASHINGTON MEWS - 8TH ST)

North

1 hr. metered parking (9am-10pm) including Sun/No parking 8am-9am (except Sun)

South

No parking 8am-6pm (M-F)

VAN DAM (GREENWICH ST - HUDSON)

North

No parking 8am-6pm (M-F)

South

No parking 8am-6pm (M-F)

VAN DAM (HUDSON - VARICK)

North

No parking 8am-6pm (M-F)

South

FNo parking 8am-6pm (M-F)

VAN DAM (VARICK - 6TH)

North

No parking 8am-6pm (M-F)

South

No parking 8am-6pm (M-F)

VARICK (KING - CHARLTON)

East

1 hr. metered parking (9am-7pm) including Sun/No parking 4am-6am (Tu, Th, Sat)

West

1 hr. metered parking (9am-7pm) including Sun/No parking [illegible]

VARICK (CHARLTON - VANDAM)

East

1 hr. metered parking (9am-7pm) including Sun/No parking 4am-6am (Tu, Th, Sat)

West

No standing 7am-10am & 4pm-7pm (except Sun)/1 hr. metered parking 10am-4pm (M-F) & 9am-7pm (Sat & Sun)

VARICK (VANDAM - SPRING)

East

No standing 4pm-7pm (except Sun)/1 hr. metered parking 10am-4pm (M-F) & 9am-7pm (Sat & Sun)

West

No standing 7am-10am & 4pm-7pm (except Sun)/1 hr. metered parking 10am-4pm (M-F) & 9am-7pm (Sat & Sun)

VARICK (SPRING - DOMINICK)

East

No standing anytime

West

No standing 7am-10am & 4pm-7pm (except Sun)/No standing except trucks loading & unloading 10am-4pm (except Sun)

VARICK (DOMINICK - BROOME)

East

No stopping anytime

West

No standing 7am-10am & 4pm-7pm (except Sun)/No standing except trucks loading & unloading 10am-4pm (except Sun)

VARICK (BROOME - WATTS)

East

2 hr. metered parking 9am-4pm (M-Sat) & 9am-7pm (Sun)/No parking 4am-6am (Tu, Th, Sat)/No standing 4pm-7pm (except Sun)

West

No parking anytime

VARICK (WATTS - GRAND)

East

2 hr. metered parking 9am-4pm (M-Sat) & 9am-7pm (Sun)/No parking 4am-6am (Tu, Th, Sat)/No parking 8am-9am (except Sun)/No standing 4pm-7pm (except Sun)

West

Two hr. metered parking (9am-7pm) including Sun//No parking 4am-6am (M, W, F)

VARICK (GRAND - CANAL)

East

2 hr. metered parking 9am-4pm (M-Sat) & 9am-7pm (Sun)/No parking 4am-6am (Tu, Th, Sat)/No standing 7am-10am & 4pm-7pm (except Sun)

West

Two hr. metered parking (9am-7pm) including Sun//No parking 4am-6am (M, W, F)

VARICK (CANAL - LAIGHT) ☹

East

No parking anytime

West

No parking anytime

VARICK (LAIGHT - ERICCSON PL)

East

No parking 8am-6pm (M-F)

West

No standing anytime (except authorized vehicles) (police vehicles only)

VARICK (ERICCSON PL - N. MOORE)

East

No parking 8am-6pm (M-F)/No standing anytime (except authorized vehicles) (police vehicles only)

West

No standing anytime (except authorized vehicles) (police vehicles only)

VARICK (N. MOORE - FRANKLIN)

East

No parking 8am-6pm (M-F)

West

No parking 8am-6pm (M-F)

VESTRY (WEST - WASHINGTON)

North

No parking 8am-6pm (M-F)

South

No parking 8am-6pm (M-F)

VESTRY (WASHINGTON - GREENWICH)

North

No parking 8am-6pm (M-F)

South

No standing anytime

VESTRY (GREENWICH - HUDSON)

North

No parking 8am-6pm (M-F)

South

No parking 8am-6pm (M-F)

VESTRY (HUDSON - VARICK)

North

No parking 8am-6pm (M-F)

South

No parking anytime

W. BROADWAY (FRANKLIN - WHITE)

East

No parking 8am-6pm (M-F)

West

No parking 8am-6pm (M-F)

W. BROADWAY (WHITE - N. MOORE)

East

No parking 6am-6pm (M-F)

West

No parking 8am-6pm (M-F)

W. BROADWAY (N. MOORE - BEACH/WALKER)

East

1 hr. metered parking (9am-7pm) including Sun/No parking 2am-6am (Tu, F)

West

No parking 8am-6pm (M-F)

W. BROADWAY (BEACH/WALKER - LISPENARD)

East

No standing anytime (except authorized vehicles)

West

No parking 8am-6pm (M-F)

W. BROADWAY (LISPENARD - CANAL)

East

No standing 7am-10am & 4pm-7pm (except Sun)/No standing except trucks loading & unloading 10am-4pm (except Sun)

West

No parking 8am-6pm (M-F)

W. BROADWAY (CANAL - GRAND)

East

No parking 8am-6pm (except Sun)

West

No parking 8am-6pm (M-F)/No standing 11pm-7am including Sun

W. BROADWAY (PRINCE - SPRING)

East

No parking 8am-6pm (M-F)

West

No parking 8am-6pm (M-F)

W. BROADWAY (SPRING - BROOME/WATTS)

East

No parking 8am-6pm (M-F)

West

No parking 8am-6pm (M-F)

W. BROADWAY (BROOME/WATTS - GRAND)

East

No parking 8am-6pm (M-F)/No standing 7am-4pm (M-F)/No standing 11pm-7am including Sun

West

No parking 8am-6pm (M-F)

WALKER (W. BROADWAY - 6TH)

North

No standing anytime

South

No standing except trucks loading & unloading 7am-7pm (M-F)

WALKER (6TH - CHURCH)

North

No standing except trucks loading & unloading 7am-4pm (M-F)/No standing 4pm-7pm (M-F)

South

No standing except trucks loading & unloading 7am-7pm (M-F)

WALKER (CHURCH - BROADWAY)

North

No standing except trucks loading & unloading 7am-4pm (M-F)/No standing 4pm-7pm (M-F)

South

No standing except trucks loading & unloading 7am-7pm (M-F)

WALKER (BROADWAY - CORTLAND)

North

No standing except trucks loading & unloading 7am-4pm (M-F)/No standing 4pm-7pm (M-F)

South

No standing except trucks loading & unloading 7am-7pm (M-F)

WALKER (CORTLAND - LAFAYETTE)

North

No standing except trucks loading & unloading 7am-4pm (M-F)/No standing 4pm-7pm (M-F)

South

No standing except trucks loading & unloading 7am-7pm (M-F)

WALKER (LAFAYETTE - CENTRE)

North

No standing except trucks loading & unloading 7am-4pm (M-F)/No standing 4pm-7pm (M-F)

South

No standing except trucks loading & unloading 7am-7pm (M-F)

WASHINGTON (14TH - 13TH)

East

No parking anytime

West

No parking 2am-4pm (M-F) except trucks loading & unloading "Ganesvoort market"

WASHINGTON (13TH - LITTLE W.12TH)

East

No parking 2am-4pm (M-F) except trucks loading & unloading "Ganesvoort market"

West

No parking 2am-4pm (M-F) except trucks loading & unloading "Ganesvoort market"

WASHINGTON (LITTLE W.12TH - GANESVOORT)

East

No parking 2am-4pm (M-F) except trucks loading & unloading "Ganesvoort market"

West

No parking 2am-4pm (M-F) except trucks loading & unloading "Ganesvoort market"

WASHINGTON (GANESVOORT - HORATIO)

East

No parking 5am-4pm (M-F)

West

No parking 5am-4pm (M-F)

WASHINGTON (HORATIO - JANE)

East

No parking 5am-4pm (M-F)

West

No parking 11am-2pm (M & Th)

WASHINGTON (JANE - W.12TH)

East

No parking 8am-6pm (M-F)/No parking 11am-2pm (Tu & F)

West

No parking 11am-2pm (M & Th)

WASHINGTON (W.12TH - BETHUNE)

East

No parking 11am-2pm (Tu & F)

West

No standing anytime

WASHINGTON (BETHUNE - BANK)

East

No parking 11am-2pm (Tu & F)

West

No parking 11am-2pm (M & Th)

WASHINGTON (BANK - W.11TH)

East

No parking 11am-2pm (Tu & F)/No parking 8am-6pm (except Sun)

West

No parking 11am-2pm (M & Th)

WASHINGTON (W.11TH - PERRY)

East

No parking 8am-6pm (M-F)/No parking 11am-2pm (Tu & F)

West

No parking 11am-2pm (M & Th)

WASHINGTON (PERRY - CHARLES)

East

No parking 8am-6pm (except Sun)

West

No parking 11am-2pm (M & Th)

WASHINGTON (CHARLES - W.10TH)

East

No parking 11am-2pm (Tu & F)

West

No parking 11am-2pm (M & Th)

WASHINGTON (W.10TH - CHRISTOPHER)

East

No parking 11am-2pm (Tu & F)

West

No parking 11am-2pm (M & Th)

WASHINGTON (CHRISTOPHER - BARROW)

East

No parking 11am-2pm (Tu & F)

West

No parking 11am-2pm (M & Th)

WASHINGTON (BARROW - MORTON)

East

No parking 11am-2pm (Tu & F)

West

No parking 11am-2pm (M & Th)

WASHINGTON (MORTON - LEROY)

East

No standing except trucks loading & unloading

West

No parking 11am-2pm (M & Th)

WASHINGTON (LEROY - CLARKSON)

East

No parking 8am-6pm (except Sun)

West

No parking 8am-6pm (M-F)

WASHINGTON (CLARKSON - W. HOUSTON)

East

No parking 8am-6pm (except Sun)

West

No standing anytime

WASHINGTON (W. HOUSTON - SPRING) ☹

East

No standing anytime

West

No standing anytime

WASHINGTON (SPRING - CANAL) ☹

East

No standing anytime

West

No standing anytime

WASHINGTON (HUBERT - LAIGHT)

East

No parking 8am-6pm (M-F)

West

No parking 8am-6pm (M-F)

WASHINGTON (LAIGHT - VESTRY)

East

No parking 8am-6pm (M-F)

West

No parking 8am-6pm (M-F)

WASHINGTON (VESTRY - DEBROSSES)

East

No parking 8am-6pm (M-F)

West

No parking 8am-6pm (M-F)

WASHINGTON (DEBROSSES - WATTS)

East

No parking 8am-6pm (M-F)

West

No parking 8am-6pm (M-F)

WASHINGTON (WATTS - CANAL)

East

No parking 8am-6pm (M-F)

West

No parking anytime

WASHINGTON MEWS (5TH - UNIVERSITY)

North

No parking anytime

South

No parking anytime

WASHINGTON PL (SHERIDAN - 6TH)

North

No parking 8am-6pm (M-F)

South

No parking 8am-11am (Tu & F)

WASHINGTON PL (6TH - WASHINGTON SQ. W.)

North

No parking 11am-2pm (M & Th)

South

No parking 11am-2pm (Tu & F)/1 hr. metered parking (9am-7pm) including Sun/No parking 8am-9am (except Sun)

WASHINGTON PL (BROADWAY - MERCER)

North

No parking 8am-6pm (M-F)

South

1 hr. metered parking (9am-7pm) including Sun/No parking 8am-9am (except Sun)

WASHINGTON PL (MERCER - GREENE)

North

No parking 8am-11am (M & Th)

South

1 hr. metered parking (9am-7pm) including Sun/No parking 8am-9am (except Sun)/No parking 8am-6pm (M-F)

WASHINGTON PL (GREENE - WASHINGTON SQ. N.)

North

No parking 8am-6pm (M-F)

South

No parking 8am-6pm (M-F)

WATTS (WEST - WASHINGTON)

North

No parking 8am-6pm (M-F)

South

No parking 8am-6pm (M-F)

WATTS (WASHINGTON - GREENWICH)

North

No parking 8am-6pm (M-F)

South

No parking 8am-6pm (M-F)

WATTS (GREENWICH - HUDSON)

North

No parking 8am-6pm (M-F)

South

No standing anytime

WATTS (W. BROADWAY - THOMPSON)

North

No standing anytime

South

No parking 7am-7pm (M-F)/No standing 4pm-7pm (M-F)

WATTS (THOMPSON - 6TH)

North

No parking 7am - 4pm (M-F)/No standing 4pm-7pm (M-F)

South

No parking 7am-7pm (M-F)/No standing 4pm-7pm (M-F)

WATTS (6TH - VARICK)

North

No standing 7am-7pm (M-F)

South

No standing 7am-7pm (M-F)

WATTS (VARICK - HOLLAND TUNNEL ACCESS) ☹

North

No parking anytime

South

No parking anytime

WAVERLY PL (BANK - W. 11TH) ☺

East

No parking 8am-11am (Tu & F)

West

No standing anytime

WAVERLY PL (W. 11TH - PERRY)

East

No parking 8am-11am (Tu & F)

West

No standing anytime

WAVERLY PL (PERRY - CHARLES)

East

1 hr. metered parking (9am-7pm) including Sun/No parking 8am-9am (except Sun)

West

No standing anytime

WAVERLY PL (CHARLES - W. 10TH)

East

No parking 8am-11am (Tu & F)

West

No standing anytime

WAVERLY PL (W. 10TH - CHRISTOPHER)

East

No parking 8am-11am (Tu & F)

West

No standing anytime

WAVERLY PL (CHRISTOPHER - GAY)

East

No parking 8am-11am (Tu & F)

West

No standing anytime

WAVERLY PL (OFFSHOOT) (GAY - CHRISTOPHER)

North

No parking 8am-11am (M & Th)

South

No parking 8am-6pm (M-F)

WAVERLY PL (OFFSHOOT) (6TH - GAY)

North

1 hr. metered parking (9am-7pm) including Sun/No parking 8am-9am (except Sun)

South

No parking 8am-6pm (M-F)

WAVERLY PL (WASHINGTON SQ. E. - 5TH)

North

No parking 8am-6pm (M-F)

South

No standing anytime

WAVERLY PL (5TH - MACDOUGAL)

North

No parking 8am-6pm (M-F)

South

No standing anytime

WAVERLY PL (MACDOUGAL - 6TH)

North

No parking 8am-6pm (M-F)

South

No parking 8am-6pm (except Sun)

WAVERLY PL (WASHINGTON SQ. E. - GREENE)

North

No parking 8am-6pm (M-F)

South

1 hr. metered parking (9am-7pm) including Sun/No parking 8am-9am (except Sun)

WAVERLY PL (GREENE - MERCER)

North

No parking 8am-6pm (M-F)

South

No parking 8am-6pm (M-F)

WAVERLY PL (MERCER - BROADWAY)

North

No parking 8am-6pm (M-F)

South

No parking 8am-6pm (M-F)

WEEHAWKEN (CHRISTOPHER - 10TH)

North

No parking 7am-7pm (except Sun)

South

No parking 7am-7pm (except Sun)

WEST (CANAL - WATTS)

East

No standing anytime

West

No standing anytime

WEST (WATTS - DEBROSSES)

East

No standing anytime

West

No standing anytime

WEST (DEBROSSES - VESTRY)

East

No standing anytime

West

No standing anytime

WEST (VESTRY - LAIGHT)

East

No standing anytime

West

No standing anytime

WEST (LAIGHT - HUBERT)

East

No parking 7am-7pm (M-F)

West

No standing anytime

WEST (CANAL - SPRING)

East

No standing anytime

West

No standing anytime

WEST (SPRING - W. HOUSTON)

East

No standing anytime

West

No standing anytime

WEST (W. HOUSTON - CLARKSON) ☹

East

No standing anytime

West

No standing anytime

WEST (CLARKSON - LEROY) ☹

East

No standing anytime

West

No standing anytime

WEST (LEROY - MORTON) ☹

East

No standing anytime

West

No standing anytime

WEST (MORTON - BARROW) ☺

East

No parking 11am-2pm (Tu & F)

West

No standing anytime

WEST (BARROW - CHRISTOPHER) ☺

East

No parking 11am-2pm (Tu & F)

West

No standing anytime

WEST (CHRISTOPHER - W. 10TH ST) ☺

East

No parking 11am-2pm (Tu & F)

West

No standing anytime

WEST (W. 10TH ST - CHARLES) ☺

East

No parking 11am-2pm (Tu & F)

West

No standing anytime

WEST (CHARLES - CHARLES LANE)

East
No parking 7am-7pm (except Sun)

West
No standing anytime

WEST (CHARLES LANE - PERRY)

East
No parking 7am-7pm (except Sun)

West
No standing anytime

WEST (PERRY - W. 11TH)

East
No parking anytime

West
No parking anytime

WEST (W. 11TH - BANK)

East
No parking 11am-2pm (Tu & F)

West
No standing anytime

WEST (BANK - BETHUNE)

East
No parking 11am-2pm (Tu & F)

West
No standing anytime

WEST (BETHUNE - W. 12TH)

East
No parking 11am-2pm (Tu & F)

West
No standing anytime

WEST (W. 12TH - JANE)

East
No parking anytime

West
No parking anytime

WEST (JANE - HORATIO)

East

No parking anytime

West

No parking anytime

WEST (HORATIO - GANESVOORT)

East

No parking anytime

West

No parking anytime

WEST (GANESVOORT - 10TH AVE)

East

No parking anytime

West

No parking anytime

WEST (10TH AVE - W. 14TH ST)

East

No parking anytime

West

No parking anytime

WHITE (CENTRE - LAFAYETTE)

North

No standing 7am-7pm (M-F) except authorized vehicles (Dept. Of Sanitation)

South

No standing 7am-7pm (M-F)

WHITE (LAFAYETTE - CORTLAND ALLEY)

North

No parking 8am-6pm (M-F)

South

No standing except trucks loading & unloading 7am-7pm (M-F)

WHITE (CORTLAND ALLEY - BROADWAY)

North

No parking anytime

South

No parking 8am-6pm (M-F)

WHITE (BROADWAY - 6TH/CHURCH)

North

No parking anytime

South

No parking 9am-6pm (M-F)

WHITE (6TH/CHURCH - W. BROADWAY)

North

No parking 8am-6pm (M-F)

South

No parking 8am-6pm (M-F)

WOOSTER (HOUSTON - PRINCE)

East

No parking 8am-6pm (M-F)

West

No parking 8am-6pm (M-F)

WOOSTER (PRINCE - SPRING)

East

No parking 8am-6pm (M-F)

West

No parking 8am-6pm (M-F)

WOOSTER (SPRING - BROOME)

East

No parking 8am-6pm (M-F)

West

No parking 8am-6pm (M-F)

WOOSTER (BROOME - GRAND)

East

No parking 8am-6pm (M-F)

West

No parking 8am-6pm (M-F)

WOOSTER (GRAND - CANAL)

East

No parking 8am-6pm (M-F)

West

No parking 8am-6pm (M-F)

YORK (6TH - ST. JOHNS LANE)

North

No parking 8am-6pm (M-F)

South

No parking 8am-6pm (M-F)

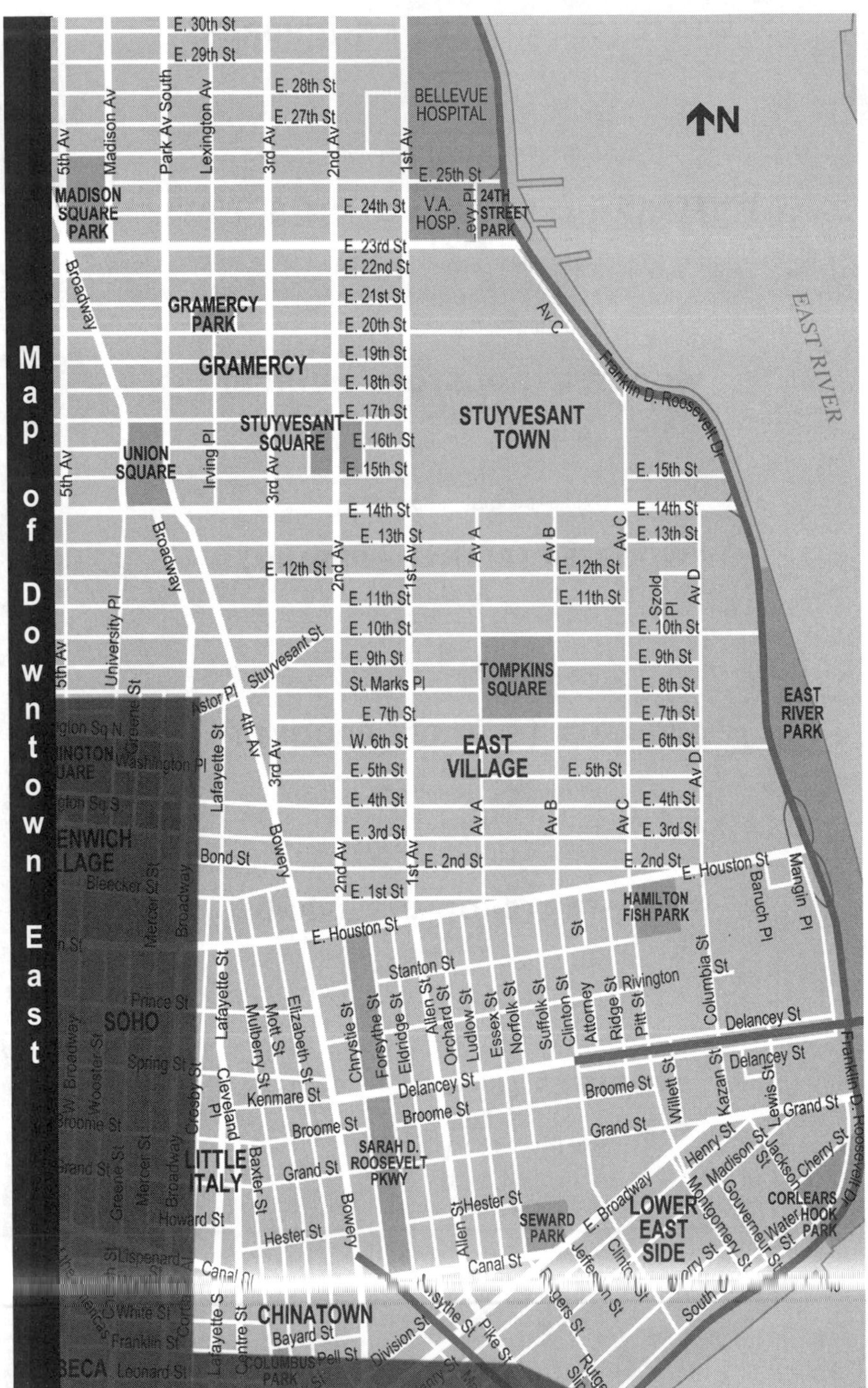
Map of Downtown East
N
E. 30th St
E. 29th St
E. 28th St
E. 27th St
E. 25th St
E. 24th St
E. 23rd St
E. 22nd St
E. 21st St
E. 20th St
E. 19th St
E. 18th St
E. 17th St
E. 16th St
E. 15th St
E. 14th St
E. 13th St
E. 12th St
E. 11th St
E. 10th St
E. 9th St
St. Marks Pl
E. 8th St
E. 7th St
W. 6th St
E. 6th St
E. 5th St
E. 4th St
E. 3rd St
E. 2nd St
E. 1st St
E. Houston St
5th Av
Madison Av
Park Av South
Lexington Av
3rd Av
2nd Av
1st Av
Levy Pl
Av A
Av B
Av C
Av D
Szold Pl
Irving Pl
University Pl
Broadway
Stuyvesant St
Astor Pl
4th Av
Lafayette St
Bowery
Bond St
Greene St
Washington Pl
Mercer St
Bleecker St
Prince St
Spring St
Broome St
Grand St
Howard St
Canal St
Lispenard St
White St
Franklin St
Leonard St
Bayard St
Pell St
Wooster St
W. Broadway
Crosby St
Cleveland Pl
Kenmare St
Mulberry St
Mott St
Elizabeth St
Baxter St
Centre St
Hester St
Chrystie St
Forsythe St
Eldridge St
Allen St
Orchard St
Ludlow St
Essex St
Norfolk St
Suffolk St
Clinton St
Attorney
Ridge St
Pitt St
Columbia St
Stanton St
Rivington
Delancey St
Willett St
Kazan St
Lewis St
Baruch Pl
Mangin Pl
Henry St
Madison St
Montgomery St
Gouverneur St
Jackson St
Cherry St
Water St
South St
E. Broadway
Jefferson St
Rutgers St
Rutger Slip
Pike St
Division St
Franklin D. Roosevelt Dr
BELLEVUE HOSPITAL
V.A. HOSP.
24TH STREET PARK
MADISON SQUARE PARK
GRAMERCY PARK
GRAMERCY
STUYVESANT SQUARE
UNION SQUARE
STUYVESANT TOWN
TOMPKINS SQUARE
EAST VILLAGE
EAST RIVER
EAST RIVER PARK
HAMILTON FISH PARK
SOHO
LITTLE ITALY
SARAH D. ROOSEVELT PKWY
CHINATOWN
COLUMBUS PARK
SEWARD PARK
LOWER EAST SIDE
CORLEARS HOOK PARK

Chapter 5 -

DOWNTOWN EAST: Street Parking Regulations

(East 30TH Street - White Street)

30TH ST (5TH-MADISON)

North

No standing except trucks loading & unloading 8am-6pm (M-F)

South

No standing except trucks loading & unloading 8am-6pm (M-F)

30TH ST (MADISON-PARK)

North

No standing except trucks loading & unloading 8am-6pm (M-F)

South

No standing except trucks loading & unloading 8am-6pm (M-F)

30TH ST (PARK-LEXINGTON)

North

No standing except trucks loading & unloading 8am-6pm (M-F)

South

No Standing 8am-6pm (Tu,Th)/No standing except trucks loading & unloading 8am-6pm (M,W,F)

30TH ST (LEXINGTON-3RD) ☺

North

No Standing 8am-6pm (M,W,F)/No standing except trucks loading & unloading 8am-6pm (Tu,Th)

South

No Standing 8am-6pm (Tu,Th,Sat)/No standing except trucks loading & unloading 8am-6pm (M,W,F)/No parking 10am-11:30am (Tu & F)/1 hr. metered parking (9am-7pm) including Sun

30TH ST (3RD-2ND) ☺

North

No parking 10am-11:30am (M & Th)/1 hr. metered parking (9am-7pm) including Sun/No parking 7am-4pm (school days)

South

No parking 10am-11:30am (Tu & F)/1 hr. metered parking (9am-7pm) including Sun

30TH ST (2ND-1ST) ☺

North

No parking 10am-11:30am (M & Th)/2 hr. metered parking (9am-10pm) including Sun

South

No parking 10am-11:30am (Tu & F)/2 hr. metered parking (9am-10pm) including Sun

29TH ST (1ST-2ND)

North

No parking 10am-11:30am (M & Th)

South

No parking 10am-11:30am (Tu & F)/2 hr. metered parking (9am-10pm) including Sun

29TH ST (2ND-3RD)

North

No parking 10am-11:30am (M & Th)/1 hr. metered parking (9am-7pm) including Sun/No parking 7am-4pm (school days)

South

No parking 10am-11:30am (Tu & F)/1 hr. metered parking (9am-7pm) including Sun

29TH ST (3RD-LEXINGTON)

North

No parking 8am-6pm (M-F)

South

No parking 10am-11:30am (Tu & F)/1 hr. metered parking (9am-7pm) including Sun/No parking 8am-6pm (except Sun)

29TH ST (LEXINGTON-PARK)

North

No standing except trucks loading & unloading 8am-7pm (except Sun)

South

No standing except trucks loading & unloading 8am-7pm (except Sun)

29TH ST (PARK-MADISON)

North

No standing except trucks loading & unloading 8am-6pm (except Sun)/No standing 8am-7pm (M-F)

South

No standing except trucks loading & unloading 8am-6pm (M-F)/No parking 7am-4pm (school days)

29TH ST (MADISON-5TH)

North

No standing except trucks loading & unloading 8am-7pm (M-F)

South

No standing except trucks loading & unloading 8am-7pm (M-F)

28TH ST (5TH-MADISON)

North

No standing except trucks loading & unloading 8am-7pm (M-F)

South

No standing except trucks loading & unloading 7am-7pm (M-F)

28TH ST (MADISON-PARK)

North

No standing except trucks loading & unloading 8am-6pm (M-F)

South

No standing except trucks loading & unloading 8am-6pm (M-F)

28TH ST (PARK-LEXINGTON)

North

No standing except trucks loading & unloading 8am-6pm (M-F)

South

No standing except trucks loading & unloading 8am-7pm (M-F)

28TH ST (LEXINGTON-3RD)

North

No parking 7am-4pm (school days)/1 hr. metered parking (9am-7pm) including Sun/No Parking 8:30am-9am (M,Tu,Th,F)

South

No standing except trucks loading & unloading 8am-6pm (M-F)/1 hr. metered parking (9am-7pm) including Sun/No Parking 8:30am-9am (M,Tu,Th,F)

28TH ST (3RD-2ND) ☺

North

No parking 8:30am-10am (M & Th)/1 hr. metered parking (9am-7pm) including Sun

South

No parking 8:30am-10am (Tu & F)/1 hr. metered parking (9am-7pm) including Sun

27TH ST (2ND-3RD) ☺

North

No parking 8:30am-10am (M & Th)/1 hr. metered parking (9am-7pm) including Sun

South

No parking 8:30am-10am (Tu & F)/1 hr. metered parking (9am-7pm) including Sun

27TH ST (3RD-LEXINGTON)

North

No parking 8am-6pm (M-F)

South

No parking 8am-6pm (M-F)/1 hr. metered parking (9am-7pm) including Sun/No Parking 8:30am-9am (M,Tu,Th,F)

27TH ST (LEXINGTON-PARK)

North

No standing except trucks loading & unloading 7am-6pm (M-F)

South

No standing except trucks loading & unloading 7am-6pm (M-F)

27TH ST (PARK-MADISON)

North

No standing except trucks loading & unloading 8am-6pm (M-F)

South

1 hr. metered parking (9am-10pm) including Sun/No parking 8am-9am (except Sun)/No standing except trucks loading & unloading 8am-7pm (M-F)

27TH ST (MADISON-5TH)

North

No standing except trucks loading & unloading 8am-7pm (M-F)

South

No standing except trucks loading & unloading 8am-7pm (M-F)

26TH ST (5TH-MADISON)

North

No standing except trucks loading & unloading 8am-7pm (M-F)

South

No standing anytime

26TH ST (MADISON-PARK)

North

1 hr. metered parking (9am-7pm) including Sun/No parking 8am-9am (except Sun)

South

No standing except trucks loading & unloading 8am-7pm (M-F)/No standing except trucks loading & unloading 7am-7pm (M-F) except authorized vehicles

26TH ST (PARK-LEXINGTON) ☺

North

No parking 11am-2pm (M & F)

South

No parking 11am-2pm (Tu & Th)

26TH ST (LEXINGTON-3RD)

North

1 hr. metered parking (9am-7pm) including Sun/No Parking 8:30am-9am (M,Tu,Th,F)/No parking 8am-6pm (M-F)

South

1 hr. metered parking (9am-7pm) including Sun/No Parking 8:30am-9am (M,Tu,Th,F)/No parking 8am-6pm (M-F)

26TH ST (3RD-2ND) ☺

North

1 hr metered parking (9am-7pm) including Sun/No parking 8:30am-10am (M & Th)

South

1 hr. metered parking (9am-7pm) including Sun/24s

26TH ST (2ND-1ST)

North

No standing anytime

South

No parking 8am-6pm (except Sun)

25TH ST (ASSER LEVY-1ST) ☺

North

No standing anytime (except authorized vehicles)

South

No parking 9:30am-11am (Tu & F)

25TH ST (1ST-2ND) ☺

North

No parking 7am-7pm (M-F)

South

No parking 9:30am-11am (Tu & F)/2 hr. metered parking (9am-7pm) including Sun

25TH ST (2ND-3RD) ☺

North

1 hr metered parking (9am-7pm) including Sun/No parking 8:30am-10am (M & Th)

South

1 hr metered parking (9am-7pm) including Sun/No parking 8:30am-10am (Tu & F)

25TH ST (3RD-LEXINGTON)

North

1 hr. metered parking (9am-7pm) including Sun/No Parking 8:30am-9am (M,Tu,Th,F)/No parking 8am-6pm (M-F)

South

No standing anytime

25TH ST (LEXINGTON-PARK)

North

No Standing 3p-6p/1 hour metered parking 9am-3pm (including Sun.)/No parking 8am-9am (except Sun)

South

No standing except trucks loading & unloading 8am-7pm (M-F)

25TH ST (PARK-MADISON)

North

No parking 7am-4pm (school days)/No standing except trucks loading & unloading 8am-6pm (M-F)

South

1 hr. metered parking (9am-7pm) including Sun/No parking 8am-9am (except Sun)

24TH ST (MADISON-PARK)

North

No standing anytime

South

No standing except trucks loading & unloading 7am-7pm (M-F)

24TH ST (PARK-LEXINGTON)

North

No standing except trucks loading & unloading 8am-7pm (M-F)

South

1 hr. metered parking (9am-7pm) including Sun/No parking 8am-9am (except Sun)

24TH ST (LEXINGTON-3RD) ☹

North

No standing anytime

South

No standing anytime

24TH ST (3RD-2ND) ☺

North

1 hr. metered parking (9am-7pm) including Sun/24n/No parking 7am-4pm (school days)

South

1 hr. metered parking (9am-7pm) including Sun/24s/No Parking 1pm-3pm school days/1 hour metered parking 9am-1pm & 3pm-7pm (including Sun.)

24TH ST (2ND-1ST-DEAD END)

North

2 hr. metered parking (8:30am-7pm) including Sun/No Parking 8am-8:30am (M,Tu,Th,F)

South

2 hr. metered parking (8:30am-7pm) including Sun/No Parking 8am-8:30am (M,Tu,Th,F)

23RD ST (FDR-ASSER LEVY)

North

No parking 9:30am-11am (M & Th)

South

No parking 9:30am-11am (Tu & F)

23RD ST (ASSER LEVY-1ST)

North

2 hr. metered parking (8:30am-7pm) including Sun/No parking 8am-8:30am (except Sun)

South

2 hr. metered parking (8am-7pm) including Sun/No parking 7:30am-8am (except Sun)

23RD ST (1ST-2ND)

North

1 hr. metered parking (8:30am-7pm) including Sun/No Parking 8am-8:30am (M,Tu,Th,F)

South

No parking 8am-6pm (M-F)

23RD ST (2ND-3RD)

North

No standing 7am-4pm (school days)/1 hr. metered parking (8:30am-7pm) including Sun/No parking 8am-8:30am (except Sun)

South

No parking 8am-6pm (M-F)

23RD ST (3RD-LEXINGTON)

North

1 hour metered parking 8:30am-4pm (including Sun.)/No parking 8am-8:30am (except Sun)

South

1 hour metered parking 10am-4pm (including Sun.)/No parking 7:30am-8am (except Sun)/No Standing 8am-10am & 4pm-6pm (M-F)

23RD ST (LEXINGTON-PARK)

North

No Standing 7am-9am & 4pm-7pm (except Sun.)/No standing except trucks loading & unloading 9am-4pm (except Sun.)

South

No Standing 9am-9pm (except Sun.)/No Standing 8am-9am & 4pm-7pm (except Sun.)

23RD ST (PARK-MADISON)

North

No standing anytime

South

No standing except trucks loading & unloading 9am-4pm (except Sun.)

23RD ST (MADISON-5TH)

North

No standing anytime

South

No standing anytime

23RD ST ST ACCESS RD. (1ST-ASSER LEVY)

North

No parking 9:30am-11am (M & Th)

South

No parking 9:30am-11am (Tu & F)

23RD ST ST ACCESS RD. (ASSER LEVY-FDR)

North

No parking 9:30am-11am (M & Th)

South

No parking 9:30am-11am (Tu & F)

22ND ST (5TH-BROADWAY)

North

No standing anytime

South

No standing anytime

22ND ST (BROADWAY-PARK)

North

No standing except trucks loading & unloading 8am-6pm (M-F)/No standing 11pm-6am (including Sun)

South

No standing except trucks loading & unloading 8am-6pm (M-F)/No standing 11pm-6am (including Sun)

22ND ST (PARK-LEXINGTON)

North

No standing except trucks loading & unloading 8am-7pm (M-F)

South

No Parking 7:30am-8am (M,Tu,Th,F)/1 hr. metered parking (8am-7pm) including Sun/No parking 8am-6pm (M-F)

22ND ST (LEXINGTON-3RD)

North

No parking 8am-6pm (M-F)/No Standing 8am-6pm (M-F) except authorized vehicles

South

No parking 8am-6pm (except Sun)

22ND ST (3RD-2ND) ☺

North

No parking 8am-6pm (M-F)

South

No parking 8am-6pm (M-F)/No parking 7am-4pm (school days)/1 hr. metered parking (9am-7pm) including Sun/No parking 9:30am-11am (Tu & F)

22ND ST (2ND-1ST) ☺

North

No parking 9:30am-11am (M & Th)

South

No parking 9:30am-11am (Tu & F)/No parking 8am-6pm (except Sun)

21ST ST (1ST-2ND) ☺

North

No parking 9:30am-11am (M & Th)

South

No parking 9:30am-11am (Tu & F)/No parking 7am-4pm (school days)/2 hr. metered parking (9am-7pm) including Sun

21ST ST (2ND-3RD) ☹

North

No standing anytime except authorized vehicles

South

No standing anytime except authorized vehicles

21ST ST (3RD-LEXINGTON)

North

2 hr. metered parking (9am-7pm) including Sun/No parking 8am-9am (except Sun)/No parking 7am-7pm (except Sun)

South

2 hr. metered parking (8am-7pm) including Sun/No parking 7:30am-8am (except Sun)/No parking 7am-7pm (except Sun)

21ST ST (LEXINGTON-PARK)

North

No standing except trucks loading & unloading 8am-6pm (M-F)

South

2 hr. metered parking (8am-7pm) including Sun/No parking 7:30am-8am (except Sun)/No parking 7am-7pm (except Sun)/No standing except trucks loading & unloading 8am-6pm (M-F)

21ST ST (PARK-BROADWAY)

North

No standing except trucks loading & unloading 8am-6pm (M-F)

South

No standing except trucks loading & unloading 8am-6pm (M-F)/No Standing 1am-7am including Sun.

21ST ST (BROADWAY-5TH)

North

No standing except trucks loading & unloading 8am-7pm (M-F)

South

No standing except trucks loading & unloading 8am-7pm (M-F)

20TH ST (5TH-BROADWAY)

North

No standing except trucks loading & unloading 8am-7pm (M-F)/No standing 11pm-6am (including Sun)

South

No standing except trucks loading & unloading 8am-7pm (M-F)/No standing 11pm-6am (including Sun)

20TH ST (BROADWAY-PARK)

North

No standing except trucks loading & unloading 8am-7pm (M-F)

South

No standing 7am-7pm (except Sun)

20TH ST (PARK-IRVING)

North

1 hr. metered parking (8am-7pm) including Sun/2 hr. metered parking (8am-7pm) including Sun/No parking 7:30am-8am (except Sun)/No parking 7am-7pm (except Sun)

South

No standing except trucks loading & unloading 8am-6pm (M-F)

20TH ST (IRVING-3RD)

North

2 hr. metered parking (8am-7pm) including Sun/No parking 7:30am-8am (except Sun)

South

No parking 8am-6pm (M-F)

20TH ST (3RD-2ND) ☺

North

No parking anytime

South

1 hr. metered parking (9am-7pm) including Sun/No parking 9:30am-11am (Tu & F)

20TH ST (2ND-1ST) ☺

North

2 hr. metered parking (9am-7pm) including Sun/No parking 9:30am-11am (M & Th)/No parking 7am-4pm (school days)

South

No parking 9:30am-11am (Tu & F)/No parking 7am-4pm (school days)

20TH ST (1ST-FDR DR.) ☺

North

No parking 9:30am-11am (M & Th)

South

No parking 9:30am-11am (Tu & F)

20TH ST ACCESS RD (1ST-FDR DR.) ☺

North

No parking 11:30am-1pm (M & Th)

South

No parking 11:30am-1pm (Tu & F)/No standing except trucks loading & unloading 7am-6pm (except Sun)

19TH ST (1ST-2ND) ☺

North

No parking 9:30am-11am (M & Th)/No parking 7am-4pm (school days)/2 hr. metered parking (9am-7pm) including Sun

South

No parking 9:30am-11am (Tu & F)/2 hr. metered parking (9am-7pm) including Sun

19TH ST (2ND-3RD) ☺

North

No parking 9:00am-11am (M & Th)

South

No parking 9:30am-11am (Tu & F)/No parking 8am-6pm (M-F)

19TH ST (3RD-IRVING) ☺

North

No Parking 8am-6pm (M,W,F)

South

1 hr. metered parking (9am-7pm) including Sun/No parking 8:30am-10am (Tu & F)

19TH ST (IRVING-PARK)

North

No parking 8am-6pm (M-F)

South

No parking 8am-6pm (M-F)/1 hr. metered parking (9am-7pm) including Sun

19TH ST (PARK-BROADWAY)

North

1 hr. metered parking (9am-7pm) including Sun/No parking 8am-9am (except Sun)/No standing except trucks loading & unloading 8am-6pm (except Sun)

South

No standing except trucks loading & unloading 8am 6pm (except Sun)

19TH ST (BROADWAY-5TH)

North

No standing except trucks loading & unloading 8am-7pm (M-F)/No parking 7am-4pm (school days)

South

No standing except trucks loading & unloading 8am-7pm (M-F)

18TH ST (5TH-BROADWAY)

North

No standing except trucks loading & unloading 8am-7pm (M-F)

South

No standing except trucks loading & unloading 7am-7pm (M-F)

18TH ST (BROADWAY-PARK)

North

No standing except trucks loading & unloading 8am-7pm (M-F)

South

No standing except trucks loading & unloading 8am-7pm (M-F)

18TH ST (PARK-IRVING)

North

1 hr. metered parking (9am-7pm) including Sun/No parking 8am-9am (except Sun)

South

No standing except trucks loading & unloading 8am-6pm (M-F)/1 hr. metered parking (9am-7pm) including Sun/No parking 8am-9am (except Sun)

18TH ST (IRVING-3RD)

North

1 hr. metered parking (9am-7pm) including Sun/No parking 8:30am-10am (M & Th)

South

No parking 8:30am-10am (Tu & F)

18TH ST (3RD-2ND)

North

1 hr. metered parking (9am-7pm) including Sun/No parking 8:30am-10am (M & Th)

South

1 hr. metered parking (9am-7pm) including Sun/No parking 8:30am-10am (Tu & F)

18TH ST (2ND-1ST)

North

No parking 10am-11:30am (M & Th)

South

No parking 10am-11:30am (Tu & F)/1 hr. metered parking (9am-7pm) including Sun

18TH ST (1ST AVE. LOOP)

North

No Parking 11am-2pm (Fri)

South

No parking anytime

17TH ST (1ST-2ND)

North

No standing except trucks loading & unloading

South

2 hr. metered parking (8:30am-7pm) including Sun/No Parking 8am-8:30am (M,Tu,Th,F)

17TH ST (2ND-RUTHERFORD)

North

No standing anytime (except authorized vehicles) 7am-7pm

South

No standing anytime

17TH ST (RUTHERFORD-3RD)

North

No parking 11:30am-1pm (M & Th)/1 hr. metered parking (9am-7pm) including Sun

South

No parking 11:30am-1pm (Tu & F)/1 hr. metered parking (9am-7pm) including Sun

17TH ST (3RD-IRVING)

North

No parking 11:30am-1pm (M & Th)/No standing except trucks loading & unloading 7am-7pm (M-F)

South

No parking 11:30am-1pm (Tu & F)/1 hr. metered parking (9am-7pm) including Sun/No parking 7am-4pm (school days)

17TH ST (IRVING-PARK)

North

1 hr. metered parking (9am-7pm) including Sun/No parking 8am-9am (except Sun)

South

No standing except trucks loading & unloading 8am-7pm (M-F)

17TH ST (PARK-UNION SQ)

North

No standing anytime

South

No standing anytime

17TH ST (UNION SQ-BROADWAY-5TH)

North

1 hr. metered parking (9am-7pm) including Sun/No parking 8am-9am (except Sun)/No standing except trucks loading & unloading 8am-6pm (M-F)

South

No standing except trucks loading & unloading 8am-6pm (M-F)

16TH ST (5TH-UNION SQ)

North

No parking 8am-6pm (M-F)

South

No parking 8am-6pm (M-F)

16TH ST (PARK-IRVING)

North

1 hr. metered parking (9am-7pm) including Sun/No parking 8am-9am (except Sun)

South

No standing except trucks loading & unloading 8am-6pm (except Sun)

16TH ST (IRVING-3RD)

North

No parking 8am-9:30am (M & Th)

South

No parking 8am-9:30am (Tu & F)/No standing except trucks loading & unloading 7am-7pm (except Sun)

16TH ST (3RD-RUTHERFORD) ☺

North

No parking 11:30am-1pm (M & Th)/1 hr. metered parking (9am-7pm) including Sun

South

No parking 11:30am-1pm (Tu & F)/No parking 7am-4pm (school days)

16TH ST (1ST-PERLMAN PL.) ☺

North

No parking anytime

South

2 hr. metered parking 9am-7pm (including Sun)/No parking 7am-4pm (school days)/No parking 11:30am-1pm (Tu & F)

15TH ST (RUTHERFORD-2ND) ☺

North

No parking 11:30am-1pm (M & Th)/2 hr. metered parking (9am-7pm) including Sun

South

No parking 11:30am-1pm (Tu & F)

15TH ST (2ND-PERLMAN) ☺

North

No parking anytime

South

No parking 11:30am-1pm (Tu & F)/No parking 7am-4pm (school days)

15TH ST (PERLMAN-1ST) ☺

North

No parking 11:30am-1pm (M & Th)/No parking 8am-6pm (M-F)

South

No parking 11:30am-1pm (Tu & F)/No parking 7am-4pm (school days)

15TH ST (RUTHERFORD-3RD) ☺

North

No parking 11:30am-1pm (M & Th)/No parking 7am-4pm (school days)

South

No parking 11:30am-1pm (Tu & F)

15TH ST (3RD-IRVING) ☺

North

No parking 11:30am-1pm (M & Th)

South

1 hr. metered parking (9:00am-7pm) including Sun/No Parking 8am-9:00am (M,Tu,Th,F)

15TH ST (IRVING-PARK)

North

No parking 8am-6pm (M-F)

South

No standing except trucks loading & unloading 7am-7pm (except Sun)

15TH ST (PARK-UNION SQ) ☹

North

No standing anytime

South

No standing anytime

15TH ST (UNION SQ-BROADWAY-5TH)

North

No standing except trucks loading & unloading 8am-7pm (M-F)/1 hr. metered parking (9am-7pm) including Sun/No parking 8am-9am (except Sun)

South

No standing except trucks loading & unloading 8am-6pm (M-F)

14TH ST (5TH-UNION SQ-UNIVERSITY PL)

North

1 hr. metered parking (9am-10pm) including Sun/No parking 8am-9am (except Sun)

South

1 hr. metered parking (9am-10pm) including Sun/No parking 8am-9am (except Sun)

14TH ST (UNION-BROADWAY)

North

No standing anytime

South

No standing anytime

14TH ST (BROADWAY-4TH) ☹

North

No standing except trucks loading & unloading

South

No standing anytime

14TH ST (4TH-IRVING)

North

No parking 8am-6pm (M-F)

South

No standing except trucks loading & unloading 7am-6pm (except Sun)/No Standing 6pm-7am (including Sun)

14TH ST (IRVING-3RD)

North

No standing except trucks loading & unloading 7am-6pm (except Sun)/No Standing 6pm-7am (including Sun)

South

No standing except trucks loading & unloading 7am-6pm (except Sun)/No Standing 6pm-7am (including Sun)

14TH ST (3RD-2ND)

North

1 hr. metered parking (8am-7pm) including Sun/No parking 7:30am-8am (except Sun)

South

1 hr. metered parking (10am-7pm) including Sun/No Parking 7am-10pm (except Sun)

14TH ST (2ND-1ST)

North

1 hr. metered parking (8am-7pm) including Sun/No parking 7:30am-8am (except Sun)

South

1 hr. metered parking (10am-7pm) including Sun/No Parking 7am-10pm (except Sun)/No parking 7am-7pm (except Sun)

14TH ST (1ST-AVE A)

North

1 hr. metered parking (8am-7pm) including Sun/No parking 7:30am-8am (except Sun)

South

1 hr. metered parking (10am-7pm) including Sun/No Parking 7am-10pm (except Sun)/No parking 7am-7pm (except Sun)/No parking 7am-4pm (school days)

14TH ST (AVE A-AVE B) ☺

North

No parking 11:30am-1pm (M & Th)

South

1 hr. metered parking (10am-7pm) including Sun/No Parking 7am-10pm (except Sun)

14TH ST (AVE B-AVE C) ☺

North

No parking 11:30am-1pm (M & Th)

South

1 hr. metered parking (10am-7pm) including Sun/No Parking 7am-10pm (except Sun)

14TH ST (AVE C-AVE D)

North

No parking 11am-12:30pm (M & F)

South

No parking 11am-12:30pm (Tu & F)

14TH ST ACCESS RD (1ST-AVE D)

North

No parking 11:30am-1pm (M & Th)

South

No parking 11:30am-1pm (Tu & F)

13TH ST (AVE D - AVE C)

North

No parking 11am-12:30pm (M & F)

South

No parking 11am-12:30pm (Tu & F)

13TH ST (DEAD END - AVE B)

North

No parking 11am-12:30pm (M & F)

South

No parking 11am-12:30pm (Tu & F)

13TH ST (AVE B - AVE A)

North

No parking 11am-12:30pm (M & F)

South

No parking 11am-12:30pm (Tu & F)

13TH ST (AVE A - 1ST AVE)

North

No parking 9am-10:30am (M & Th)/No standing 7am-4pm (school days) (except M.I.U. vehicles)

South

No parking 9am-10:30am (Tu & F)

13TH ST (1ST AVE - 2ND AVE)

North

No parking 9am-10:30am (M & Th)/2 hr. metered parking (9am-7pm) including Sun/No standing except authorized vehicles (Ear, Eye & Throat Hospital doctor's vehicles)

South

No parking 9am-10:30am (Tu & F)/No standing 7am-7pm (M-F) except authorized vehicles (Ear, Eye & Throat Hospital doctor's vehicles)

13TH ST (2ND AVE - 3RD AVE) ☺

North

2 hr. metered parking (9am-7pm) including Sun/No parking 9am-10:30am (M & Th)

South

2 hr. metered parking (9am-7pm) including Sun/No parking 9am-10:30am (Tu & F)

13TH ST (3RD AVE - 4TH AVE) ☺

North

2 hr. metered parking (9am-7pm) including Sun/No parking 9am-10:30am (M & Th)/No parking 7am-6pm (M-F)

South

2 hr. metered parking (9am-7pm) including Sun/No parking 9am-10:30am (Tu & F)/No parking 7am-6pm (M-F)

13TH ST (4TH AVE - BROADWAY)

North

No standing 7am -7pm including Sun

South

No standing 7am -7pm including Sun

13TH ST (BROADWAY - UNIVERSITY)

North

No standing 7am -7pm including Sun

South

1 hr. metered parking (9am-7pm) including Sun/No standing 7pm - 9am including Sun (night regulation)/No standing except trucks loading & unloading 9am-7pm (including Sun)

13TH ST (UNIVERSITY - 5TH)

North

No parking 8am-6pm (M-F)/No standing 8am - 9am (M-F)

South

No parking 8am-6pm (M-F)/No standing 8am - 9am (M-F)

12TH ST (5TH - UNIVERSITY)

North

1 hr. metered parking (9am-7pm) including Sun/No parking 8am-9am (M-F)/No parking 8am-6pm (M-F)

South

1 hr. metered parking (9am-7pm) including Sun/No parking 8am-9am (M-F)/No parking 8am-6pm (M-F)

12TH ST (UNIVERSITY - BROADWAY)

North

No parking 8am-9am (M-F)/No parking 8am-6pm (M-F)

South

No parking 8am-9am (M-F)/No parking 8am-6pm (M-F)

12TH ST (BROADWAY - 4TH AVE)

North

No parking 8am-6pm (M-F)

South

No parking 8am-6pm (M-F)/No parking 7am-6pm (M-F)

12TH ST (4TH AVE - 3RD AVE)

North

No parking 7am-6pm (M-F)/No parking 10pm-6am (Th, F, Sat)

South

No parking 7am-6pm (M-F)/No parking 10pm-6am (Th, F, Sat)

12TH ST (3RD AVE - 2ND AVE)

North

No parking 9am-10:30am (M & Th)

South

No parking 9am-10:30am (Tu & F)

12TH ST (2ND AVE - 1ST AVE)

North

No parking 9am-10:30am (M & Th)/2 hr. metered parking (9am-7pm) including Sun

South

No parking 9am-10:30am (Tu & F)/2 hr. metered parking (9am-7pm) including Sun/No parking 7am-4pm (school days)

12TH ST (1ST AVE - AVE A)

North

No parking 9am-10:30am (M & Th)/No parking 8am-6pm (M-F)

South

No parking 9am-10:30am (Tu & F)/No parking 7am-4pm (school days)

12TH ST (AVE A - AVE B)

North

No parking 11am-12:30pm (M & F)

South

No parking 11am-12:30pm (Tu & F)

12TH ST (AVE B - AVE C) ☺

North

No parking 11am-12:30pm (M & F)/No parking 8am-6pm (M-F)

South

No parking 11am-12:30pm (Tu & F)/No parking 8am-6pm (except Sun)/No parking 7am-4pm (school days)

12TH ST (SZOLD - AVE D) ☺

North

No parking 11am-12:30pm (M & F)/No parking 7am-4pm (school days)

South

No parking 11am-12:30pm (Tu & F)/No parking 7am-4pm (school days)

11TH ST (AVE C - AVE B) ☺

North

No parking 11am-12:30pm (M & F)

South

No parking 11am-12:30pm (Tu & F)

11TH ST (AVE B - AVE A) ☺

North

No parking 11am-12:30pm (M & F)

South

No parking 11am-12:30pm (Tu & F)

11TH ST (AVE A - 1ST AVE) ☺

North

No parking 9am-10:30am (M & Th)/No parking 7am-4pm (school days)

South

No parking 9am-10:30am (Tu & F)

11TH ST (1ST AVE - 2ND AVE) ☺

North

2 hr. metered parking (9am-7pm) including Sun/No parking 9am-10:30am (M & Th)

South

2 hr. metered parking (9am-7pm) including Sun/No parking 9am-10:30am (Tu & F)

11TH ST (2ND AVE - 3RD AVE) ☺

North

2 hr. metered parking (9am-7pm) including Sun/No parking 9am-10:30am (M & Th)

South

2 hr. metered parking (9am-7pm) including Sun/No parking 9am-10:30am (Tu & F)

11TH ST (3RD AVE - 4TH AVE) ☺

North

No parking 9am-10:30am (M & Th)

South

No parking 9am-10:30am (Tu & F)

11TH ST (BROADWAY - UNIVERSITY)

North

No standing except trucks loading & unloading 8am-6pm (M-F)

South

No parking 8am-6pm (M-F)/1 hr. metered parking (9am-7pm) including Sun/No parking 8am-9am (except Sun)

11TH ST (UNIVERSITY - 5TH) ☺

North

No parking 8am-11am (M & Th)

South

No parking 8am-11am (Tu & F)

10TH ST (5TH - UNIVERSITY) ☺

North

No parking 8am-11am (M & Th)

South

No parking 8am-11am (Tu & F)

10TH ST (UNIVERSITY - BROADWAY)

North

1 hr. metered parking (9am-7pm) including Sun/No parking 8am-9am (except Sun)/No parking 8am-6pm (M-F)

South

No parking 8am-6pm (M-F)

10TH ST (BROADWAY - 4TH AVE)

North

No parking 8am-6pm (M-F)

South

2 hr. metered parking (9am-7pm) including Sun

10TH ST (4TH AVE - 3RD AVE) ☺

North

2 hr. metered parking (9am-7pm) including Sun/No parking 9am-10:30am (M & Th)

South

2 hr. metered parking (9am-7pm) including Sun/No parking 9am-10:30am (Tu & F)

10TH ST (3RD AVE - STUVESANT) ☺

North

2 hr. metered parking (9am-7pm) including Sun/No parking 9am-10:30am (M & Th)

South

No parking 9am-10:30am (Tu & F)

10TH ST (STUVESANT - 2ND AVE) ☺

North

No parking anytime

South

2 hr. metered parking (9am-7pm) including Sun/No parking 9am-10:30am (Tu & F)

10TH ST (2ND AVE - 1ST AVE)

North

2 hr. metered parking (9am-7pm) including Sun/No parking 7am-6pm (M-F)

South

2 hr. metered parking (9am-7pm) including Sun/No parking 7am-6pm (M-F)

10TH ST (1ST AVE - AVE A)

North

No parking 7am-6pm (M-F)

South

No parking 7am-6pm (M-F)

10TH ST (AVE A - AVE B)

North

No parking 8am-6pm (M-F)

South

No parking anytime

10TH ST (AVE B - AVE C)

North

No parking 8am-6pm (M-F)

South

No parking anytime

10TH ST (AVE C - SZOLD)

North

No standing 7am-6pm (M-F)

South

No standing except trucks loading & unloading 8am-6pm (M-F)

10TH ST (SZOLD - AVE D)

North

No standing anytime

South

No standing except trucks loading & unloading 8am-6pm (M-F)

10TH ST LOOP (AVE D - FDR DR) ☺

North

No parking 11am-12:30pm (M & F)

South

No parking 11am-12:30pm (Tu & F)

9TH ST (AVE D - AVE C) ☺

North

No parking 11am-12:30pm (M & F)

South

No parking 11am-12:30pm (Tu & F)/No parking 7am-6pm (school days)

9TH ST (AVE C - AVE B) ☺

North

No parking 11am-12:30pm (M & F)/No parking 8am-6pm (M-F)

South

No parking 11am-12:30pm (Tu & F)

9TH ST (AVE A - 1ST AVE) ☺

North

No parking 9am-10:30am (M & Th)

South

No parking 9am-10:30am (Tu & F)

9TH ST (1ST AVE - 2ND AVE) ☺

North

No parking 9am-10:30am (M & Th)/2 hr. metered parking (9am-7pm) including Sun

South

No parking 9am-10:30am (Tu & F)/2 hr. metered parking (9am-7pm) including Sun

9TH ST (2ND AVE - STUVESANT) ☺

North

No parking 7am-6pm (except Sun)

South

No parking 9am-10:30am (Tu & F)/2 hr. metered parking (9am-7pm) including Sun

9TH ST (STUVESANT - 3RD AVE) ☹

North

No parking anytime

South

No parking anytime

9TH ST (3RD AVE - 4TH AVE) ☹

North

No parking anytime

South

No parking anytime

9TH ST (3RD - 4TH AVE)

North

No parking 8am-6pm (M-F)

South

No parking 8am-6pm (M-F)

9TH ST (WANAMAKER PL) (4TH AVE - BROADWAY)

North

No parking anytime

South

No parking 8am-6pm (M-F)

9TH ST (BROADWAY - UNIVERSITY)

North

No parking anytime

South

1 hr. metered parking (9am-7pm) including Sun/No parking 8am-9am (except Sun)

9TH ST (UNIVERSITY - 5TH)

North

No parking anytime

South

No parking 8am-6pm (except Sun)

8TH ST (5TH - UNIVERSITY)

North

No standing 11pm-6am (including Sun)/1 hr. metered parking (9am-10pm) including Sun/No parking 8am-9am (except Sun)

South

No standing 11pm-6am (including Sun)/1 hr. metered parking (9am-10pm) including Sun/No parking 8am-9am (except Sun)

8TH ST (UNIVERSITY - GREENE)

North

No standing 11pm-6am (including Sun)/1 hr. metered parking (9am-10pm) including Sun/No parking 8am-9am (except Sun)

South

No standing 11pm-6am (including Sun)/1 hr. metered parking (9am-10pm) including Sun/No parking 8am-9am (except Sun)

8TH ST (GREENE - MERCER)

North

No standing 11pm-6am (including Sun)/1 hr. metered parking (9am-10pm) including Sun/No parking 8am-9am (except Sun)

South

No standing 11pm-6am (including Sun)/1 hr. metered parking (9am-10pm) including Sun/No parking 8am-9am (except Sun)

8TH ST (MERCER - BROADWAY)

North

No standing 11pm-6am (including Sun)/1 hr. metered parking (9am-10pm) including Sun/No parking 8am-9am (except Sun)

South

No standing anytime

8TH ST (BROADWAY - 4TH AVE)

North

No standing 8am - 4pm (M-F)

South

No standing anytime

8TH ST/ST. MARKS (4TH AVE - 3RD AVE)

North

No standing 8am-6pm (M-F) except authorized vehicles

South

No standing 8am-6pm (M-F) except authorized vehicles

8TH ST (AVE B - AVE C) ☺

North

No parking 11am-12:30pm (M & F)

South

No parking 11am-12:30pm (Tu & F)

8TH ST (AVE C - AVE D) ☺

North

No parking 11am-12:30pm (M & F)

South

No parking 11am-12:30pm (Tu & F)

8TH ST/ST. MARKS (3RD AVE - 2ND AVE) ☹

North

No standing except trucks loading & unloading

South

No standing except trucks loading & unloading

8TH ST/ST. MARKS (2ND AVE - 1ST AVE) ☺

North

No parking anytime

South

2 hr. metered parking (9am-7pm) including Sun/No parking 9am-10:30am (Tu & F)

8TH ST/ST. MARKS (1ST AVE - AVE A) ☺

North

No standing anytime

South

No parking 9am-10:30am (Tu & F)/No parking 7am-4pm (school days)

7TH ST (AVE D - AVE C) ☺

North

No parking 11am-12:30pm (M & F)

South

No parking 11am-12:30pm (Tu & F)

7TH ST (AVE C - AVE B) ☺

North

No parking 11am-12:30pm (M & F)/No parking 7am-4pm (school days)

South

No parking 11am-12:30pm (Tu & F)

7TH ST (AVE B - AVE A) ☺

North

No parking 11am-12:30pm (M & F)

South

No parking 11am-12:30pm (Tu & F)

7TH ST (AVE A - 1ST AVE) ☺

North

No parking anytime

South

No parking 9am-10:30am (Tu & F)

7TH ST (1ST AVE - 2ND AVE)

North

2 hr. metered parking (9am-7pm) including Sun/No parking 9am-10:30am (M & Th)

South

2 hr. metered parking (9am-7pm) including Sun/No parking 9am-10:30am (Tu & F)

7TH ST (2ND AVE - 3RD AVE)

North

2 hr. metered parking (9am-7pm) including Sun/No parking 9am-10:30am (M & Th)

South

2 hr. metered parking (9am-7pm) including Sun/No parking 9am-10:30am (Tu & F)

6TH ST (COOPER SQ - 2ND AVE)

North

2 hr. metered parking (9am-7pm) including Sun/No parking 9am-10:30am (M & Th)/No parking 7am-4pm (school days)

South

2 hr. metered parking (9am-7pm) including Sun/27s

6TH ST (2ND AVE - 1ST AVE)

North

2 hr. metered parking (9am-7pm) including Sun/No parking 9am-10:30am (M & Th)

South

2 hr. metered parking (9am-7pm) including Sun/27s

6TH ST (1ST AVE - AVE A)

North

No parking 9am-10:30am (M & Th)/No parking 8am-6pm (M-F)

South

No parking 9am-10:30am (Tu & F)

6TH ST (AVE A - AVE B)

North

No parking 11am-12:30pm (M & F)

South

No parking 11am-12:30pm (Tu & F)

6TH ST (AVE B - AVE C)

North

No parking 11am-12:30pm (M & F)

South

No parking 11am-12:30pm (Tu & F)/No parking 7am-4pm (school days)

6TH ST (AVE C- AVE D) ☺

North

No parking 11am-12:30pm (M & F)

South

No parking 11am-12:30pm (Tu & F)

6TH ST (AVE D - FDR DR) ☺

North

No parking 11am-12:30pm (M & F)

South

No parking 11am-12:30pm (Tu & F)

5TH ST (AVE D - AVE C) ☺

North

No parking 11am-12:30pm (M & F)

South

No parking 11am-12:30pm (Tu & F)

5TH ST (AVE C - DEAD END) ☺

North

No parking 11am-12:30pm (M & F)

South

No parking 11am-12:30pm (Tu & F)

5TH ST (AVE B - AVE A) ☺

North

No parking 11am-12:30pm (M & F)

South

No parking 11am-12:30pm (Tu & F)

5TH ST (1ST AVE - 2ND AVE) ☺

North

No parking 9am-10:30am (M & Th)

South

No parking 9am-10:30am (Tu & F)

5TH ST (2ND AVE - COOPER SQ) ☺

North

No parking 9am-10:30am (M & Th)

South

No parking 9am-10:30am (Tu & F)

4TH ST (LAFAYETTE - COOPER SQ/BOWERY)

North

No standing 10pm-6am including Sun/No parking 8am-6pm (except Sun)

South

No standing 10pm-6am including Sun/No standing except trucks loading & unloading 7am-7pm (M-F)

4TH ST (COOPER SQ/BOWERY - 2ND AVE)

North

2 hr. metered parking (9am-7pm) including Sun/No parking 9am-10:30am (M & Th)

South

2 hr. metered parking (9am-7pm) including Sun/No parking 9am-10:30am (Tu & F)/No parking 8am-6pm (M-F)

4TH ST (2ND AVE - 1ST AVE)

North

2 hr. metered parking (9am-7pm) including Sun/No parking 9am-10:30am (M & Th)/No parking 7am-4pm (school days)

South

2 hr. metered parking (9am-7pm) including Sun/No parking 9am-10:30am (Tu & F)/No parking 7am-6pm (M-F)

4TH ST (1ST AVE - AVE A)

North

No parking 9am-10:30am (M & Th)

South

No parking 9am-10:30am (Tu & F)/No parking 7am-4pm (school days)

4TH ST (AVE A - AVE B)

North

No parking 11am-12:30pm (M & F)

South

No parking 11am-12:30pm (Tu & F)/No parking 8am-6pm (M-F)

4TH ST (AVE B - AVE C)

North

No parking 11am-12:30pm (M & F)/No parking 7am-4pm (school days)

South

No parking 11am-12:30pm (Tu & F)

4TH ST (AVE C- AVE D)

North

No parking 11am-12:30pm (M & F)/No parking 7am-4pm (school days)

South

No parking 11am-12:30pm (Tu & F)/No standing except trucks loading & unloading 7am-7pm (M-F)

3RD ST (AVE D - AVE C) ☺

North

No parking 11am-12:30pm (M & F)

South

No parking 11am-12:30pm (Tu & F)

3RD ST (AVE C - AVE B) ☺

North

No parking 11am-12:30pm (M & F)/No parking 8am-6pm (M-F)

South

No parking 11am-12:30pm (Tu & F)

3RD ST (AVE B - AVE A) ☺

North

No parking 11am-12:30pm (M & F)

South

No parking 11am-12:30pm (Tu & F)

3RD ST (AVE A - 1ST AVE) ☺

North

No parking 9am-10:30am (M & Th)/No parking 7am-4pm (school days)

South

No parking 9am-10:30am (Tu & F)

3RD ST (1ST AVE - 2ND AVE) ☺

North

No parking 9am-10:30am (M & Th)

South

No parking 9am-10:30am (Tu & F)

3RD ST (2ND AVE - BOWERY) ☺

North

No parking 9am-10:30am (M & Th)/No standing except trucks loading & unloading 8am-6pm (M-F)

South

No parking 9am-10:30am (Tu & F)

3RD ST (BOWERY - LAFAYETTE)

North

No parking 8am-6pm (M-F)

South

No parking 8am-6pm (M-F)

2ND ST (AVE D - AVE C)

North

No parking 11am-12:30pm (M & F)/No parking 8am-6pm (M-F)

South

No parking 11am-12:30pm (Tu & F)

2ND ST (AVE C - AVE B)

North

No parking 11am-12:30pm (M & F)

South

No parking 11am-12:30pm (Tu & F)

2ND ST (AVE B - AVE A)

North

No parking 11am-12:30pm (M & F)

South

No parking 11am-12:30pm (Tu & F)

2ND ST (AVE A - 1ST AVE)

North

No parking 9am-10:30am (M & Th)

South

No parking 9am-10:30am (Tu & F)/No parking 8am-6pm (except Sun)

2ND ST (1ST AVE - 2ND AVE)

North

No parking 9am-10:30am (M & Th)/No parking 7am-4pm (school days)

South

No parking 9am-10:30am (Tu & F)

2ND ST (2ND AVE - BOWERY)

North

No parking 9am-10:30am (M & Th)

South

No parking 9am-10:30am (Tu & F)

1ST ST (AVE B - AVE A)

North

2 hr. metered parking (9am-7pm) including Sun/No standing 11pm - 9am including Sun

South

No parking anytime

1ST ST (AVE A - LUDLOW)

North

2 hr. metered parking (9am-7pm) including Sun/No standing 11pm - 9am including Sun

South

1 hr. metered parking (9am-7pm) including Sun/No standing 11pm - 9am including Sun

1ST ST (LUDLOW - ORCHARD)

North

No parking 8am-9am (M, Th)

South

1 hr. metered parking (9am-7pm) including Sun/No standing 11pm - 9am including Sun

1ST ST (ORCHARD - 1ST AVE)

North

2 hr. metered parking (9am-7pm) including Sun/No standing 11pm - 9am including Sun

South

No standing 11pm - 9am including Sun

1ST ST (1ST AVE - 2ND AVE)

North

No parking 10am-11:30am (M & Th)

South

No parking 10am-11:30am (Tu & F)/No parking 8am-6pm (M-F)

1ST ST (2ND AVE - BOWERY)

North

No parking 10am-11:30am (M & Th)

South

No parking 10am-11:30am (Tu & F)

1ST AVE (HOUSTON - 1TH)

East

No parking anytime

West

1 hr. metered parking (8:30am-7pm) including Sun/No parking 8am-8:30am (except Sun)

1ST AVE (1TH - 2ND ST)

East

1 hr. metered parking (9am-7pm) including Sun/No parking 8:30am-9am (except Sun)

West

1 hr. metered parking (8:30am-7pm) including Sun/No parking 8am-8:30am (except Sun)

1ST AVE (2ND ST - 3TH) ☺

East

No parking 8:30am-9am (except Sun)

West

1 hr. metered parking (8:30am-7pm) including Sun/No parking 8am-8:30am (except Sun)

1ST AVE (3TH - 4TH) ☺

East

No parking 8:30am-9am (except Sun)

West

1 hr. metered parking (8:30am-7pm) including Sun/No parking 8am-8:30am (except Sun)

1ST AVE (4TH - 5TH) ☺

East

No parking 8:30am-9am (except Sun)

West

1 hr. metered parking (8:30am-7pm) including Sun/No parking 8am-8:30am (except Sun)

1ST AVE (5TH - 6TH) ☺

East

No parking 8:30am-9am (except Sun)

West

1 hr. metered parking (8:30am-7pm) including Sun/No parking 8am-8:30am (except Sun)

1ST AVE (6TH - 7TH)

East

1 hr. metered parking (9am-7pm) including Sun/No parking 8:30am-9am (except Sun)

West

1 hr. metered parking (8:30am-7pm) including Sun/No parking 8am-8:30am (except Sun)

1ST AVE (7TH - ST MARKS PL)

East

1 hr. metered parking (9am-7pm) including Sun/No parking 8:30am-9am (except Sun)

West

1 hr. metered parking (8:30am-7pm) including Sun/No parking 8am-8:30am (except Sun)

1ST AVE (ST MARKS PL - 9TH)

East

1 hr. metered parking (9am-7pm) including Sun/No parking 8:30am-9am (except Sun)

West

1 hr. metered parking (8:30am-7pm) including Sun/No parking 8am-8:30am (except Sun)

1ST AVE (9TH - 10TH)

East

1 hr. metered parking (9am-7pm) including Sun/No parking 8:30am-9am (except Sun)

West

1 hr. metered parking (8:30am-7pm) including Sun/No parking 8am-8:30am (except Sun)

1ST AVE (10TH -11TH)

East

1 hr. metered parking (9am-7pm) including Sun/No parking 8:30am-9am (except Sun)

West

1 hr. metered parking (8:30am-7pm) including Sun/No parking 8am-8:30am (except Sun)

1ST AVE (11TH - 12TH)

East

1 hr. metered parking (9am-7pm) including Sun/No parking 8:30am-9am (except Sun)

West

No parking 8am-8:30am (except Sun)/No parking 7am-4pm (school days)

1ST AVE (12TH - 13TH)

East

1 hr. metered parking (9am-7pm) including Sun/No parking 8:30am-9am (except Sun)

West

1 hr. metered parking (8:30am-7pm) including Sun/No parking 8am-8:30am (except Sun)

1ST AVE (13TH - 14TH)

East

1 hr. metered parking (9am-7pm) including Sun/No parking 8:30am-9am (except Sun)

West

1 hr. metered parking (8:30am-7pm) including Sun/No parking 8am-8:30am (except Sun)

1ST AVE (14TH-15TH)

East

1 hr. metered parking (8:30am-7pm) including Sun/No parking 8am-8:30am (except Sun)

West

No standing except trucks loading & unloading 7am-7pm (M-F)

1ST AVE (15TH-16TH)

East

1 hr. metered parking (8:30am-7pm) including Sun/No parking 8am-8:30am (except Sun)

West

1 hr. metered parking (9am-7pm) including Sun/No parking 8:30am-9am (except Sun)

1ST AVE (16TH-17TH)

East

1 hr. metered parking (8:30am-7pm) including Sun/No parking 8am-8:30am (except Sun)

West

1 hr. metered parking (9am-7pm) including Sun/No parking 8:30am-9am (except Sun)

1ST AVE (17TH-18TH)

East

1 hr. metered parking (8:30am-7pm) including Sun/No parking 8am-8:30am (except Sun)

West

1 hr. metered parking (9am-7pm) including Sun/No parking 8:30am-9am (except Sun)

1ST AVE (18TH-19TH)

East

1 hr. metered parking (8:30am-7pm) including Sun/No parking 8am-8:30am (except Sun)

West

1 hr. metered parking (9am-7pm) including Sun/No parking 8:30am-9am (except Sun)

1ST AVE (19TH-20TH)

East

No standing anytime

West

1 hr. metered parking (9am-7pm) including Sun/No parking 8:30am-9am (except Sun)

1ST AVE (20TH-21ST)

East

No standing anytime

West

1 hr. metered parking (9am-7pm) including Sun/No parking 8:30am-9am (except Sun)/No standing except trucks loading & unloading 7am-4pm (M-F)/1 hr. metered parking 4pm-7pm (M-F) & 9am-7pm (Sa & Sun)

1ST AVE (21ST-22ND)

East

2 hr. metered parking (8:30am-7pm) including Sun/No parking 8am-8:30am (except Sun)

West

1 hr. metered parking (9am-7pm) including Sun/No parking 8:30am-9am (except Sun)

1ST AVE (22ND-23RD)

East

2 hr. metered parking (8:30am-7pm) including Sun/No parking 8am-8:30am (except Sun)

West

1 hr. metered parking (9am-7pm) including Sun/No parking 8:30am-9am (except Sun)

1ST AVE (23RD-24TH)

East

No parking anytime

West

1 hr. metered parking (9am-7pm) including Sun/No parking 8:30am-9am (except Sun)

1ST AVE (24TH-25TH)

East

1 hr. metered parking (8:30am-7pm) including Sun/No parking 8am-8:30am (except Sun)

West

1 hr. metered parking (9am-7pm) including Sun/No parking 8:30am-9am (except Sun)

1ST AVE (25TH-26TH)

East

No standing anytime

West

1 hr. metered parking (9am-7pm) including Sun/No parking 8:30am-9am (except Sun)/No standing anytime (except authorized vehicles) 7am-7pm

1ST AVE (26TH-27TH)

East

No standing anytime

West

No standing anytime

1ST AVE (27TH-28TH)

East

No standing anytime (except authorized vehicles)

West

1 hr. metered parking (9am-7pm) including Sun/No parking 8:30am-9am (except Sun)

1ST AVE (28TH-29TH)

East

No standing anytime (except authorized vehicles)

West

1 hr. metered parking (9am-7pm) including Sun/No parking 8:30am-9am (except Sun)

1ST AVE (29TH-30TH)

East

No standing anytime (except authorized vehicles)

West

No standing anytime (except authorized vehicles)

1ST AVE ACCESS RD. (14TH-15TH)

East

No parking 11:30am-1pm (Tu & F)

West

No parking 11:30am-1pm (M & Th)

1ST AVE ACCESS RD. (15TH-16TH)

East

No parking 11:30am-1pm (Tu & F)

West

No parking 11:30am-1pm (M & Th)

1ST AVE ACCESS RD. (16TH-17TH)

East

No parking 11:30am-1pm (Tu & F)

West

No parking 11:30am-1pm (M & Th)

1ST AVE ACCESS RD. (17TH-18TH)

East

No parking 11:30am-1pm (Tu & F)

West

No parking 11:30am-1pm (M & Th)

1ST AVE ACCESS RD. (18TH-19TH)

East

No parking 11:30am-1pm (Tu & F)

West

No parking 11:30am-1pm (M & Th)

1ST AVE ACCESS RD. (19TH-20TH)

East

No parking 11:30am-1pm (Tu & F)

West

No parking 11:30am-1pm (M & Th)

1ST AVE ACCESS RD. (20TH-21ST)

East

No parking 11:30am-1pm (Tu & F)

West

No parking 11:30am-1pm (M & Th)

2ND AVE (30TH-29TH)

East

1 hr. metered parking (8:30am-10pm) including Sun

West

One hr. metered parking 10am-4pm & 7pm-10pm (M-F) & 9am-10pm (Sa & Sun)/No Stopping 7am-10am & 4pm-7pm (M-F)

2ND AVE (29TH-28TH)

East

1 hr. metered parking (8:30am-10pm) including Sun

West

One hr. metered parking (10am-4pm & 7pm-10pm) incl. Sun/No Stopping 7am-10am & 4pm-7pm (M-F)

2ND AVE (28TH-27TH)

East

1 hr. metered parking (8:30am-10pm) including Sun

West

One hr. metered parking (10am-4pm & 7pm-10pm) incl. Sun/No Stopping 7am-10am & 4pm-7pm (M-F)

2ND AVE (27TH-26TH)

East

1 hr. metered parking (8:30am-10pm) including Sun

West

One hr. metered parking (10am-4pm & 7pm-10pm) incl. Sun/No Stopping 7am-10am & 4pm-7pm (M-F)

2ND AVE (26TH-25TH)

East

1 hr. metered parking (8:30am-10pm) including Sun

West

One hr. metered parking (10am-4pm & 7pm-10pm) incl. Sun/No Stopping 7am-10am & 4pm-7pm (M-F)

2ND AVE (25TH-24TH)

East

1 hr. metered parking (8:30am-10pm) including Sun

West

1 hr. metered parking (10am-4pm & 7pm-10pm) including Sun/No Stopping 7am-10am & 4pm-7pm (M-F)

2ND AVE (24TH-23RD)

East

No standing except trucks loading & unloading 9am-7pm (except Sun)/No parking 8:30am-9am (except Sun)

West

1 hr. metered parking (10am-4pm & 7pm-10pm) including Sun/No Stopping 7am-10am & 4pm-7pm (M-F)

2ND AVE (23RD-22ND)

East

1 hr. metered parking (8:30am-10pm) including Sun

West

1 hr. metered parking (10am-4pm & 7pm-10pm) including Sun/No Stopping 7am-10am & 4pm-7pm (M-F)

2ND AVE (22ND-21ST)

East

1 hr. metered parking (8:30am-10pm) including Sun

West

1 hr. metered parking (10am-4pm & 7pm-10pm) including Sun/No Stopping 7am-10am & 4pm-7pm (M-F)

2ND AVE (21ST-20TH)

East

1 hr. metered parking (8:30am-10pm) including Sun

West

1 hr. metered parking (10am-4pm & 7pm-10pm) including Sun/No Stopping 7am-10am & 4pm-7pm (M-F)

2ND AVE (20TH-19TH)

East

1 hr. metered parking (8:30am-10pm) including Sun

West

1 hr. metered parking (10am-4pm & 7pm-10pm) including Sun/No Stopping 7am-10am & 4pm-7pm (M-F)

2ND AVE (19TH-18TH)

East

1 hr. metered parking (8:30am-10pm) including Sun

West

1 hr. metered parking (10am-4pm & 7pm-10pm) including Sun/No Stopping 7am-10am & 4pm-7pm (M-F)

2ND AVE (18TH-17TH)

East

1 hr. metered parking (8:30am-10pm) including Sun

West

1 hr. metered parking (10am-4pm & 7pm-10pm) including Sun/No Stopping 7am-10am & 4pm-7pm (M-F)

2ND AVE (17TH-16TH)

East

2 hr. metered parking (8:30am-10pm) including Sun

West

2 hr. metered parking (10am-4pm & 7pm-10pm) including Sun/No Stopping 7am-10am & 4pm-7pm (M-F)

2ND AVE (16TH-15TH)

East

2 hr. metered parking (8:30am-10pm) including Sun

West

2 hr. metered parking (10am-4pm & 7pm-10pm) including Sun/No Stopping 7am-10am & 4pm-7pm (M-F)

2ND AVE (15TH-14TH)

East

1 hr. metered parking (10am-4pm & 7pm-10pm) including Sun/No parking 7am-6pm (except Sun)

West

1 hr. metered parking (10am-4pm & 7pm-10pm) including Sun

2ND AVE (14TH - 13TH)

East

1 hour metered parking 8:30am-10pm including Sun/No parking 8am-8:30am (except Sun)

West

1 hr. metered parking (9am-10pm) including Sun/No parking 8:30am-9am (except Sun)

2ND AVE (13TH - 12TH)

East

1 hour metered parking 8:30am-10pm including Sun/No parking 8am-8:30am (except Sun)

West

1 hr. metered parking (9am-10pm) including Sun/No parking 8:30am-9am (except Sun)

2ND AVE (12TH - 11TH)

East

1 hour metered parking 8:30am-10pm including Sun/No parking 8am-8:30am (except Sun)

West

1 hr. metered parking (9am-10pm) including Sun/No parking 8:30am-9am (except Sun)

2ND AVE (11TH - 10TH)

East

1 hour metered parking 8:30am-10pm including Sun/No parking 8am-8:30am (except Sun)

West

1 hr. metered parking (9am-10pm) including Sun/No parking 8:30am-9am (except Sun)

2ND AVE (10TH - 9TH)

East

1 hour metered parking 8:30am-10pm including Sun/No parking 8am-8:30am (except Sun)

West

1 hr. metered parking (9am-10pm) including Sun/No parking 8:30am-9am (except Sun)

2ND AVE (9TH - ST MARKS PL)

East

1 hour metered parking 8:30am-10pm including Sun/No parking 8am-8:30am (except Sun)

West

No parking anytime

2ND AVE (ST MARKS PL - 7TH)

East

1 hour metered parking 8:30am-10pm including Sun/No parking 8am-8:30am (except Sun)

West

1 hr. metered parking (9am-10pm) including Sun/No parking 8:30am-9am (except Sun)

2ND AVE (7TH - 6TH)

East

1 hour metered parking 8:30am-10pm including Sun/No parking 8am-8:30am (except Sun)

West

1 hr. metered parking (9am-10pm) including Sun/No parking 8:30am-9am (except Sun)

2ND AVE (6TH - 5TH)

East

1 hour metered parking 8:30am-10pm including Sun/No parking 8am-8:30am (except Sun)

West

1 hr. metered parking (9am-10pm) including Sun/No parking 8:30am-9am (except Sun)

2ND AVE (5TH - 4TH)

East

1 hour metered parking 8:30am-10pm including Sun/No parking 8am-8:30am (except Sun)

West

1 hr. metered parking (9am-10pm) including Sun/No parking 8:30am-9am (except Sun)

2ND AVE (4TH - 3TH)

East

1 hour metered parking 8:30am-10pm including Sun/No parking 8am-8:30am (except Sun)

West

1 hr. metered parking (9am-10pm) including Sun/No parking 8:30am-9am (except Sun)

2ND AVE (3TH - 2ND ST)

East

1 hour metered parking 8:30am-10pm including Sun/No parking 8am-8:30am (except Sun)

West

1 hr. metered parking (9am-10pm) including Sun/No parking 8:30am-9am (except Sun)

2ND AVE (2ND ST - 1ST ST) ☺

East

No parking 8am-8:30am (except Sun)

West

1 hr. metered parking (9am-10pm) including Sun/No parking 8:30am-9am (except Sun)

2ND AVE (1ST ST - HOUSTON)

East

No parking 8am-6pm (M-F)

West

No parking 8am-6pm (M-F)

3RD AVE (7TH - 6TH)

East

1 hr. metered parking (8:30am-7pm) including Sun/No parking 8am-8:30am (except Sun)

West

No standing anytime

3RD AVE (6TH - 5TH)

East

1 hr. metered parking (8am-7pm) including Sun/No parking 7:30am-8am (except Sun)

West

No parking 7am-7pm (except Sun)

3RD AVE (5TH - 4TH) ☺

East

No parking 7:30am-8am (except Sun)

West

No parking 7am-7pm (except Sun)

3RD AVE (7TH - ST. MARKS PL/8TH)

East

1 hr. metered parking (8:30am-7pm) including Sun/No parking 8am-8:30am (except Sun)

West

1 hr. metered parking (8am-7pm) including Sun/No parking 7:30am-8am (except Sun)

3RD AVE (ST. MARKS PL/8TH - 9TH)

East

No standing anytime

West

No standing 8am-6pm (M-F) except authorized vehicles (DEP)

3RD AVE (9TH -10TH)

East

1 hr. metered parking (8:30am-7pm) including Sun/No parking 8am-8:30am (except Sun)

West

1 hr. metered parking (8am-7pm) including Sun/No parking 7:30am-8am (except Sun)

3RD AVE (10TH -11TH)

East

1 hr. metered parking (8:30am-7pm) including Sun/No parking 8am-8:30am (except Sun)

West

1 hr. metered parking (8am-7pm) including Sun/No parking 7:30am-8am (except Sun)

3RD AVE (11TH - 12TH)

East

1 hr. metered parking (8:30am-7pm) including Sun/No parking 8am-8:30am (except Sun)

West

1 hr. metered parking (8am-7pm) including Sun/No parking 7:30am-8am (except Sun)

3RD AVE (12TH - 13TH)

East

1 hr. metered parking (8:30am-7pm) including Sun/No parking 8am-8:30am (except Sun)

West

1 hr. metered parking (8am-7pm) including Sun/No parking 7:30am-8am (except Sun)

3RD AVE (13TH - 14TH)

East

1 hr. metered parking (9am-7pm) including Sun/No parking 8am-9am (except Sun)

West

No standing anytime

3RD AVE (14TH-15TH)

East

No parking 8am-8:30am (except Sun)/1 hr. metered parking (8:30am-10pm) including Sun

West

No parking 7:30am-8am (except Sun)/1 hr. metered parking (8am-10pm) including Sun

3RD AVE (15TH-16TH)

East

No parking 8am-8:30am (except Sun)/1 hr. metered parking (8:30am-10pm) including Sun

West

No parking 7:30am-8am (except Sun)/1 hr. metered parking (8am-10pm) including Sun

3RD AVE (16TH-17TH)

East

No parking 8am-8:30am (except Sun)/1 hr. metered parking (8:30am-10pm) including Sun/No standing except trucks loading & unloading 7am-7pm (except Sun)

West

No parking 7:30am-8am (except Sun)/1 hr. metered parking (8am-10pm) including Sun

3RD AVE (17TH-18TH)

East

No parking 8am-8:30am (except Sun)/1 hr. metered parking (8:30am-10pm) including Sun

West

No parking 7:30am-8am (except Sun)/1 hr. metered parking (8am-10pm) including Sun

3RD AVE (18TH-19TH)

East

No parking 8am-8:30am (except Sun)/1 hr. metered parking (8:30am-10pm) including Sun

West

No parking 7:30am-8am (except Sun)/1 hr. metered parking (8am-10pm) including Sun

3RD AVE (19TH-20TH)

East

No parking 8am-8:30am (except Sun)/1 hr. metered parking (8:30am-10pm) including Sun

West

No parking 7:30am-8am (except Sun)/1 hr. metered parking (8am-10pm) including Sun

3RD AVE (20TH-21ST)

East

No parking 8am-8:30am (except Sun)/1 hr. metered parking (8:30am-10pm) including Sun

West

No parking 7:30am-8am (except Sun)/1 hr. metered parking (8am-10pm) including Sun

3RD AVE (21ST-22ND)

East

No parking 8am-8:30am (except Sun)/1 hr. metered parking (8:30am-10pm) including Sun

West

No parking 7:30am-8am (except Sun)/1 hr. metered parking (8am-10pm) including Sun

3RD AVE (22ND-23RD)

East

No standing except trucks loading & unloading 8am-6pm (except Sun)

West

No parking 7:30am-8am (except Sun)/1 hr. metered parking (8am-10pm) including Sun

3RD AVE (23RD-24TH)

East

No standing anytime

West

No standing anytime

3RD AVE (24TH-25TH)

East

No parking 8am-8:30am (except Sun)/1 hr. metered parking (8:30am-10pm) including Sun

West

No parking 7:30am-8am (except Sun)/1 hr. metered parking (8am-10pm) including Sun

3RD AVE (25TH-26TH)

East

No parking 8am-8:30am (except Sun)/1 hr. metered parking (8:30am-10pm) including Sun

West

No parking 7:30am-8am (except Sun)/1 hr. metered parking (8am-10pm) including Sun

3RD AVE (26TH-27TH)

East

No parking 8am-8:30am (except Sun)/1 hr. metered parking (8:30am-10pm) including Sun

West

No parking 7:30am-8am (except Sun)/1 hr. metered parking (8am-10pm) including Sun

3RD AVE (27TH-28TH)

East

No parking 8am-8:30am (except Sun)/1 hr. metered parking (8:30am-10pm) including Sun

West

No parking 7:30am-8am (except Sun)/1 hr. metered parking (8am-10pm) including Sun

3RD AVE (28TH-29TH)

East

No parking 8am-8:30am (except Sun)/1 hr. metered parking (8:30am-10pm) including Sun

West

No parking 7:30am-8am (except Sun)/1 hr. metered parking (8am-10pm) including Sun

3RD AVE (29TH-30TH)

East

No parking 8am-8:30am (except Sun)/1 hr. metered parking (8:30am-10pm) including Sun

West

No parking 7:30am-8am (except Sun)/1 hr. metered parking (8am-10pm) including Sun

4TH AVE (8TH ST - 9TH ST)

East

No standing anytime

West

No standing anytime

4TH AVE (9TH ST - 10TH ST)

East

No parking 7am-6pm (except Sun)

West

No parking 8am-6pm (M-F)

4TH AVE/LAFAYETTE (10TH ST - 11TH ST)

East

1 hr. metered parking (8am-7pm) including Sun/No parking 7:30am-8am (except Sun)

West

No parking 8am-6pm (M-F)

4TH AVE (11TH ST - 12TH ST)

East

No parking 7am-7pm (except Sun)

West

No parking 8am-6pm (M-F)/No parking 7am-4pm (school days)/1 hr. metered parking (9am-7pm) including Sun/No parking 8am-9am (except Sun)

4TH AVE (12TH ST - 13TH ST)

East

1 hr. metered parking (8am-7pm) including Sun/No parking 7:30am-8am (except Sun)

West

No parking 7am-7pm (M-F)

4TH AVE (13TH ST - 14TH ST)

East

No standing anytime

West

No parking 7am-7pm (M-F)

ALLEN (HOUSTON - STANTON)

East

2 hr. metered parking (9am-7pm) including Sun/No parking Midnite-3am (Tu,Th,Sat)

West

2 hr. metered parking (9am-7pm) including Sun/No parking Midnite-3am (M,W,F)

ALLEN (STANTON - RIVINGTON)

East

2 hr. metered parking (9am-7pm) including Sun/No parking Midnite-3am (Tu,Th,Sat)

West

2 hr. metered parking (9am-7pm) including Sun/No parking Midnite-3am (M,W,F)

ALLEN (RIVINGTON - DELANCEY)

East

2 hr. metered parking (9am-7pm) including Sun/No parking Midnite-3am (Tu,Th,Sat)

West

1 hr. metered parking (9am-4pm) including Sun/No standing 4pm-7pm (except Sun)/No parking Midnite-3am (M,W,F)

ALLEN (DELANCEY - BROOME)

East

2 hour metered parking 9am-4pm including Sun/No standing 4pm-7pm including Sun/No parking Midnite-3am (Tu,Th,Sat)

West

2 hour metered parking 10am-7pm including Sun/No standing 7am-10am (except Sunday) except trucks loading and unloading/No standing except trucks loading & unloading 7am-7pm (M-F)/No parking Midnite-3am (M,W,F)

ALLEN (BROOME - GRAND)

East

2 hr. metered parking (9am-7pm) including Sun/No parking Midnite-3am (Tu,Th,Sat)

West

2 hour metered parking 10am-7pm including Sun/No standing 7am-10am (except Sunday) except trucks loading and unloading/No parking Midnite-3am (M,W,F)

ALLEN (GRAND - HESTER)

East

2 hr. metered parking (9am-7pm) including Sun/No parking Midnite-3am (Tu,Th,Sat)

West

2 hr. metered parking (9am-7pm) including Sun/No parking Midnite-3am (M,W,F)

ALLEN (HESTER - CANAL)

East

2 hr. metered parking (9am-7pm) including Sun/No parking Midnite-3am (Tu,Th,Sat)

West

No standing except trucks loading & unloading 7am-7pm (except Sun)/No parking Midnite-3am (M,W,F)

ASSER LEVY (23RD-24TH) ☺

East

No parking 7am-7pm (including Sun)/No parking 11:30am-1pm (Tu & F)

West

No standing anytime (except authorized vehicles)

ASSER LEVY (24TH-25TH)

East

No parking 7am-7pm (including Sun)/No parking 11:30am-1pm (Tu & F)

West

No standing anytime (except authorized vehicles)

ASTOR (4TH AVE - 3RD AVE)

North

No parking anytime

South

No parking anytime

ATTORNEY (DELANCEY NORTH - RIVINGTON)

East

No parking 9am-10:30am (Tu & F)/No parking 7am-4pm (school days)

West

No parking 9am-10:30am (M & Th)

ATTORNEY (HOUSTON - STANTON)

East

No parking 7am-6pm (except Sun)

West

No parking 7am-6pm (M-F)

ATTORNEY (STANTON - DEAD END)

East

No parking 9am-10:30am (Tu & F)

West

No parking 9am-10:30am (M & Th)

AVE A (14TH ST - 13TH ST)

East

1 hr. metered parking (9am-7pm) including Sun/No parking 8:30am-9am (except Sun)

West

1 hr. metered parking (8:30am-7pm) including Sun/No parking 8am-8:30am (except Sun)

AVE A (13TH ST - 12TH ST)

East

1 hr. metered parking (9am-7pm) including Sun/No parking 8:30am-9am (except Sun)

West

1 hr. metered parking (8:30am-7pm) including Sun/No parking 8am-8:30am (except Sun)

AVE A (12TH ST - 11TH ST)

East

1 hr. metered parking (9am-7pm) including Sun/No parking 8:30am-9am (except Sun)

West

1 hr. metered parking (8:30am-7pm) including Sun/No parking 8am-8:30am (except Sun)

AVE A (11TH ST - 10TH ST)

East

No parking 8:30am-9am (except Sun)

West

No parking 8am-8:30am (except Sun)

AVE A (10TH ST - 9TH ST)

East

2 hr. metered parking (9am-7pm) including Sun/No parking 8:30am-9am (except Sun)

West

1 hr. metered parking (8:30am-7pm) including Sun/No parking 8am-8:30am (except Sun)

AVE A (9TH ST - ST. MARKS PL)

East

2 hr. metered parking (9am-7pm) including Sun/No parking 8:30am-9am (except Sun)

West

1 hr. metered parking (8:30am-7pm) including Sun/No parking 8am-8:30am (except Sun)

AVE A (ST. MARKS PL - 7TH ST)

East

2 hr. metered parking (9am-7pm) including Sun/No parking 8:30am-9am (except Sun)

West

1 hr. metered parking (8:30am-7pm) including Sun/No parking 8am-8:30am (except Sun)

AVE A (7TH ST - 6TH ST)

East

1 hr. metered parking (9am-7pm) including Sun/No parking 8:30am-9am (except Sun)

West

1 hr. metered parking (8:30am-7pm) including Sun/No parking 8am-8:30am (except Sun)

AVE A (6TH ST - 5TH ST)

East

1 hr. metered parking (9am-7pm) including Sun/No parking 8:30am-9am (except Sun)

West

1 hr. metered parking (8:30am-7pm) including Sun/No parking 8am-8:30am (except Sun)

AVE A (5TH ST - 4TH ST)

East

1 hr. metered parking (9am-7pm) including Sun/No parking 8:30am-9am (except Sun)

West

1 hr. metered parking (8:30am-7pm) including Sun/No parking 8am-8:30am (except Sun)

AVE A (4TH ST - 3RD ST)

East

1 hr. metered parking (9am-7pm) including Sun/No parking 8:30am-9am (except Sun)

West

1 hr. metered parking (8:30am-7pm) including Sun/No parking 8am-8:30am (except Sun)

AVE A (3RD ST - 2ND ST)

East

1 hr. metered parking (9am-7pm) including Sun/No parking 8:30am-9am (except Sun)

West

1 hr. metered parking (8:30am-7pm) including Sun/No parking 8am-8:30am (except Sun)

AVE A (2ND ST - 1ST ST)

East

1 hr. metered parking (9am-7pm) including Sun/No parking 8:30am-9am (except Sun)

West

1 hr. metered parking (8:30am-7pm) including Sun/No parking 8am-8:30am (except Sun)

AVE B (HOUSTON - 2ND ST) ☺

East

No parking 11am-12:30pm (M & F)

West

No parking 11am-12:30pm (M & Th)

AVE B (2ND ST - 3RD ST) ☺

East

No parking 11am-12:30pm (M & F)

West

No parking 11am-12:30pm (M & Th)

AVE B (3RD ST - 4TH ST) ☺

East

No parking 11am-12:30pm (M & F)

West

No parking 11am-12:30pm (M & Th)

AVE B (4TH ST - 5TH ST) ☺

East

No parking 11am-12:30pm (M & F)/No standing anytime (except authorized vehicles)

West

No parking 11am-12:30pm (M & Th)

AVE B (5TH ST - 6TH ST) ☺

East

No parking 11am-12:30pm (M & F)

West

No parking 11am-12:30pm (M & Th)

AVE B (6TH ST - 7TH ST) ☺

East

No parking 11am-12:30pm (M & F)

West

No parking 11am-12:30pm (M & Th)

AVE B (7TH ST - 8TH ST) ☺

East

No parking 11am-12:30pm (M & F)

West

No parking 11am-12:30pm (M & Th)

AVE B (8TH ST - 9TH ST) ☺

East

No parking 7am-6pm (except Sun)

West

No parking 11am-12:30pm (M & Th)

AVE B (9TH ST - 10TH ST)

East

No parking 11am-12:30pm (M & F)

West

No parking 11am-12:30pm (M & Th)

AVE B (10TH ST -11TH ST)

East

No parking 11am-12:30pm (M & F)

West

No parking 11am-12:30pm (M & Th)

AVE B (11TH ST - 12TH ST)

East

No parking 11am-12:30pm (M & F)

West

No parking 11am-12:30pm (M & Th)

AVE B (12TH ST - 13TH ST)

East

No parking 11am-12:30pm (M & F)

West

No parking 11am-12:30pm (M & Th)

AVE B (13TH ST - 14TH ST)

East

No parking 8am-6pm (except Sun)

West

No parking 11am-12:30pm (M & Th)

AVE C (14TH ST - 13TH ST)

East

No parking 11am-12:30pm (M & F)

West

No parking 11am-12:30pm (M & Th)

AVE C (13TH ST - 12TH ST)

East

No parking 11am-12:30pm (M & F)

West

No parking 11am-12:30pm (M & Th)

AVE C (12TH ST - 11TH ST)

East

No parking 11am-12:30pm (M & F)

West

No parking 11am-12:30pm (M & Th)

AVE C (11TH ST - 10TH ST)

East

No parking anytime

West

No parking 11am-12:30pm (M & Th)

AVE C (10TH ST - 9TH ST)

East

No parking 11am-12:30pm (M & F)

West

No parking 11am-12:30pm (M & Th)

AVE C (9TH ST - 8TH ST)

East

No parking 11am-12:30pm (M & F)

West

No parking 11am-12:30pm (M & Th)

AVE C (8TH ST - 7TH ST)

East

No parking 11am-12:30pm (M & F)

West

No parking 11am-12:30pm (M & Th)

AVE C (7TH ST - 6TH ST)

East

No parking 11am-12:30pm (M & F)

West

No parking 11am-12:30pm (M & Th)

AVE C (6TH ST - 5TH ST)

East

No parking 7am-7pm (except Sun)

West

No parking 11am-12:30pm (M & Th)

AVE C (5TH ST - 4TH ST)

East

No parking 11am-12:30pm (M & F)

West

No parking 11am-12:30pm (M & Th)

AVE C (4TH ST - 3RD ST)

East

No parking 11am-12:30pm (M & F)

West

No parking 11am-12:30pm (M & Th)

AVE C (3RD ST - 2ND ST)

East

No parking 11am-12:30pm (M & F)

West

No parking 11am-12:30pm (M & Th)

AVE C (2ND ST - HOUSTON)

East

No parking anytime

West

No parking anytime

AVE D (HOUSTON/2ND ST - 3RD ST)

East

No parking 11am-12:30pm (M & F)

West

No parking 11am-12:30pm (M & Th)

AVE D (3RD ST - 4TH ST)

East

No parking 11am-12:30pm (M & F)

West

No parking 11am-12:30pm (M & Th)

AVE D (4TH ST - 5TH ST)

East

No parking 11am-12:30pm (M & F)

West

No parking 11am-12:30pm (M & Th)

AVE D (5TH ST - 6TH ST)

East

No parking 11am-12:30pm (M & F)

West

No parking 11am-12:30pm (M & Th)

AVE D (6TH ST - 7TH ST)

East

No parking 11am-12:30pm (M & F)

West

No parking 11am-12:30pm (M & Th)

AVE D (7TH ST - 8TH ST)

East

No parking 11am-12:30pm (M & F)

West

No parking 11am-12:30pm (M & Th)

AVE D (8TH ST - 9TH ST)

East

No parking 11am-12:30pm (M & F)

West

No parking 11am-12:30pm (M & Th)

AVE D (9TH ST - 10TH ST)

East

No parking 11am-12:30pm (M & F)

West

No parking 11am-12:30pm (M & Th)

AVE D (12TH ST - 13TH ST)

East

No parking 11am-12:30pm (M & F)

West

No standing anytime

AVE D (13TH ST - 14TH ST)

East

No parking 11am-12:30pm (M & F)

West

No standing anytime

BARUCH PL (HOUSTON - STANTON) ☺

East

No parking 11am-12:30pm (M & F)

West

No parking 11am-12:30pm (M & Th)

BARUCH ST (HOUSTON - RIVINGTON) ☺

East

No parking 11am-12:30pm (M & F)

West

No parking 11am-12:30pm (M & Th)

BARUCH ST (RIVINGTON - DELANCEY NORTH) ☺

East

No parking 11am-12:30pm (M & F)

West

No parking 11am-12:30pm (M & Th)

BARUCH ST (DELANCEY N. - DELANCEY S.) ☺

East

No parking 9am-10:30am (Tu & F)

West

No parking 9am-10:30am (M & Th)

BAYARD (MULBERRY - MOTT)

North

No standing except trucks loading & unloading

South

No standing 7am-8am except Sun/No standing except trucks loading & unloading 8am-6pm (except Sun)

BAYARD (MOTT - ELIZABETH)

North

No standing except trucks loading & unloading

South

No standing 7am-8am except Sun/No standing except trucks loading & unloading 8am-6pm (except Sun)

BLEECKER (MULBERRY - MOTT)

North

No parking 7am-6pm (except Sun)

South

No parking 7am-6pm (except Sun)

BLEECKER (MOTT - ELIZABETH)

North

No parking 7am-6pm (except Sun)

South

No parking 7am-6pm (except Sun)

BLEECKER (ELIZABETH - BOWERY)

North

No parking 7am-6pm (except Sun)

South

No parking 8am-6pm (M-F)/No standing 11pm-6am (including Sun)

BOND (BOWERY - LAFAYETTE)

East

No parking 8am-6pm (M-F)

West

No parking 8am-6pm (M-F)

BOWERY (1ST ST - 2ND ST)

East

No parking 8am-6pm (M-F)

West

No standing except trucks loading & unloading 8am-6pm (except Sun)

BOWERY (2ND ST - 3RD ST)

East

No parking 8am-6pm (M-F)

West

No parking 8am-6pm (except Sun)

BOWERY (3RD ST - 4TH ST)

East

No parking 8am-6pm (except Sun)

West

No parking 8am-6pm (M-F)/1 hr. metered parking (9am-7pm) including Sun/No parking 8am-9am (except Sun)

BOWERY (4TH ST - 5TH ST) ☺

East

No parking 7:30am-8am (M, Th)

West

No parking 7am-7pm (except Sun)

BOWERY (5TH ST - 6TH ST)

East

No parking 8am-6pm (except Sun)/1 hr. metered parking (8am-7pm) including Sun/No parking 7:30am-8am (except Sun)

West

No parking 7am-7pm (except Sun)

BOWERY (BLEECKER - 1ST ST)

East

No parking 8am-6pm (except Sun)

West

No standing except trucks loading & unloading 8am-6pm (M-F)

BOWERY (1ST ST - HOUSTON)

East

No parking 8am-6pm (except Sun)

West

No standing except trucks loading & unloading 8am-6pm (M-F)

BOWERY (HOUSTON - STANTON)

East

No standing except trucks loading & unloading 7am-7pm (except Sun)/No parking Midnite-3am (Tu,Th,Sat)

West

1 hr. metered parking (9am-4pm) including Sun/No standing 4pm-7pm (M-F)/No parking Midnite-3am (M,W,F)

BOWERY (STANTON - PRINCE)

East

No standing except trucks loading & unloading 7am-7pm (except Sun)/No parking Midnite-3am (Tu,Th,Sat)

West

1 hr. metered parking (9am-4pm) including Sun/No standing 4pm-7pm (M-F)/No parking Midnite-3am (M,W,F)

BOWERY (PRINCE - RIVINGTON)

East

No standing except trucks loading & unloading 7am-7pm (except Sun)/No parking Midnite-3am (Tu,Th,Sat)

West

No standing except trucks loading & unloading 7am-7pm (except Sun)/No parking Midnite-3am (M,W,F)

BOWERY (RIVINGTON - SPRING)

East

No standing except trucks loading & unloading 7am-7pm (except Sun)/No parking Midnite-3am (Tu,Th,Sat)

West

No standing except trucks loading & unloading 7am-7pm (except Sun)/No parking Midnite-3am (M,W,F)

BOWERY (SPRING - KENMARE/DELANCEY)

East

No standing except trucks loading & unloading 7am-7pm (except Sun)/No parking Midnite-3am (Tu,Th,Sat)

West

No parking 9am-4pm (except Sun) except trucks loading and unloading/No standing 4pm-7pm (M-F)/No parking Midnite-3am (M,W,F)

BOWERY (KENMARE/DELANCEY - BROOME)

East

No standing except trucks loading & unloading 7am-7pm (except Sun)/No parking Midnite-3am (Tu,Th,Sat)

West

1 hr. metered parking (10am-4pm) including Sun/No parking 7am-10am (except Sun)/No standing 4pm-7pm (M-F)/No parking Midnite-3am (M,W,F)

BOWERY (BROOME - GRAND)

East

1 hour metered parking 10am-7pm including Sun/No parking 7am-10am (except Sunday)/No parking Midnite-3am (Tu,Th,Sat)

West

1 hr. metered parking (10am-4pm) including Sun/No parking 7am-10am (except Sun)/No standing 4pm-7pm (M-F)/No parking Midnite-3am (M,W,F)

BOWERY (GRAND - HESTER)

East

No standing except trucks loading & unloading 7am-7pm (except Sun)/No parking Midnite-3am (Tu,Th,Sat)

West

1 hr. metered parking (10am-4pm) including Sun/No parking 7am-10am (except Sun)/No standing 4pm-7pm (M-F)/No parking Midnite-3am (M,W,F)

BOWERY (HESTER - CANAL)

East

No standing except trucks loading & unloading/No parking Midnite-3am (Tu,Th,Sat)

West

1 hr. metered parking (9am-4pm) including Sun/No standing 4pm-7pm (M-F)/No parking Midnite-3am (M,W,F)

BOWERY (CANAL - BAYARD)

East

No standing anytime

West

1 hour metered parking 7:30am - 7pm including Sun/No parking 7am-7:30am (except Sun)

BOWERY (BAYARD - PELL)

East

1 hour metered parking 7:30am - 7pm including Sun/No parking 7am-7:30am (except Sun)

West

No standing except trucks loading & unloading 7am-7pm (except Sun)

BOWERY (PELL - DIVISION/DOYERS) ☹

East

No parking anytime

West

No standing except trucks loading & unloading

BROADWAY (23RD-22ND)

East

1 hr. metered parking (9am-7pm) including Sun/No parking 8am-9am (except Sun)

West

No standing anytime

BROADWAY (22ND-21ST)

East

1 hr. metered parking (9am-7pm) including Sun/No parking 8am-9am (except Sun)

West

1 hr. metered parking (9am-7pm) including Sun/No parking 8am-9am (except Sun)

BROADWAY (21ST-20TH)

East

No parking 8am-6pm (M-F)

West

No parking 8am-6pm (M-F)

BROADWAY (20TH-19TH)

East

No parking 8am-6pm (M-F)

West

No parking 8am-6pm (M-F)

BROADWAY (19TH-18TH)

East

No standing except trucks loading & unloading 8am-6pm (M-F)

West

No standing except trucks loading & unloading 8am-6pm (M-F)

BROADWAY (18TH-17TH)

East

No parking 8am-6pm (M-F)

West

No standing anytime

BROADWAY [UNION SQUARE] (17TH-16TH)

East

No Parking 4:30am-6am (M,W,F)/No standing except trucks loading & unloading 7am-7pm (M-F)

West

No standing anytime

BROADWAY [UNION SQUARE] (16TH-15TH)

East

No Parking 4:30am-6am (M,W,F)/No standing except trucks loading & unloading 7am-7pm (M-F)

West

No standing anytime

BROADWAY [UNION SQUARE] (15TH-14TH) ☹

East

No standing anytime

West

No standing anytime

BROADWAY (14TH - 13TH)

North

No standing anytime

South

No standing except trucks loading & unloading 7am-7pm (M-F)/No standing 1am-7am including Sun

BROADWAY (13TH - 12TH)

North

No standing except trucks loading & unloading 7am-4pm (M-F)/No standing 4pm-7pm (M-F)/No standing 1am-7am including Sun

South

No standing except trucks loading & unloading 7am-7pm (M-F)/No standing 1am-7am including Sun

BROADWAY (12TH - 11TH)

North

No standing except trucks loading & unloading 7am-4pm (M-F)/No standing 4pm-7pm (M-F)/No standing 1am-7am including Sun

South

No standing except trucks loading & unloading 7am-7pm (M-F)/No standing 1am-7am including Sun

BROADWAY (11TH - 10TH)

North

No standing except trucks loading & unloading 7am-4pm (M-F)/No standing 4pm-7pm (M-F)/No standing 1am-7am including Sun

South

No standing except trucks loading & unloading 7am-7pm (M-F)/No standing 1am-7am including Sun

BROADWAY (10TH - 9TH)

North

No standing except trucks loading & unloading 7am-4pm (M-F)/No standing 4pm-7pm (M-F)/No standing 1am-7am including Sun

South

No standing except trucks loading & unloading 7am-7pm (M-F)/No standing 1am-7am including Sun

BROADWAY (9TH - 8TH)

North

No standing 7am-4pm including sun except trucks loading and unloading/No standing 4pm-7pm including Sun/No standing 1am-7am including Sun

South

No standing except trucks loading & unloading 7am-7pm (M-F)/No standing 1am-7am including Sun

BROOME (LEWIS - CANNON)

North

No parking anytime (except authorized vehicles)

South

No parking anytime (except authorized vehicles)

BROOME (CANNON - A. KAZAN)

North

No parking anytime

South

No parking anytime

BROOME (A. KAZAN - SHERRIF) ☹

North

No parking anytime

South

No parking anytime

BROOME (SHERRIF - WILLET) ☹

North

No parking anytime

South

No parking anytime

BROOME (CHYRSTIE - BOWERY) ☹

North

No standing anytime

South

No standing except trucks loading & unloading

BROOME (BOWERY - ELIZABETH)

North

No standing except trucks loading & unloading 8am-6pm (except Sun)

South

1 hr. metered parking (9am-7pm) including Sun/No parking 8am-9am (except Sun)

BROOME (ELIZABETH - MOTT)

North

No standing except trucks loading & unloading 8am-6pm (except Sun)

South

No parking 8am-6pm (except Sun)

BROOME (MOTT - MULBERRY)

North

No standing except trucks loading & unloading 8am-6pm (except Sun)

South

1 hr. metered parking (9am-7pm) including Sun/No parking 8am-9am (except Sun)

BROOME (MULBERRY - CLEVELAND PL)

North

No standing except trucks loading & unloading 7am-7pm (M-F)

South

No standing except trucks loading & unloading 8am-6pm (except Sun)

BROOME (FORSYTH - ELDRIDGE)

North

No parking 7am-7pm (M-F)/1 hour parking 9am-7pm (Sat, Sun)/No parking Midnite-3am (M,W,F)

South

No parking anytime

BROOME (ELDRIDGE - ALLEN)

North

No parking Midnite-3am (M,W,F)

South

No parking anytime

BROOME (ALLEN - ORCHARD)

North

1 hr. metered parking (9am-7pm) including Sun/No parking Midnite-3am (M,W,F)

South

No parking anytime

BROOME (ORCHARD - LUDLOW)

North

1 hr. metered parking (9am-7pm) including Sun/No parking Midnite-3am (M,W,F)

South

No parking anytime

BROOME (LUDLOW - ESSEX)

North

2 hr. metered parking (9am-7pm) including Sun/No parking Midnite-3am (M,W,F)

South

No parking anytime

BROOME (ESSEX - NORFOLK)

North

No parking 8am-9:30am (M & Th)

South

No parking 8am-6pm (M-F)

BROOME (NORFOLK - SUFFOLK)

North

No parking 8am-9:30am (M & Th)

South

No parking 8am-9:30am (Tu & F)

BROOME (SUFFOLK - CLINTON) ☺

North

No parking 8am-9:30am (M & Th)

South

No parking 8am-9:30am (Tu & F)

BROOME (CLINTON - RIDGE) ☺

North

No parking 8am-9:30am (M & Th)

South

No parking 8am-9:30am (Tu & F)

BROOME (RIDGE - PITT) ☺

North

No parking 8am-9:30am (M & Th)

South

No parking 8am-9:30am (Tu & F)

CANAL (BAXTER - MULBERRY)

North

No standing 7am-10am & 4pm-7pm including Sun - other times - No standing except trucks loading & unloading

South

No standing 7am-10am & 4pm-7pm including Sun - other times - No standing except trucks loading & unloading

CANAL (MULBERRY - MOTT)

North

No standing 7am-10am & 4pm-7pm including Sun - other times - No standing except trucks loading & unloading

South

No standing 7am-10am & 4pm-7pm including Sun - other times - No standing except trucks loading & unloading

CANAL (MOTT - ELIZABETH)

North

No standing 7am-10am & 4pm-7pm including Sun - other times - No standing except trucks loading & unloading

South

No standing 7am-10am & 4pm-7pm including Sun - other times - No standing except trucks loading & unloading

CANAL (ELIZABETH - BOWERY)

North

No standing 7am-10am & 4pm-7pm including Sun - other times - No standing except trucks loading & unloading

South

No standing 7am-10am & 4pm-7pm including Sun - other times - No standing except trucks loading & unloading

CANAL (BOWERY - CHRYSTIE)

North

No standing anytime

South

No standing anytime

CANAL (CHRYSTIE - FORSYTH)

North

2 hr. metered parking (8am-7pm) including Sun/No parking 7:30am-8am (except Sun)

South

2 hr. metered parking (8am-7pm) including Sun/No parking 7:30am-8am (except Sun)

CANAL (FORSYTH - ELDRIDGE)

North

2 hr. metered parking (8am-7pm) including Sun/No parking 7:30am-8am (except Sun)

South

2 hr. metered parking (8am-7pm) including Sun/No parking 7:30am-8am (except Sun)

CANAL (ELDRIDGE - ALLEN/PIKE)

North

No standing anytime (except authorized vehicles)

South

No standing anytime (except authorized vehicles)

CANAL (E. BROADWAY - ESSEX)

North

No parking anytime

South

No parking anytime

CANAL (ESSEX - LUDLOW)

North

1 hr. metered parking (8:30am-7pm) including Sun/No parking 8am-8:30am (except Sun)

South

2 hr. metered parking (8am-7pm) including Sun/No parking 7:30am-8am (except Sun)

CANAL (LUDLOW - ORCHARD)

North

1 hr. metered parking (8:30am-7pm) including Sun/No parking 8am-8:30am (except Sun)

South

2 hr. metered parking (8am-7pm) including Sun/No parking 7:30am-8am (except Sun)

CANAL (ORCHARD - ALLEN/PIKE)

North

1 hr. metered parking (8:30am-7pm) including Sun/No parking 8am-8:30am (except Sun)

South

2 hr. metered parking (8am-7pm) including Sun/No parking 7:30am-8am (except Sun)

CANNON (DELANCEY SOUTH - BROOME)

East

No parking anytime

West

No parking anytime

CHERRY (FDR SOUTH - JACKSON)

North

No parking 11am-12:30pm (M & F)

South

No parking 11am-12:30pm (Tu & F)

CHERRY (MONTGOMERY - CLINTON)

North

No parking 11am-12:30pm (M & F)

South

No parking 11am-12:30pm (Tu & F)/No parking 7am-4pm (school days)

CHERRY (CLINTON - RUTGERS)

North

No parking 11am-12:30pm (M & F)

South

No parking 11am-12:30pm (Tu & F)

CHRYSTIE (CANAL - HESTER)

East

2 hour parking (no meters!) 10am-7pm including Sun/No standing 7am-10am (except Sun)

West

No standing except trucks loading & unloading 8am-7pm (except Sun)/No parking 8am-9am (except Sun)

CHRYSTIE (HESTER - GRAND)

East

2 hour parking (no meters!) 10am-7pm including Sun/No standing 7am-10am (except Sun)

West

No standing except trucks loading & unloading 8am-7pm (except Sun)/No parking 8am-9am (except Sun)

CHRYSTIE (GRAND - BROOME)

East

2 hr. metered parking (9am-7pm) including Sun/No parking Midnite-3am (Tu,Th,Sat)

West

No standing except trucks loading & unloading 8am-6pm (M-F)/No parking Midnite-3am (M,W,F)

CHRYSTIE (BROOME - DELANCEY)

East

2 hr. metered parking (9am-7pm) including Sun/No parking Midnite-3am (Tu,Th,Sat)

West

No standing except trucks loading & unloading 8am-6pm (M-F)/No parking Midnite-3am (M,W,F)

CHRYSTIE (DELANCEY - RIVINGTON)

East

2 hr. metered parking (9am-7pm) including Sun/No parking Midnite-3am (Tu,Th,Sat)

West

No standing except trucks loading & unloading 8am-6pm (M-F)/No parking Midnite-3am (M,W,F)

CHRYSTIE (RIVINGTON - STANTON)

East

No parking Midnite-3am (Tu,Th,Sat)

West

No parking Midnite-3am (M,W,F)/No parking 8am-6pm (M-F)

CHRYSTIE (STANTON - HOUSTON)

East

No parking Midnite-3am (Tu,Th,Sat)

West

No parking Midnite-3am (M,W,F)

CLEVELAND MARKET PL (BROOME - GRAND)

East

No standing anytime

West

No standing anytime

CLINTON (SOUTH - WATER)

East

No parking 11am-12:30pm (M & F)

West

No parking 11am-12:30pm (M & Th)

CLINTON (WATER - CHERRY)

East

No parking 11am-12:30pm (M & F)

West

No parking 11am-12:30pm (M & Th)

CLINTON (CHERRY - MADISON)

East

No parking 11am-12:30pm (M & F)

West

No parking 11am-12:30pm (M & Th)

CLINTON (MADISON - HENRY)

East

No parking 11am-12:30pm (M & F)

West

No standing 7am-7pm except doctor's vehicles

CLINTON (HENRY - E. BROADWAY) ☺

East

No parking 11am-12:30pm (M & F)

West

No parking 11am-12:30pm (M & Th)

CLINTON (E. BROADWAY - GRAND) ☺

East

No parking 8am-9:30am (Tu & F)

West

No parking 8am-9:30am (M & Th)/No standing except trucks loading & unloading 7am-4pm (except Sun)

CLINTON (GRAND - BROOME)

East

No parking anytime

West

No parking 8am-6pm (M-F)

CLINTON (BROOME - DELANCEY) ☹

East

No parking anytime

West

No parking anytime

CLINTON (HOUSTON - STANTON) ☺

East

No parking anytime

West

No standing 7am-10am (except Sun)

CLINTON (STANTON - RIVINGTON)

East

No parking anytime

West

1 hour metered parking 10am -7pm including Sun/No standing 10am -7pm including Sun except trucks loading and unloading/No standing 7am-10am (except Sun)

CLINTON (RIVINGTON - DELANCEY)

East

No parking anytime

West

1 hour metered parking 10am -7pm including Sun/No standing 7am -7pm including Sun except trucks loading and unloading/No standing 7am-10am (except Sun)

COLUMBIA (GRAND - BROOME)

East

No parking anytime

West

No parking 9am-10:30am (M & Th)

COLUMBIA (BROOME - DELANCEY SOUTH)

East

No parking anytime

West

No parking 9am-10:30am (M & Th)

COLUMBIA (DELANCEY SOUTH - DELANCEY NORTH)

East

No parking anytime

West

No parking anytime

COLUMBIA (HOUSTON - STANTON)

East

No parking 11am-12:30pm (M & F)

West

No parking 11am-12:30pm (M & Th)/No parking 7am-4pm (school days) except Board of Ed

COLUMBIA (STANTON - RIVINGTON)

East

No parking 11am-12:30pm (M & F)

West

No parking 11am-12:30pm (M & Th)

COLUMBIA (RIVINGTON - DELANCEY NORTH)

East

No parking 11am-12:30pm (M & F)

West

No parking 11am-12:30pm (M & Th)/No parking 7am-4pm (school days) except Board of Ed

COOPER SQ (6TH ST - 7TH ST)

East

No standing anytime

West

No parking 7am-7pm (except Sun)

DELANCEY (CHRYSTIE - FORSYTH)

North

2 hr. metered parking (9am-7pm) including Sun/No parking Midnite-3am (M,W,F)

South

2 hr. metered parking (9am-7pm) including Sun/No parking Midnite-3am (Tu,Th,Sat)

DELANCEY (FORSYTH - ELDRIDGE)

North

1 hr. metered parking (9am-7pm) including Sun/No parking Midnite-3am (M,W,F)

South

1 hr. metered parking (9am-7pm) including Sun/No parking Midnite-3am (Tu,Th,Sat)

DELANCEY (ELDRIDGE - ALLEN)

North

1 hr. metered parking (9am-7pm) including Sun/No parking Midnite-3am (M,W,F)

South

1 hr. metered parking (10am-4pm) including Sun/No standing 7am-10am & 4pm-7pm (M-F)/No parking Midnite-3am (Tu,Th,Sat)

DELANCEY (ALLEN - ORCHARD)

North

No standing anytime

South

No parking Midnite-3am (Tu,Th,Sat)

DELANCEY (ORCHARD - LUDLOW)

North

1 hour metered parking 10am-7pm including Sun/No standing 7am-10am (M-F)/No parking Midnite-3am (M,W,F)

South

1 hr. metered parking (10am-4pm) including Sun/No standing 7am-10am & 4pm-7pm (M-F)/No parking Midnite-3am (Tu,Th,Sat)

DELANCEY (LUDLOW - ESSEX)

North

1 hour metered parking 10am-7pm including Sun/No standing 7am-10am (M-F)/No parking Midnite-3am (M,W,F)

South

1 hr. metered parking (10am-4pm) including Sun/No standing 7am-10am & 4pm-7pm (M-F)/No parking Midnite-3am (Tu,Th,Sat)

DELANCEY (ESSEX - NORFOLK)

North

1 hour metered parking 10am-7pm including Sun/No standing 7am-10am (M-F)/No parking Midnite-3am (M,W,F)

South

1 hr. metered parking (10am-4pm) including Sun/No standing 7am-10am & 4pm-7pm (M-F)/No parking Midnite-3am (Tu,Th,Sat)

DELANCEY (NORFOLK - SUFFOLK)

North

1 hour metered parking 10am-7pm including Sun/No standing 7am-10am (M-F)/No parking Midnite-3am (M,W,F)

South

1 hr. metered parking (10am-4pm) including Sun/No standing 7am-10am & 4pm-7pm (M-F)/No parking Midnite-3am (Tu,Th,Sat)

DELANCEY (SUFFOLK - CLINTON)

North

No parking anytime

South

No parking anytime

DELANCEY NORTH (E. RIVER DR - BARUCH)

North

No parking 9am-10:30am (M & Th)

South

No parking anytime

DELANCEY NORTH (BARUCH - COLUMBIA)

North

No parking 9am-10:30am (M & Th)

South

No parking anytime

DELANCEY NORTH (COLUMBIA - SHERRIF)

North

No parking 9am-10:30am (M & Th)

South

No parking anytime

DELANCEY NORTH (SHERRIF - WILLET)

North

No parking 9am-10:30am (M & Th)

South

No parking anytime

DELANCEY NORTH (WILLET - PITT)

North

No parking 9am-10:30am (M & Th)

South

No parking anytime

DELANCEY NORTH (PITT - RIDGE)

North

No parking 9am-10:30am (M & Th)/No standing except trucks loading & unloading 7am-7pm (except Sun)

South

No parking anytime

DELANCEY NORTH (RIDGE - ATTORNEY)

North

No parking 9am-10:30am (M & Th)

South

No parking anytime

DELANCEY NORTH (ATTORNEY - CLINTON)

North

1 hour parking (no meters) 9am - 7pm (except Sun)/No parking 8:30am-9am (except Sun)

South

No parking anytime

DELANCEY SOUTH (CLINTON - RIDGE)

North

No parking 8am-11am (M, W, F)

South

No parking 8am-9:30am (Tu & F)

DELANCEY SOUTH (RIDGE - PITT)

North

No parking anytime

South

No parking anytime

DELANCEY SOUTH (PITT - WILLET)

North

No parking 8am-9:30am (M & Th)

South

No parking 8am-9:30am (Tu & F)

DELANCEY SOUTH (WILLET - SHERRIF)

North

No parking 8am-9:30am (M & Th)

South

No parking 8am-9:30am (Tu & F)

DELANCEY SOUTH (SHERRIF - A. KAZAN)

North

No parking 8am-9:30am (M & Th)

South

No parking 8am-9:30am (Tu & F)

DELANCEY SOUTH (A. KAZAN - CANNON)

North

No parking 8am-9:30am (M & Th)

South

No parking 8am-9:30am (Tu & F)

DELANCEY SOUTH (CANNON - LEWIS)

North

No parking 9am-10:30am (M & Th)

South

No parking 9am-10:30am (Tu & F)

DELANCEY SOUTH (LEWIS - E. RIVER DR)

North

No parking 9am-10:30am (M & Th)

South

No parking 9am-10:30am (Tu & F)

E. BROADWAY (BOWERY - CATHERINE)

North

No standing anytime

South

No standing anytime

E. BROADWAY (CATHERINE - MARKET)

North

No standing except trucks loading & unloading 7am-7pm (except Sun)/No parking Midnite-3am (M,W,F)

South

No standing except trucks loading & unloading 7am-7pm (except Sun)/No parking Midnite-3am (Tu,Th,Sat)

E. BROADWAY (MARKET - FORSYTH)

North

No standing except trucks loading & unloading 7am-7pm (except Sun)/No parking Midnite-3am (M,W,F)

South

No standing anytime

E. BROADWAY (FORSYTH - PIKE)

North

No standing except trucks loading & unloading 7am-7pm (except Sun)/No parking Midnite-3am (M,W,F)

South

No standing except trucks loading & unloading 7am-7pm (except Sun)/No parking Midnite-3am (Tu,Th,Sat)

E. BROADWAY (PIKE - RUTGERS)

North

No parking 8am-6pm (except Sun)

South

1 hr. metered parking (8:30am-7pm) including Sun/No parking 8am-8:30am (except Sun)

E. BROADWAY (RUTGERS - STRAUS SQ)

North

No standing anytime

South

No standing except trucks loading & unloading

E. BROADWAY (STRAUS SQ - JEFFERSON)

North

1 hr. metered parking (8:30am-7pm) including Sun/No parking 8am-8:30am (except Sun)

South

1 hr. metered parking (8:30am-7pm) including Sun/No parking 8am-8:30am (except Sun)

E. BROADWAY (JEFFERSON - CLINTON)

North

No parking 8am-9:30am (M & Th)

South

1 hr. metered parking (8:30am-7pm) including Sun/No parking 8am-8:30am (except Sun)

E. BROADWAY (CLINTON - MONTGOMERY) ☺

North

No parking 8am-9:30am (M & Th)

South

No parking 8am-9:30am (Tu & F)

E. BROADWAY (MONTGOMERY - S. DICKSTEIN PLAZA (PITT)) ☺

North

No parking 8am-9:30am (M & Th)

South

No parking 8am-9:30am (Tu & F)

E. BROADWAY (S. DICKSTEIN PLAZA (PITT) - GRAND) ☺

North

No parking 8am-9:30am (M & Th)

South

No parking 8am-9:30am (Tu & F)

ELDRIDGE (MANHATTAN BRIDGE ENTRANCE - CANAL)

East

No parking anytime

West

2 hr. metered parking (9am-7pm) including Sun/No parking 8:30am-9am (except Sun)

ELDRIDGE (CANAL - HESTER)

East

2 hr. metered parking (9am-7pm) including Sun/No parking 8:30am-9am (except Sun)/No parking 7am-7pm (except Sun)

West

No parking 8am-6pm (M-F)

ELDRIDGE (HESTER - GRAND)

East

2 hr. metered parking (9am-7pm) including Sun/No parking 8:30am-9am (except Sun)

West

No parking 7am-7pm (M-F)

ELDRIDGE (GRAND - BROOME)

East

2 hr. metered parking (9am-7pm) including Sun/No parking 8:30am-9am (except Sun)

West

No parking 7am-7pm (M-F)/1 hour parking 9am-7pm (Sat, Sun)

ELDRIDGE (BROOME - DELANCEY)

East

2 hr. metered parking (9am-7pm) including Sun/No parking 8:30am-9am (except Sun)

West

No parking 7am-7pm (M-F)/1 hour parking 9am-7pm (Sat, Sun)

ELDRIDGE (DELANCEY - RIVINGTON) ☺

East

No parking 8am-9:30am (Tu & F)

West

No parking 8am-6pm (M-F)/1 hour parking (no meters!) 10am-7pm (except Sun)

ELDRIDGE (RIVINGTON - STANTON) ☺

East

No parking 8am-9:30am (Tu & F)

West

No parking 8am-9:30am (M & Th)

ELDRIDGE (STANTON - HOUSTON) ☺

East

No parking 8am-9:30am (Tu & F)

West

No parking 8am-9:30am (M & Th)

ELIZABETH (BAYARD - CANAL)

East

No standing except trucks loading & unloading 8am-6pm (except Sun)

West

No standing anytime (except authorized vehicles)

ELIZABETH (CANAL - HESTER)

East

No parking 7am-10am (except Sun)/1 hr. metered parking (10am-7pm) including Sun

West

No parking 8am-6pm (M-F)

ELIZABETH (HESTER - GRAND)

East

1 hr. metered parking (9am-7pm) including Sun/No parking 8am-9am (except Sun)

West

No parking 8am-6pm (M-F)

ELIZABETH (GRAND - BROOME)

East

1 hr. metered parking (9am-7pm) including Sun/No parking 8am-9am (except Sun)

West

No parking 8am-6pm (M-F)

ELIZABETH (BROOME - KENMARE)

East

No parking 8am-6pm (M-F)

West

No parking 8am-6pm (M-F)

ELIZABETH (KENMARE - SPRING)

East

No parking 7am-6pm (except Sun)

West

No parking 8am-6pm (M-F)

ELIZABETH (SPRING - PRINCE)

East

No parking 8am-6pm (M-F)

West

No parking 8am-6pm (except Sun)

ELIZABETH (PRINCE - HOUSTON) ☺

East

No parking 8am-6pm (except Sun)

West

No parking 8am-11am (M & Th)

ELIZABETH (HOUSTON - BLEECKER) ☺

East

No parking 8am-11am (Tu & F)

West

No parking 8am-11am (M & Th)

ESSEX (HOUSTON - STANTON)

East

2 hr. metered parking (9am-7pm) including Sun/No parking Midnite-3am (Tu,Th,Sat)/No parking 7am-4pm (school days)

West

1 hr. metered parking (9am-7pm) including Sun/No parking Midnite-3am (M,W,F)

ESSEX (STANTON - RIVINGTON)

East

1 hr. metered parking (9am-7pm) including Sun/No parking Midnite-3am (Tu,Th,Sat)

West

1 hr. metered parking (9am-7pm) including Sun/No parking Midnite-3am (M,W,F)

ESSEX (RIVINGTON - DELANCEY)

East

1 hr. metered parking (9am-7pm) including Sun/No parking Midnite-3am (Tu,Th,Sat)

West

1 hr. metered parking (9am-7pm) including Sun/No parking Midnite-3am (M,W,F)

ESSEX (DELANCEY - BROOME)

East

1 hr. metered parking (9am-7pm) including Sun/No parking Midnite-3am (Tu,Th,Sat)

West

1 hr. metered parking (9am-7pm) including Sun/No parking Midnite-3am (M,W,F)

ESSEX (BROOME - GRAND)

East

2 hr. metered parking (9am-7pm) including Sun/No parking Midnite-3am (Tu,Th,Sat)

West

2 hr. metered parking (9am-7pm) including Sun/No parking Midnite-3am (M,W,F)

ESSEX (GRAND - HESTER)

East

2 hr. metered parking (9am-7pm) including Sun/No parking Midnite-3am (Tu,Th,Sat)

West

2 hr. metered parking (9am-7pm) including Sun/No parking Midnite-3am (M,W,F)

ESSEX (HESTER - CANAL)

East

2 hr. metered parking (9am-7pm) including Sun/No parking Midnite-3am (Tu,Th,Sat)

West

2 hr. metered parking (9am-7pm) including Sun/No parking Midnite-3am (M,W,F)

FDR (14TH ST - 10TH ST)

East

No parking anytime

West

No parking anytime

FDR (10TH ST - 6TH ST)

East

No parking anytime

West

No parking anytime

FDR (6TH ST - HOUSTON)

East

No parking anytime

West

No parking anytime

FDR ACCESS RD (10TH ST - 6TH ST)

East

No parking anytime

West

No parking 11am-12:30pm (M & Th)

FDR ACCESS RD (HOUSTON - DELANCEY NORTH)

East

No parking anytime

West

No parking 11am-12:30pm (M & Th)

FDR ACCESS RD (DELANCEY SOUTH - GRAND)

East

No parking anytime

West

No parking 9am-10:30am (M & Th)

FDR ACCESS RD (GRAND - CHERRY)

East

No parking anytime

West

No parking 11am-12:30pm (M & Th)

FDR SOUTH ACCESS RD (GRAND - CHERRY)

East

No parking 11am-12:30pm (M & F)

West

No parking 11am-12:30pm (M & Th)

FORSYTH (CANAL - DEAD END)

East

No parking 7am-4pm (M-F)

West

No parking 7am-4pm (M-F)

FORSYTH (HESTER - GRAND)

East

1 hr. metered parking (9am-7pm) including Sun/No parking Midnite-3am (Tu,Th,Sat)

West

2 hr. metered parking (9am-7pm) including Sun/No parking Midnite-3am (M,W,F)

FORSYTH (GRAND - BROOME)

East

1 hr. metered parking (9am-7pm) including Sun/No parking Midnite-3am (Tu,Th,Sat)

West

2 hr. metered parking (9am-7pm) including Sun/No parking Midnite-3am (M,W,F)

FORSYTH (BROOME - DELANCEY)

East

1 hr. metered parking (9am-7pm) including Sun/No parking Midnite-3am (Tu,Th,Sat)

West

2 hr. metered parking (9am-7pm) including Sun/No parking Midnite-3am (M,W,F)

FORSYTH (DELANCEY - RIVINGTON)

East

No parking Midnite-3am (Tu,Th,Sat)

West

No parking Midnite-3am (M,W,F)

FORSYTH (RIVINGTON - STANTON)

East

No parking Midnite-3am (Tu,Th,Sat)

West

No parking Midnite-3am (M,W,F)

FORSYTH (STANTON - HOUSTON) 

East

No parking Midnite-3am (Tu,Th,Sat)/No parking 7am-4pm (school days)

West

No parking Midnite-3am (M,W,F)

GOUVENUER (FDR DR - WATER) 

East

No parking 11am-12:30pm (M & F)

West

No parking 11am-12:30pm (M & Th)

GOUVENUER (WATER - MADISON) 

East

No parking 11am-12:30pm (M & F)

West

No parking anytime

GOUVENUER SLIP (SOUTH - WATER) 

East

No parking 11am-12:30pm (M & F)

West

No parking anytime

GRAND (FDR SOUTH - MADISON) 

North

No parking 9am-10:30am (M & Th)

South

No parking 9am-10:30am (Tu & F)

GRAND (MADISON - LEWIS) 

North

No parking 9am-10:30am (M & Th)

South

No parking 9am-10:30am (Tu & F)

GRAND (LEWIS/JACKSON - COLUMBIA) 

North

No parking 9am-10:30am (M & Th)

South

No standing anytime

GRAND (COLUMBIA - E. BROADWAY)

North

1 hr. metered parking (8:30am-7pm) including Sun/No parking 8am-8:30am (except Sun)

South

1 hr. metered parking (8:30am-7pm) including Sun/No parking 8am-8:30am (except Sun)

GRAND (E. BROADWAY - WILLET)

North

1 hr. metered parking (8:30am-7pm) including Sun/No parking 8am-8:30am (except Sun)

South

1 hr. metered parking (8:30am-7pm) including Sun/No parking 8am-8:30am (except Sun)

GRAND (WILLET - PITT) ☺

North

No parking 8am-9:30am (M & Th)

South

No parking 8am-9:30am (Tu & F)

GRAND (PITT - RIDGE) ☺

North

No parking 8am-9:30am (M & Th)

South

No parking 8am-9:30am (Tu & F)

GRAND (RIDGE - CLINTON)

North

No standing anytime

South

No parking 8am-9:30am (Tu & F)

GRAND (CLINTON - SUFFOLK)

North

2 hr. metered parking (8:30am-7pm) including Sun/No parking 8am-8:30am (except Sun)

South

2 hr. metered parking (8am-7pm) including Sun/No parking 7:30am-8am (except Sun)

GRAND (SUFFOLK - NORFOLK) ☺

North

2 hr. metered parking (8:30am-7pm) including Sun/No parking 8am-8:30am (except Sun)

South

No parking 8am-9:30am (Tu & F)

GRAND (NORFOLK - ESSEX)

North

2 hr. metered parking (8:30am-7pm) including Sun/No parking 8am-8:30am (except Sun)

South

1 hr. metered parking (8:30am-7pm) including Sun/No parking 8am-8:30am (except Sun)

GRAND (ESSEX - LUDLOW)

North

No parking 8am-6pm (M-F)/No parking Midnite-3am (M,W,F)

South

1 hr. metered parking (9am-7pm) including Sun/No parking Midnite-3am (Tu,Th,Sat)

GRAND (LUDLOW - ORCHARD)

North

1 hr. metered parking (9am-7pm) including Sun/No parking Midnite-3am (M,W,F)

South

1 hr. metered parking (9am-7pm) including Sun/No parking Midnite-3am (Tu,Th,Sat)

GRAND (ORCHARD - ALLEN)

North

1 hr. metered parking (9am-7pm) including Sun/No parking Midnite-3am (M,W,F)

South

1 hr. metered parking (9am-7pm) including Sun/No parking Midnite-3am (Tu,Th,Sat)

GRAND (ALLEN - ELDRIDGE)

North

1 hr. metered parking (9am-7pm) including Sun/No parking Midnite-3am (M,W,F)

South

1 hr. metered parking (9am-7pm) including Sun/No parking Midnite-3am (Tu,Th,Sat)

GRAND (ELDRIDGE - FORSYTH)

North

1 hr. metered parking (9am-7pm) including Sun/No parking Midnite-3am (M,W,F)

South

1 hr. metered parking (9am-7pm) including Sun/No parking Midnite-3am (Tu,Th,Sat)

GRAND (FORSYTH - CHRYSTIE/BOWERY)

North

No standing anytime (taxis only)

South

1 hr. metered parking (9am-7pm) including Sun/No parking Midnite-3am (Tu,Th,Sat)

GRAND (CENTRE - BAXTER)

North

No parking anytime

South

No parking 8am-6pm (except Sun)

GRAND (BAXTER - MULBERRY)

North

No standing except trucks loading & unloading 8am-6pm (except Sun)

South

No standing except trucks loading & unloading 8am-6pm (except Sun)

GRAND (MULBERRY - MOTT)

North

1 hr. metered parking (9am-7pm) including Sun/No parking 8am-9am (except Sun)

South

No standing except trucks loading & unloading 8am-6pm (except Sun)

GRAND (MOTT - ELIZABETH)

North

1 hr. metered parking (9am-7pm) including Sun/No parking 8am-9am (except Sun)

South

No standing except trucks loading & unloading 8am-6pm (except Sun)

GRAND (ELIZABETH - BOWERY/CHRYSTIE)

North

1 hr. metered parking (9am-7pm) including Sun/No parking 8am-9am (except Sun)

South

No standing except trucks loading & unloading 8am-6pm (except Sun)

HENRY (PIKE - RUTGERS) ☺

North

No parking 11am-12:30pm (M & F)

South

No parking 11am-12:30pm (Tu & F)/No parking 8am-6pm (M-F)/No parking 7am-4pm (school days)

Armonk Public Library

Amount paid: 4.00
Payment date: 5/2/2009,
13:30
Title: Only human [DVD]

Amount paid: $2.00
Payment date: 5/2/2009,
13:30
Title: Persepolis [DVD]

Armonk Public Library

Amount paid: 4.00
Payment date: 5/2/2009,
13:30
Title: Only human [DVD]

Amount paid: $2.00
Payment date: 5/2/2009,
13:30
Title: Persepolis [DVD]

HENRY (RUTGERS - JEFFERSON)

North

No parking 11am-12:30pm (M & F)

South

No parking 11am-12:30pm (Tu & F)

HENRY (JEFFERSON - CLINTON)

North

No parking 11am-12:30pm (M & F)

South

No parking 11am-12:30pm (Tu & F)

HENRY (CLINTON - MONTGOMERY)

North

No parking 11am-12:30pm (M & F)/No parking 7am-4pm (school days)

South

No parking 11am-12:30pm (Tu & F)

HENRY (MONTGOMERY - JACKSON/GRAND/LEWIS)

North

No parking 11am-12:30pm (Tu & F)

South

No parking 11am-12:30pm (M & F)/No standing except trucks loading & unloading 7am-4pm (except Sun)

HESTER (FORSYTH - ELDRIDGE)

North

2 hr. metered parking (9am-7pm) including Sun/No parking Midnite-3am (M,W,F)

South

No parking Midnite-3am (Tu,Th,Sat)/No parking 7am-4pm (school days)

HESTER (ELDRIDGE - ALLEN)

North

2 hr. metered parking (9am-7pm) including Sun/No parking Midnite-3am (M,W,F)

South

2 hr. metered parking (9am-7pm) including Sun/No parking Midnite-3am (Tu,Th,Sat)

HESTER (ALLEN - ORCHARD)

North

No parking 7am-7pm (M-F)/1 hour parking 9am-7pm (Sat, Sun)/No parking Midnite-3am (M,W,F)

South

1 hour parking (no meters) 9am-7pm including Sun/No parking Midnite-3am (Tu,Th,Sat)

HESTER (ORCHARD - LUDLOW)

North

No parking Midnite-3am (M,W,F)/No parking 7am-4pm (school days)

South

No parking Midnite-3am (Tu,Th,Sat)/No parking 7am-4pm (school days)

HESTER (LUDLOW - ESSEX)

North

No parking 7am-7pm (M-F)/1 hour parking 9am-7pm (Sat, Sun)/No parking Midnite-3am (M,W,F)

South

1 hour parking (no meters) 9am-7pm including Sun/No parking Midnite-3am (Tu,Th,Sat)

HESTER (CHYRSTIE - BOWERY)

North

1 hr. metered parking (9am-7pm) including Sun/No parking Midnite-3am (M,W,F)

South

No standing 7am-7pm (except Sun)/No parking Midnite-3am (Tu,Th,Sat)

HESTER (BOWERY - ELIZABETH)

North

1 hr. metered parking (9am-7pm) including Sun/No parking 8am-9am (except Sun)

South

No parking 8am-6pm (except Sun)

HESTER (ELIZABETH - MOTT)

North

2 hr. metered parking (9am-7pm) including Sun/No parking 8am-9am (except Sun)

South

No parking anytime

HESTER (MOTT - MULBERRY)

North

2 hr. metered parking (9am-7pm) including Sun/No parking 8am-9am (except Sun)

South

No parking 8am-6pm (except Sun)

HESTER (MULBERRY - BAXTER)

North

No parking 8am-6pm (M-F)/No parking 7am-4pm (school days)

South

1 hr. metered parking (9am-7pm) including Sun/No parking 8am-9am (except Sun)/No parking 7am-4pm (school days)

HESTER (BAXTER - CENTRE)

North

No parking 8am-6pm (M-F)

South

No parking 8am-6pm (except Sun)

HOUSTON ACCESS RD (AVE D - AVE C)

North

No parking 9am-10:30am (M & Th)

South

No parking 9am-10:30am (Tu & F)

HOUSTON (FDR DR - BARUCH)

North

No parking 9am-10:30am (M & Th)

South

No parking 9am-10:30am (Tu & F)/No parking 7am-4pm (school days)

HOUSTON (BARUCH - COLUMBIA)

North

No parking 9am-10:30am (M & Th)

South

No parking 9am-10:30am (Tu & F)

HOUSTON (COLUMBIA - PITT/AVE C)

North

No parking 9am-10:30am (M & Th)

South

No parking 9am-10:30am (Tu & F)

HOUSTON (PITT/AVE C - RIDGE)

North

No parking 9am-10:30am (M & Th)

South

No parking 9am-10:30am (Tu & F)

HOUSTON (RIDGE - ATTORNEY)

North

No parking 9am-10:30am (M & Th)

South

2 hr. metered parking (8am-7pm) including Sun/No parking 7:30am-8am (except Sun)

HOUSTON (ATTORNEY - CLINTON)

North

No parking 9am-10:30am (M & Th)

South

2 hr. metered parking (8am-7pm) including Sun/No parking 7:30am-8am (except Sun)

HOUSTON (CLINTON - SUFFOLK)

North

No parking 9am-10:30am (M & Th)

South

2 hr. metered parking (8am-7pm) including Sun/No parking 7:30am-8am (except Sun)

HOUSTON (SUFFOLK - NORFOLK)

North

No parking 9am-10:30am (M & Th)

South

2 hr. metered parking (8am-7pm) including Sun/No parking 7:30am-8am (except Sun)

HOUSTON (NORFOLK - AVE A/ESSEX)

North

No parking 9am-10:30am (M & Th)

South

2 hr. metered parking (8am-7pm) including Sun/No parking 7:30am-8am (except Sun)

HOUSTON (AVE A/ESSEX - LUDLOW)

North

1 hr. metered parking (9am-7pm) including Sun/No parking 3am-6am (M,W,F)

South

No standing anytime

HOUSTON (LUDLOW - ORCHARD)

North

1 hr. metered parking (9am-7pm) including Sun/No parking 3am-6am (M,W,F)

South

1 hr. metered parking (9am-7pm) including Sun/No parking 3am-6am (Tu,Th,Sat)

HOUSTON (ORCHARD - ALLEN)

North

1 hr. metered parking (9am-7pm) including Sun/No parking 3am-6am (M,W,F)

South

1 hr. metered parking (9am-7pm) including Sun/No parking 3am-6am (Tu,Th,Sat)

HOUSTON (ALLEN - ELDRIDGE)

North

2 hr. metered parking (9am-7pm) including Sun/No parking 3am-6am (M,W,F)

South

No standing except trucks loading & unloading

HOUSTON (ELDRIDGE - FORSYTH)

North

2 hr. metered parking (9am-7pm) including Sun/No parking 3am-6am (M,W,F)

South

No parking 8am-6pm (M-F)/No parking 3am-6am (Tu,Th,Sat)

HOUSTON (FORSYTH - CHRYSTIE/2ND AVE)

North

2 hr. metered parking (9am-7pm) including Sun/No parking 3am-6am (M,W,F)

South

No standing anytime

HOUSTON (CHRYSTIE/2ND AVE - BOWERY)

North

No standing anytime

South

No parking 3am-6am (Tu,Th,Sat)

HOUSTON (BOWERY - ELIZABETH)

North

No parking 8am-11am (M & Th)

South

No parking 8am-11am (Tu & F)

HOUSTON (ELIZABETH - MOTT)

North

No parking 8am-11am (M & Th)

South

No parking 8am-11am (Tu & F)

HOUSTON (MOTT - MULBERRY)

North

No parking 8am-6pm (M-F)

South

No parking 8am-11am (Tu & F)

HOUSTON (MULBERRY - LAFAYETTE) ☹

North

No standing anytime

South

No standing anytime

HOUSTON (LAFAYETTE - CROSBY) ☹

North

No standing anytime

South

No standing anytime

HOUSTON (CROSBY - BROADWAY) ☹

North

No standing anytime

South

No standing anytime

IRVING (14TH-15TH)

East

No parking 8am-7pm (except Sun)

West

No parking 8am-7pm (except Sun)

IRVING (15TH-16TH)

East

1 hr. metered parking (8am-7pm) including Sun/No parking 7:30am-8am (except Sun)

West

No standing except trucks loading & unloading 8am-6pm (except Sun)

IRVING (16TH-17TH)

East

No parking 8am-6pm (M-F)

West

1 hr. metered parking (9am-7pm) including Sun/No parking 8am-9am (except Sun)

IRVING (17TH-18TH)

East

1 hr. metered parking (8am-7pm) including Sun/No parking 7:30am-8am (except Sun)

West

1 hr. metered parking (9am-7pm) including Sun/No parking 8am-9am (except Sun)

IRVING (18TH-19TH)

East

1 hr. metered parking (8am-7pm) including Sun/No parking 7:30am-8am (except Sun)

West

No parking 8am-6pm (M-F)

IRVING (19TH-20TH)

East

No parking 8:30am-10am (Tu & F)

West

No parking 8am-6pm (M-F)

JACKSON (SOUTH - WATER)

East

No parking 11am-12:30pm (M & F)

West

No parking 11am-12:30pm (M & Th)

JACKSON (WATER - CHERRY)

East

No parking 11am-12:30pm (M & F)

West

No parking 11am-12:30pm (M & Th)

JACKSON (CHERRY - MADISON)

East

No parking 11am-12:30pm (M & F)

West

No parking 11am-12:30pm (M & Th)

JACKSON (MADISON - GRAND/HENRY)

East

No parking 11am-12:30pm (M & F)

West

No parking 11am-12:30pm (M & Th)

JEFFERSON (E. BROADWAY - HENRY)

East

No parking 11am-12:30pm (M & F)

West

No parking 11am-12:30pm (M & Th)

JEFFERSON (HENRY - MADISON) ☺

East

No parking 11am-12:30pm (M & F)/No standing anytime (Doctor's vehicles only)

West

No parking 11am-12:30pm (M & Th)

KENMARE (CLEVELAND - MULBERRY)

North

No standing 7am-10am (except Sun)/No standing except trucks loading & unloading 10am-7pm (except Sun)

South

No standing except trucks loading & unloading 7am-4pm (except Sun)/No standing 4pm-7pm (except Sun)

KENMARE (MULBERRY - MOTT)

North

No standing 7am-10am (except Sun)/No standing except trucks loading & unloading 10am-7pm (except Sun)

South

No standing except trucks loading & unloading 7am-4pm (except Sun)/No standing 4pm-7pm (except Sun)

KENMARE (MOTT - ELIZABETH)

North

No standing 7am-10am (except Sun)/No standing except trucks loading & unloading 10am-7pm (except Sun)

South

No standing except trucks loading & unloading 7am-4pm (except Sun)/No standing 4pm-7pm (except Sun)

KENMARE (ELIZABETH - BOWERY)

North

No standing 7am-10am (except Sun)/No standing except trucks loading & unloading 10am-7pm (except Sun)

South

No standing except trucks loading & unloading 7am-4pm (except Sun)/No standing 4pm-7pm (except Sun)

LAFAYETTE (8TH ST - WANAMAKER) ☹

East

No standing anytime

West

No standing anytime

LAFAYETTE (WANAMAKER - 10TH ST)

East

No parking 7am-6pm (except Sun)

West

No parking 8am-6pm (M-F)

LEWIS (DELANCEY - BROOME)

East

No parking 9am-10:30am (Tu & F)

West

No parking 9am-10:30am (M & Th)/No parking 7am-4pm (school days)

LEWIS (BROOME - GRAND)

East

No parking 9am-10:30am (Tu & F)

West

No parking 9am-10:30am (M & Th)

LEXINGTON (30TH-29TH)

East

1 hr. metered parking (8am-7pm) including Sun/No parking 7:30am-8am (except Sun)

West

1 hr. metered parking (8am-7pm) including Sun/No parking 7:30am-8am (except Sun)

LEXINGTON (29TH-28TH)

East

No Standing anytime except Taxis

West

1 hr. metered parking (8am-7pm) including Sun/No parking 7:30am-8am (except Sun)

LEXINGTON (28TH-27TH)

East

No standing 7am-7pm (except Sun) except authorized vehicles/No parking 8:30am-9am (except Sun)

West

No Standing anytime

LEXINGTON (27TH-26TH)

East

No parking 8am-7pm (except Sun)

West

1 hr. metered parking (8am-7pm) including Sun/No parking 7:30am-8am (except Sun)

LEXINGTON (26TH-25TH)

East

No Standing 7am-7pm (except Sun) except authorized vehicles

West

No standing anytime

LEXINGTON (25TH-24TH)

East

1 hr. metered parking (8am-7pm) including Sun/No parking 7:30am-8am (except Sun)/No parking 8am-6pm (except Sun)

West

No parking 8am-7pm (except Sun)

LEXINGTON (24TH-23RD)

East

1 hr. metered parking (8am-7pm) including Sun/No parking 7:30am-8am (except Sun)

West

1 hr. metered parking (8am-7pm) including Sun/No parking 7:30am-8am (except Sun)

LEXINGTON (23RD-22ND)

East

1 hr. metered parking (8am-7pm) including Sun/No parking 7:30am-8am (except Sun)

West

1 hr. metered parking (8am-7pm) including Sun/No parking 7:30am-8am (except Sun)

LEXINGTON (22ND-21ST)

East

1 hr. metered parking (8am-7pm) including Sun/No parking 7:30am-8am (except Sun)

West

No parking 8am-6pm (M-F)

LUDLOW (HOUSTON - STANTON)

East

1 hr. metered parking (9am-7pm) including Sun/No parking Midnite-3am (Tu,Th,Sat)/No parking 7am-7pm (except Sun)

West

No parking 7am-7pm (M-F)/1 hour parking 9am-7pm (Sat, Sun)/No parking Midnite-3am (M,W,F)

LUDLOW (STANTON - RIVINGTON)

East

1 hr. metered parking (9am-7pm) including Sun/No parking Midnite-3am (Tu,Th,Sat)/No parking 7am-7pm (except Sun)

West

No parking 7am-7pm (M-F)/1 hour parking 9am-7pm (Sat, Sun)/No parking Midnite-3am (M,W,F)

LUDLOW (RIVINGTON - DELANCEY)

East

No standing except trucks loading & unloading 7am-7pm (including Sun)/No parking Midnite-3am (Tu,Th,Sat)

West

No standing except trucks loading & unloading 7am-7pm (including Sun)/No parking Midnite-3am (M,W,F)

LUDLOW (DELANCEY - BROOME)

East

2 hr. metered parking (9am-7pm) including Sun/No parking Midnite-3am (Tu,Th,Sat)

West

No parking 7am-7pm (M-F)/No parking Midnite-3am (M,W,F)

LUDLOW (BROOME - GRAND)

East

No parking 7am-6pm (M-F)/1 hour parking 9am-7pm (Sat, Sun)/No parking Midnite-3am (Tu,Th,Sat)

West

No parking 7am-7pm (M-F)/1 hour parking 9am-7pm (Sat, Sun)/No parking Midnite-3am (M,W,F)

LUDLOW (GRAND - HESTER)

East

1 hr. metered parking (9am-7pm) including Sun/No parking Midnite-3am (Tu,Th,Sat)/No parking 8am-6pm (M-F)/No parking 8am-7pm (M-F)

West

No parking 7am-7pm (M-F)/No parking Midnite-3am (M,W,F)

LUDLOW (HESTER - CANAL)

East

1 hr. metered parking (9am-7pm) including Sun/No parking Midnite-3am (Tu,Th,Sat)

West

No parking anytime

MADISON (23RD-24TH)

East

No standing anytime

West

1 hr. metered parking (8am-7pm) including Sun/No parking 7:30am-8am (except Sun)

MADISON (24TH-25TH)

East

No standing anytime

West

1 hr. metered parking (8am-7pm) including Sun/No parking 7:30am-8am (except Sun)

MADISON (25TH-26TH)

East

No standing 7am-7pm (M-F) except authorized vehicles

West

1 hr. metered parking (8am-7pm) including Sun/No parking 7:30am-8am (except Sun)

MADISON (26TH-27TH)

East

No standing anytime

West

No standing except trucks loading & unloading 7am-3:30pm (except Sun)/No standing anytime (except authorized vehicles)

MADISON (27TH-28TH)

East

No standing anytime

West

No standing except trucks loading & unloading 7am-7pm (except Sun)/No standing except trucks loading & unloading 7am-3:30pm (except Sun)/No Standing 3:30pm-7pm (except buses)

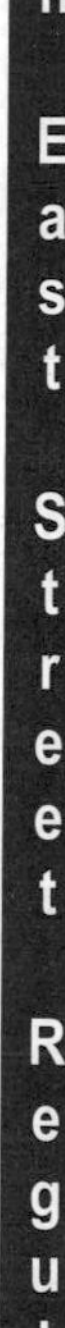

MADISON (28TH-29TH)

East

No standing 7am-10am & 4pm-7pm (except Sun)/No standing except trucks loading & unloading 10am-4pm (except Sun)

West

No standing except trucks loading & unloading 7am-7pm (except Sun)/No standing except trucks loading & unloading 7am-3:30pm (except Sun)/No Standing 3:30pm-7pm (except buses)

MADISON (29TH-30TH)

East

No standing 7am-10am & 4pm-7pm (except Sun)/No standing except trucks loading & unloading 10am-4pm (except Sun)

West

No standing except trucks loading & unloading 7am-7pm (except Sun)/No standing except trucks loading & unloading 7am-3:30pm (except Sun)/No Standing 3:30pm-7pm (except buses)

MADISON (GRAND - JACKSON) ☺

North

No standing 7am-7pm (except Sun) except ambulances

South

No parking 11am-12:30pm (Tu & F)

MADISON (JACKSON - GOVENUER) ☺

North

No parking 11am-12:30pm (M & F)

South

No parking 11am-12:30pm (Tu & F)

MADISON (GOUVENUER - MONTGOMERY) ☺

North

No parking anytime

South

No parking 11am-12:30pm (Tu & F)

MADISON (MONTGOMERY - CLINTON) ☺

North

No parking 11am-12:30pm (M & F)

South

No parking 11am-12:30pm (Tu & F)

MADISON (CLINTON - JEFFERSON)

North

No parking anytime except ambulettes

South

No parking 11am-12:30pm (Tu & F)

MADISON (JEFFERSON - RUTGERS)

North

No parking 11am-12:30pm (M & F)

South

No parking 11am-12:30pm (Tu & F)

MADISON (RUTGERS - PIKE)

North

No parking anytime

South

No parking 11am-12:30pm (Tu & F)/No parking 8am-6pm (M-F)

MANGIN (STANTON - HOUSTON)

East

No parking 11am-12:30pm (M & F)

West

No standing anytime

MONTGOMERY (E. BROADWAY - HENRY)

East

No parking 11am-12:30pm (M & F)

West

No parking 11am-12:30pm (M & Th)

MONTGOMERY (HENRY - MADISON)

East

No parking 11am-12:30pm (M & F)

West

No parking 11am-12:30pm (M & Th)/No parking 7am-4pm (school days)

MONTGOMERY (MADISON - CHERRY)

East

No parking 11am-12:30pm (M & F)

West

No parking 11am-12:30pm (M & Th)

MONTGOMERY (CHERRY - WATER)

East

No parking 11am-12:30pm (M & F)

West

No parking 7am-4pm (school days)

MONTGOMERY (WATER - SOUTH)

East

No parking 11am-12:30pm (M & F)

West

No parking 7am-4pm (school days)

MOSCO (MOTT - MULBERRY)

North

No standing anytime

South

No standing anytime

MOTT (BLEECKER - HOUSTON)

East

No parking 8am-6pm (M-F)

West

No standing except trucks loading & unloading

MOTT (HOUSTON - PRINCE)

East

No parking 8am-6pm (M-F)

West

No standing anytime

MOTT (PRINCE - SPRING)

East

No parking 8am-11am (Tu & F)

West

No parking 8am-11am (M & Th)/No parking 7am-4pm (school days)

MOTT (SPRING - KENMORE)

East

No parking 8am-6pm (except Sun)

West

No standing except trucks loading & unloading 7am-6pm (except Sun)

MOTT (KENMORE - BROOME)

East

No standing except trucks loading & unloading 7am-6pm (except Sun)

West

No standing except trucks loading & unloading 8am-6pm (except Sun)

MOTT (BROOME - GRAND)

East

No parking anytime

West

1 hr. metered parking (9am-7pm) including Sun/No parking 8am-9am (except Sun)

MOTT (GRAND - HESTER)

East

No parking 9am-6pm (except Sun) except trucks loading and unloading/No parking 8am-9am (except Sun)

West

1 hr. metered parking (9am-7pm) including Sun/No parking 8am-9am (except Sun)

MOTT (HESTER - CANAL)

East

1 hr. metered parking (9am-7pm) including Sun/No parking 8am-9am (except Sun)

West

No parking 8am-6pm (M-F)

MOTT (CANAL - BAYARD)

East

1 hour metered parking 7:30am-midnite including Sun/No parking 7am-7:30am (except Sunday)

West

No standing 7am-8am except Sun & No parking any other times

MULBERRY (MOSCO - BAYARD)

East

No parking 8am-6pm (M-F)/1 hour parking 9am-10pm (Sat, Sun)

West

No standing 7am-7pm (M-F) except authorized vehicles/No standing except trucks loading & unloading 8am-6pm (except Sun)

MULBERRY (BAYARD - CANAL)

East

No parking 8am-6pm (M-F)/1 hour parking 9am-10pm (Sat, Sun)

West

No standing except trucks loading & unloading 8am-6pm (except Sun)/No parking 8am-9am (except Sun)

MULBERRY (CANAL - HESTER)

East

No parking 7am-10am (except Sun) except trucks loading and unloading/2 hour metered parking 10am-10pm including Sun/No parking 5pm-11pm (Fri), 10am-11:30pm (Sat) & 10am-11pm (Sun & holidays) -**May 4-Oct 8**

West

No parking 7am-10am (except Sun) except trucks loading and unloading/2 hour metered parking 10am-10pm including Sun/No parking 5pm-11pm (Fri), 10am-11:30pm (Sat) & 10am-11pm (Sun & holidays) -**May 4-Oct 8**

MULBERRY (HESTER - GRAND)

East

No parking 8am-6pm (except Sun)/No parking 5pm-11pm (Fri), 10am-11:30pm (Sat) & 10am-11pm (Sun & holidays) -**May 4-Oct 8**

West

2 hr. metered parking (9am-7pm) including Sun/No parking 8am-9am (except Sun)/No parking 5pm-11pm (Fri), 10am-11:30pm (Sat) & 10am-11pm (Sun & holidays) -**May 4-Oct 8**

MULBERRY (GRAND - BROOME)

East

No parking 8am-6pm (except Sun)/No parking 5pm-11pm (Fri), 10am-11:30pm (Sat) & 10am-11pm (Sun & holidays) -**May 4-Oct 8**

West

2 hr. metered parking (9am-7pm) including Sun/No parking 8am-9am (except Sun)/No parking 5pm-11pm (Fri), 10am-11:30pm (Sat) & 10am-11pm (Sun & holidays) -**May 4-Oct 8**

MULBERRY (BROOME - KENMARE)

East

No standing except trucks loading & unloading 8am-6pm (M-F) except authorized vehicles

West

No standing except trucks loading & unloading 7am-7pm (except Sun)

MULBERRY (KENMARE - SPRING)

East

No parking 8am-6pm (except Sun)

West

No parking 8am-6pm (M-F)

MULBERRY (SPRING - PRINCE) ☺

East

No parking 8am-6pm (M-F)

West

No parking 8am-6pm (M-F)/No parking 8am-11am (M & Th)

MULBERRY (PRINCE - JERSEY)

East

No parking 8am-6pm (except Sun)

West

No standing except trucks loading & unloading 7am-7pm (M-F)

MULBERRY (JERSEY - HOUSTON)

East

No parking 8am-6pm (except Sun)

West

No parking 8am-6pm (M-F)/No parking 8am-midnite including Sun

MULBERRY (HOUSTON - BLEECKER)

East

No parking 8am-11am (Tu & F)

West

No parking 8am-6pm (M-F)

NORFOLK (GRAND - BROOME)

East

No parking anytime

West

No parking 8am-9:30am (M & Th)

NORFOLK (BROOME - DELANCEY)

East

No standing 4pm-7pm (except Sun)/1 hour parking 9am-7pm (Sat, Sun)/No parking 7am-4pm (M-F)

West

No parking 8am-9:30am (M & Th)

NORFOLK (DELANCEY - RIVINGTON)

East

No standing 7am-10am (except Sun)/No standing 10am-6pm (except Sunday) except trucks loading and unloading

West

1 hour metered parking 9am-4pm including Sun/No parking 8:30am-9am (except Sun)/No parking 7am-7pm (except Sun)

NORFOLK (RIVINGTON - STANTON)

East

No parking 7am-4pm (school days)

West

No parking 9am-10:30am (M & Th)

NORFOLK (STANTON - HOUSTON) ☺

East

No parking 9am-10:30am (Tu & F)

West

No parking 9am-10:30am (M & Th)/No parking 7am-4pm (school days)

ORCHARD (CANAL - HESTER)

East

No parking 7am-7pm (M-F)/1 hour parking 9am-7pm (Sat, Sun)/No parking Midnite-3am (Tu,Th,Sat)

West

2 hr. metered parking (9am-7pm) including Sun/No parking Midnite-3am (M,W,F)

ORCHARD (HESTER - GRAND)

East

No parking 7am-7pm (M-F)/1 hour parking 9am-7pm (Sat, Sun)/No parking Midnite-3am (Tu,Th,Sat)

West

2 hr. metered parking (9am-7pm) including Sun/No parking Midnite-3am (M,W,F)

ORCHARD (GRAND - BROOME)

East

No parking 7am-7pm (M-F)/No parking Midnite-3am (Tu,Th,Sat)

West

2 hr. metered parking (9am-7pm) including Sun/No parking Midnite-3am (M,W,F)

ORCHARD (BROOME - DELANCEY)

East

No parking 7am-7pm (M-F)/No parking Midnite-3am (Tu,Th,Sat)

West

2 hr. metered parking (9am-7pm) including Sun/No parking Midnite-3am (M,W,F)

ORCHARD (DELANCEY - RIVINGTON)

East

No parking 7am-7pm (M-F)/No parking Midnite-3am (Tu,Th,Sat)/No standing 8am-6pm Sundays

West

2 hr. metered parking (9am-7pm) including Sun/No parking Midnite-3am (M,W,F)/No standing 8am-6pm Sundays

ORCHARD (RIVINGTON - STANTON)

East

No parking 7am-7pm (M-F)/No parking Midnite-3am (Tu,Th,Sat)/No standing 8am-6pm Sundays

West

2 hr. metered parking (9am-7pm) including Sun/No parking Midnite-3am (M,W,F)/No standing 8am-6pm Sundays

ORCHARD (STANTON - HOUSTON)

East

No parking 7am-7pm (M-F)/No parking Midnite-3am (Tu,Th,Sat)/No standing 8am-6pm Sundays

West

2 hr. metered parking (9am-7pm) including Sun/No parking Midnite-3am (M,W,F)/No standing 8am-6pm Sundays

PARK (17TH-18TH)

East

No standing except trucks loading & unloading 7am-7pm (M-F)/No Parking 4:30am-6am (M,W,F)

West

No standing except trucks loading & unloading 7am-7pm (M-F)/No Parking 4:30am-6am (Tu,Th,Sat)

PARK (18TH-19TH)

East

No standing except trucks loading & unloading 7am-7pm (M-F)/No Parking 4:30am-6am (M,W,F)

West

No standing except trucks loading & unloading 7am-7pm (M-F)/No Parking 4:30am-6am (Tu,Th,Sat)

PARK (19TH-20TH)

East

No standing except trucks loading & unloading 7am-7pm (M-F)/No Parking 4:30am-6am (M,W,F)

West

No standing except trucks loading & unloading 7am-7pm (M-F)/No Parking 4:30am-6am (Tu,Th,Sat)

PARK (20TH-21ST)

East

No standing except trucks loading & unloading 7am-7pm (M-F)/No Parking 4:30am-6am (M,W,F)

West

No standing except trucks loading & unloading 7am-7pm (M-F)/No Parking 4:30am-6am (Tu,Th,Sat)

PARK (21ST-22ND)

East

No standing except trucks loading & unloading 7am-7pm (M-F)/No Parking 4:30am-6am (M,W,F)

West

No standing except trucks loading & unloading 7am-7pm (M-F)/No Parking 4:30am-6am (Tu,Th,Sat)

PARK (22ND-23RD)

East

No standing except trucks loading & unloading 7am-7pm (M-F)/No Parking 4:30am-6am (M,W,F)

West

No parking 8am-6pm (M-F)/No Parking 4:30am-6am (Tu,Th,Sat)

PARK (23RD-24TH)

East

No standing except trucks loading & unloading 7am-7pm (M-F)/No Parking 4:30am-6am (M,W,F)

West

No parking 8am-6pm (M-F)/No Parking 4:30am-6am (Tu,Th,Sat)

PARK (24TH-25TH)

East

No standing except trucks loading & unloading 7am-7pm (M-F)/No Parking 4:30am-6am (M,W,F)

West

No standing except trucks loading & unloading 7am-7pm (M-F)/No Parking 4:30am-6am (Tu,Th,Sat)

PARK (25TH-26TH)

East

No standing except trucks loading & unloading 7am-7pm (M-F)/No Parking 4:30am-6am (M,W,F)

West

No standing except trucks loading & unloading 7am-7pm (M-F)/No Parking 4:30am-6am (Tu,Th,Sat)

PARK (26TH-27TH)

East

No standing except trucks loading & unloading 7am-7pm (M-F)/No Parking 4:30am-6am (M,W,F)

West

No standing except trucks loading & unloading 7am-7pm (M-F)/No Parking 4:30am-6am (Tu,Th,Sat)

PARK (27TH-28TH)

East

No standing except trucks loading & unloading 7am-7pm (M-F)/No Parking 4:30am-6am (M,W,F)

West

No standing except trucks loading & unloading 7am-7pm (M-F)/No Parking 4:30am-6am (Tu,Th,Sat)

PARK (28TH-29TH)

East

No standing except trucks loading & unloading 7am-7pm (M-F)/No Parking 4:30am-6am (M,W,F)

West

No standing except trucks loading & unloading 7am-7pm (M-F)/No Parking 4:30am-6am (Tu,Th,Sat)

PARK (29TH-30TH)

East

No standing except trucks loading & unloading 7am-7pm (M-F)/No Parking 4:30am-6am (M,W,F)

West

No standing except trucks loading & unloading 7am-7pm (M-F)/No Parking 4:30am-6am (Tu,Th,Sat)

PELL (BOWERY - DOYERS)

North

No standing except trucks loading & unloading

South

No standing anytime

PELL (DOYERS -MOTT)

North

No standing except trucks loading & unloading

South

No standing anytime

PERLMAN (15TH-16TH)

East

No parking anytime (except authorized vehicles)

West

No parking anytime (except authorized vehicles)

PERLMAN (16TH-17TH)

East

No parking anytime (except authorized vehicles)

West

No parking anytime (except authorized vehicles)

PIKE (CANAL - DIVISION)

East

No parking anytime

West

1 hr. metered parking (9am-7pm) including Sun/No parking Midnite-3am (M,W,F)

PIKE (DIVISION - E. BROADWAY)

East

No parking anytime

West

2 hr. metered parking (8am-7pm) including Sun/No parking 7:30am-8am (except Sun)

PIKE (E. BROADWAY - HENRY)

East

No parking anytime

West

2 hr. metered parking (8am-7pm) including Sun/No parking 7:30am-8am (except Sun)

PITT (GRAND - BROOME)

East

No parking 8am-6pm (M-F)

West

No parking 8am-9:30am (M & Th)

PITT (BROOME - DELANCEY SOUTH)

East

No standing anytime

West

No standing anytime

PITT (DELANCEY SOUTH - DELANCEY NORTH)

East

No standing anytime

West

No standing except trucks loading & unloading 7am-7pm (except Sun)

PITT (DELANCEY NORTH - RIVINGTON)

East

No parking 9am-10:30am (Tu & F)

West

No parking 9am-10:30am (M & Th)

PITT (RIVINGTON - STANTON)

East

No parking 9am-10:30am (Tu & F)

West

No parking 9am-10:30am (M & Th)/No parking 7am-4pm (school days) except Board of Education

PITT (STANTON - HOUSTON) ☺

East

No parking 8am-6pm (except Sun)

West

No parking 9am-10:30am (M & Th)

PRINCE (BOWERY - ELIZABETH) ☺

North

No parking 8am-6pm (M-F)/No parking 8am-11am (M & Th)

South

No parking 7am-6pm (except Sun)

PRINCE (ELIZABETH - MOTT) ☺

North

No parking 8am-11am (M & Th)

South

No parking 7am-6pm (except Sun)

PRINCE (MOTT - MULBERRY) ☺

North

No parking 8am-11am (M & Th)

South

No parking 7am-6pm (except Sun)

PRINCE (MULBERRY - LAFAYETTE) ☺

North

No parking 8am-11am (M & Th)

South

No parking 7am-6pm (except Sun)

RIDGE (DELANCEY SOUTH - BROOME) ☺

East

No parking 8am-9:30am (Tu & F)/No parking 7am-4pm (school days)

West

No parking 8am-9:30am (M & Th)

RIDGE (HOUSTON - STANTON) ☺

East

No parking 9am-10:30am (Tu & F)

West

No parking 9am-10:30am (M & Th)

RIDGE (STANTON - RIVINGTON)

East

No parking 9am-10:30am (Tu & F)

West

No parking 9am-10:30am (M & Th)/No parking 7am-4pm (school days) except Board of Ed

RIDGE (RIVINGTON - DELANCEY NORTH)

East

No parking 9am-10:30am (Tu & F)/No standing except trucks loading & unloading 7am-7pm (except Sun)

West

No parking 9am-10:30am (M & Th)/No parking 7am-4pm (school days) except Board of Ed

RIVINGTON (COLUMBIA - BARUCH)

North

No parking anytime

South

No parking anytime

RIVINGTON (PITT - RIDGE)

North

No parking 9am-10:30am (M & Th)

South

No parking 9am-10:30am (Tu & F)

RIVINGTON (RIDGE - ATTORNEY)

North

No parking 9am-10:30am (M & Th)/No parking 7am-4pm (school days)

South

No standing 7am-4pm (school days)/No parking other times

RIVINGTON (ATTORNEY - CLINTON)

North

1 hr. metered parking (9am-7pm) including Sun/No parking 8:30am-9am (except Sun)

South

No parking 8am-6pm (M-F)

RIVINGTON (CLINTON - SUFFOLK)

North

1 hr. metered parking (9am-7pm) including Sun/No parking 8:30am-9am (except Sun)

South

No parking anytime

RIVINGTON (SUFFOLK - NORFOLK)

North

1 hr. metered parking (9am-7pm) including Sun/No parking 8:30am-9am (except Sun)

South

No parking anytime

RIVINGTON (NORFOLK - ESSEX)

North

1 hr. metered parking (9am-7pm) including Sun/No parking 8:30am-9am (except Sun)/No standing except trucks loading & unloading 8am-6pm (except Sun)

South

No parking anytime

RIVINGTON (ESSEX - LUDLOW)

North

No standing 10am-7pm including Sun except trucks loading and unloading/No parking Midnite-3am (M,W,F)

South

No parking anytime

RIVINGTON (LUDLOW - ORCHARD)

North

1 hr. metered parking (9am-7pm) including Sun/No parking Midnite-3am (M,W,F)

South

No parking anytime

RIVINGTON (ORCHARD - ALLEN) ☺

North

No parking Midnite-3am (M,W,F)

South

No parking anytime

RIVINGTON (ALLEN - ELDRIDGE)

North

No parking Midnite-3am (M,W,F)

South

No parking anytime

RIVINGTON (ELDRIDGE - FORSYTH)

North

No parking Midnite-3am (M,W,F)

South

No standing anytime (except authorized vehicles)/1 hour parking 9am-7pm (Sat, Sun)/No parking 7am-7pm (M-F)/No parking Midnite-3am (Tu,Th,Sat)

RUTGERS (CHERRY - MADISON)

East

No parking 11am-12:30pm (M & F)

West

No parking 11am-12:30pm (M & Th)

RUTGERS (MADISON - HENRY)

East

No parking 11am-12:30pm (M & F)

West

No parking 11am-12:30pm (M & Th)

RUTGERS (HENRY - E. BROADWAY)

East

2 hr. metered parking (8am-7pm) including Sun/No parking 7:30am-8am (except Sun)

West

No parking 11am-12:30pm (M & Th)

RUTGERS (E. BROADWAY - CANAL)

East

No standing anytime

West

No standing anytime

RUTHERFORD (15TH-16TH)

East

No parking anytime

West

No parking anytime

RUTHERFORD (16TH-17TH)

East

No parking anytime

West

No parking anytime

S. DICKSTEIN PLAZA (GRAND - E. BROADWAY) ☺

East

No parking 8am-9:30am (Tu & F)

West

No parking 8am-9:30am (M & Th)

S. DICKSTEIN PLAZA (E. BROADWAY - HENRY/MONTGOMERY) ☺

East

No parking 8am-9:30am (Tu & F)

West

No parking 8am-9:30am (M & Th)

SHERRIF (DELANCEY SOUTH - DELANCEY NORTH) ☺

East

No parking 9am-10:30am (Tu & F)

West

No parking 9am-10:30am (M & Th)

SOUTH (JACKSON - MONTGOMERY) ☹

East

No parking anytime

West

No parking anytime

SOUTH (MONTGOMERY - CLINTON)

East

No parking anytime

West

No standing 8am-6pm (M-F)

SOUTH (CLINTON - RUTGERS)

East

No parking anytime

West

No standing 7am-7pm (M-F)

SPRING (LAFAYETTE - MULBERRY)

North

No parking 8am-11am (M & Th)

South

No parking 7am-6pm (except Sun)

SPRING (MULBERRY - MOTT)

North

No parking 7am-6pm (M-F)

South

No parking 7am-6pm (except Sun)

SPRING (MOTT - ELIZABETH)

North

No parking 8am-11am (M & Th)

South

No parking 7am-6pm (except Sun)

SPRING (ELIZABETH - BOWERY)

North

No parking 8am-11am (M & Th)

South

No parking 7am-6pm (except Sun)

STANTON (FORSYTH - ELDRIDGE)

North

No parking Midnite-3am (M,W,F)/No parking 7am-4pm (school days)

South

No parking Midnite-3am (Tu,Th,Sat)

STANTON (ELDRIDGE - ALLEN)

North

No parking anytime

South

No parking Midnite-3am (Tu,Th,Sat)

STANTON (ALLEN - ORCHARD)

North

No parking anytime

South

1 hr. metered parking (9am-7pm) including Sun/No parking Midnite-3am (Tu,Th,Sat)

STANTON (ORCHARD - LUDLOW)

North

No parking anytime

South

1 hr. metered parking (9am-7pm) including Sun/No parking Midnite-3am (Tu,Th,Sat)

STANTON (LUDLOW - ESSEX)

North

No parking anytime

South

1 hr. metered parking (9am-7pm) including Sun/No parking Midnite-3am (Tu,Th,Sat)

STANTON (ESSEX - NORFOLK)

North

No parking anytime

South

No parking 9am-10:30am (Tu & F)

STANTON (NORFOLK - SUFFOLK)

North

No parking 8am-6pm (except Sun)

South

No parking 9am-10:30am (Tu & F)/No parking 7am-4pm (school days)

STANTON (SUFFOLK - CLINTON)

North

No parking anytime

South

No parking 9am-10:30am (Tu & F)

STANTON (CLINTON - ATTORNEY)

North

No parking anytime

South

No parking 9am-10:30am (Tu & F)

STANTON (ATTORNEY - RIDGE)

North

No parking anytime

South

No parking 9am-10:30am (Tu & F)

STANTON (RIDGE - PITT)

North

No parking anytime

South

No parking 9am-10:30am (Tu & F)

STANTON (PITT - DEAD END)

North

No parking 9am-10:30am (M & Th)

South

No parking anytime

STANTON (SHERRIF - COLUMBIA)

North

No parking anytime

South

No parking anytime

STANTON (BARUCH PL - MANGIN)

North

No parking 11am-12:30pm (M & F)/No parking 7am-4pm (school days) except Board of Ed

South

No parking 11am-12:30pm (Tu & F)

ST. MARKS (4TH AVE - 3RD AVE)

North

No standing 8am-6pm (M-F) except authorized vehicles

South

No standing 8am-6pm (M-F) except authorized vehicles

ST. MARKS (3RD AVE - 2ND AVE)

North

No standing except trucks loading & unloading

South

No standing except trucks loading & unloading

ST. MARKS (2ND AVE - 1ST AVE)

North

No parking anytime

South

2 hr. metered parking (9am-7pm) including Sun/No parking 9am-10:30am (Tu & F)

ST. MARKS (1ST AVE - AVE A)

North

No standing anytime

South

No parking 9am-10:30am (Tu & F)/No parking 7am-4pm (school days)

STUVESANT (3RD AVE - 2ND AVE)

East

No parking 9am-10:30am (M & Th)

West

No parking 9am-10:30am (Tu & F)

SUFFOLK (GRAND - BROOME)

East

No parking anytime

West

No parking 8am-9:30am (M & Th)

SUFFOLK (BROOME - DELANCEY)

East

No standing 7am-1pm (M-F)

West

No parking 8am-9:30am (M & Th)

SUFFOLK (DELANCEY - RIVINGTON)

East

No parking anytime

West

1 hour metered parking 9am-4pm including Sun/No parking 8:30am-9am (except Sun)/No parking 7am-7pm (except Sun)

SUFFOLK (RIVINGTON - STANTON)

East

No parking 9am-10:30am (Tu & F)

West

No standing 4pm-7pm (M-F)

SUFFOLK (STANTON - HOUSTON)

East

No parking 9am-10:30am (Tu & F)

West

No standing 4pm-7pm (M-F)

SZOLD (10TH ST - 11TH ST)

East

No parking 11am-12:30pm (M & F)

West

No parking 11am-12:30pm (M & Th)

SZOLD (11TH ST - 12TH ST)

East

No parking 11am-12:30pm (M & F)/No parking 7am-4pm (school days)

West

No parking 11am-12:30pm (M & Th)

TARAS SCHEUNKO PL (7TH ST - 6TH ST)

East

No parking 9am-10:30am (Tu & F)

West

No parking 9am-10:30am (M & Th)

UNION SQUARE (17TH-16TH)

East

No standing anytime

West

No standing anytime

UNION SQUARE (16TH-15TH)

East

No standing anytime

West

No standing anytime

UNION SQUARE (15TH-14TH)

East

No standing anytime

West

No standing anytime

UNIVERSITY PL (8TH ST - 9TH ST)

North

No parking 8am - 4pm (M-F)/No standing 4pm-6pm (M-F)

South

No parking 8am - 4pm (M-F)/No standing 4pm-6pm (M-F)

UNIVERSITY PL (9TH ST - 10TH ST)

North

No parking 8am - 4pm (M-F)/No standing 4pm-6pm (M-F)

South

No parking 8am - 4pm (M-F)/No standing 4pm-6pm (M-F)

UNIVERSITY PL (10TH ST - 11TH ST)

North

No parking 8am - 4pm (M-F)/No standing 4pm-6pm (M-F)

South

No parking 8am - 4pm (M-F)/No standing 4pm-6pm (M-F)

UNIVERSITY PL (11TH ST - 12TH ST)

North

No parking 8am - 4pm (M-F)/No standing 4pm-6pm (M-F)

South

No parking 8am - 4pm (M-F)/No standing 4pm-6pm (M-F)

UNIVERSITY PL (12TH ST - 13TH ST)

North

No parking 8am - 4pm (M-F)/No standing 4pm-6pm (M-F)

South

No parking 8am - 4pm (M-F)/No standing 4pm-6pm (M-F)

UNIVERSITY PL (13TH ST - 14TH ST)

North

No parking 8am - 4pm (M-F)/No standing 4pm-6pm (M-F)

South

No standing anytime

WATER (MONTGOMERY - GOUVENUER) ☺

North

No parking 11am-12:30pm (M & F)

South

No parking 11am-12:30pm (Tu & F)

WATER (GOUVENUER - JACKSON) ☺

North

No parking 11am-12:30pm (M & F)

South

No parking 11am-12:30pm (Tu & F)

WILLET (DELANCEY NORTH - DELANCEY SOUTH) ☺

East

No parking 9am-10:30am (Tu & F)

West

No parking 9am-10:30am (M & Th)

WILLET (DELANCEY SOUTH - BROOME) ☺

East

No parking 8am-9:30am (Tu & F)

West

No parking 8am-9:30am (M & Th)

WILLET (BROOME - GRAND) ☺

East

No parking 8am-9:30am (Tu & F)

West

No parking 8am-9:30am (M & Th)

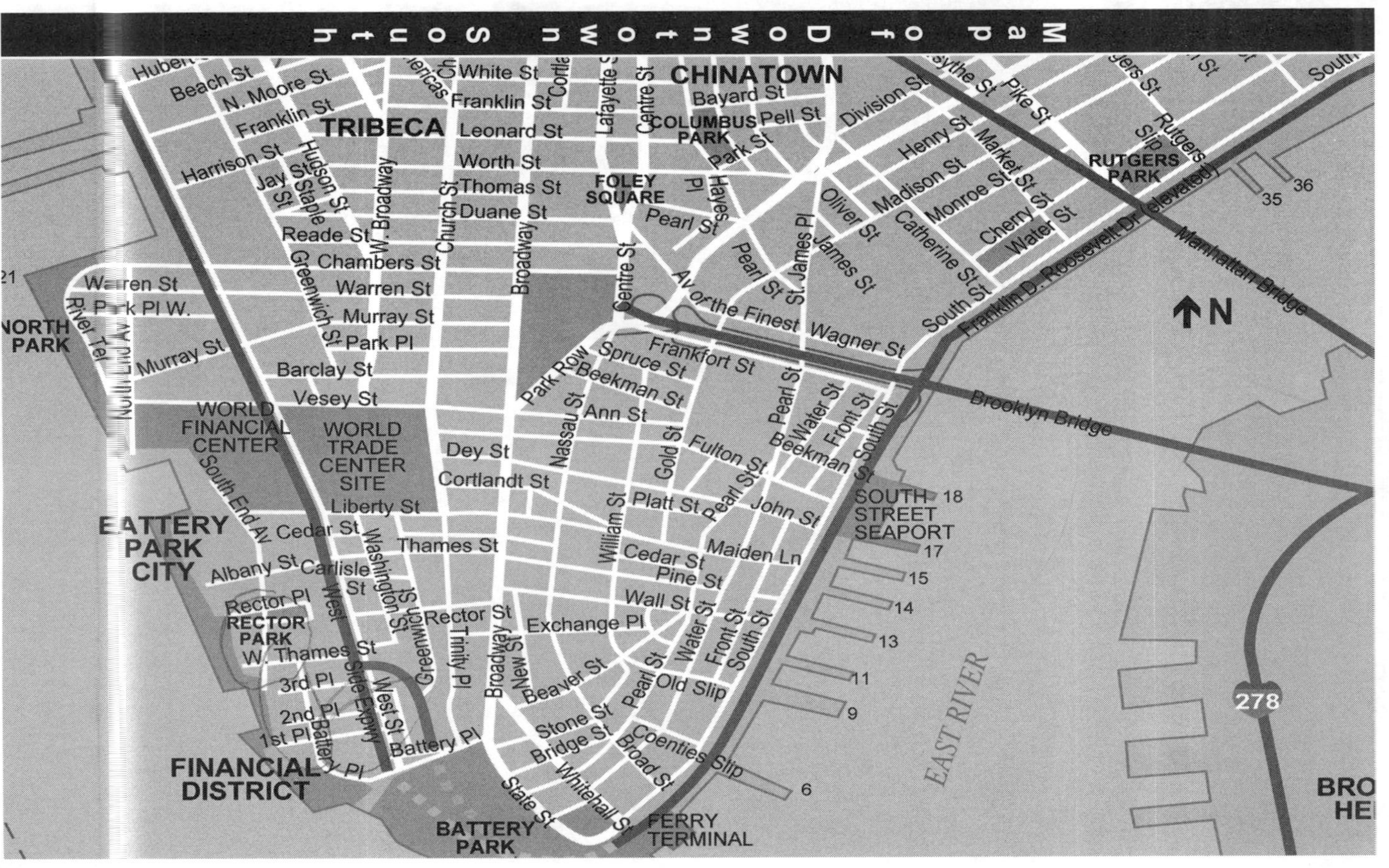
Map of Downtown South
CHINATOWN
COLUMBUS PARK
FOLEY SQUARE
TRIBECA
RUTGERS PARK
SOUTH STREET SEAPORT
EAST RIVER
WORLD TRADE CENTER SITE
WORLD FINANCIAL CENTER
BATTERY PARK CITY
RECTOR PARK
FINANCIAL DISTRICT
BATTERY PARK
FERRY TERMINAL
NORTH PARK
Manhattan Bridge
Brooklyn Bridge
Franklin D. Roosevelt Dr (elevated)
278
N
Broadway
W. Broadway
Church St
Centre St
Lafayette St
Pearl St
Park Row
Av of the Finest
St. James Pl
James St
Oliver St
Catherine St
Madison St
Monroe St
Cherry St
Water St
Market St
Henry St
Pike St
Division St
Rutgers Slip
Bayard St
Pell St
Park St
Hayes Pl
Worth St
Thomas St
Duane St
Leonard St
Franklin St
White St
Reade St
Chambers St
Warren St
Murray St
Park Pl
Park Pl W.
River Ter
Barclay St
Vesey St
Hudson St
Staple St
Jay St
Harrison St
Greenwich St
N. Moore St
Beach St
Frankfort St
Spruce St
Beekman St
Ann St
Nassau St
Fulton St
Gold St
John St
Platt St
Maiden Ln
Cedar St
Pine St
Wall St
William St
Exchange Pl
Beaver St
Stone St
Bridge St
Whitehall St
State St
New St
Broad St
Coenties Slip
Old Slip
Front St
South St
Dey St
Cortlandt St
Liberty St
Thames St
Rector St
Trinity Pl
Washington St
Carlisle St
Albany St
Rector Pl
W. Thames St
West St
West Side Expwy
Battery Pl
1st Pl
2nd Pl
3rd Pl
South End Av
Wagner St
18
17
15
14
13
11
9
6
35
36

Chapter 6 -

DOWNTOWN SOUTH:

Street Parking Regulations

(White Street - Battery Park)

1ST PL (LITTLE WEST - BATTERY PL) ☹

North

No parking anytime

South

No parking anytime

1ST PL (BATTERY PL - DEAD END) ☹

North

No parking anytime

South

No parking anytime

2ND PL (LITTLE WEST - BATTERY PL) ☹

North

No parking anytime

South

No parking anytime

2ND PL (BATTERY PL - DEAD END) ☹

North

No parking anytime

South

No parking anytime

3RD PL (LITTLE WEST - BATTERY PL) ☹

North

No parking anytime

South

No parking anytime

3RD PL (BATTERY PL - DEAD END) ☹

North

No parking anytime

South

No parking anytime

ALBANY (SOUTH END - DEAD END) ☺

North

No parking 9am-10:30am (M & Th)

South

No parking 9am-10:30am (Tu & F)

ALBANY (SOUTH END - WEST)

North

No standing anytime

South

No standing anytime

ALBANY (WEST - WASHINGTON)

North

1 hr. metered parking (9am-7pm) including Sun

South

No standing except trucks loading & unloading 8am-6pm (M-F)

ALBANY (WASHINGTON - GREENWICH)

North

No standing anytime

South

No standing except trucks loading & unloading 7am-7pm (M-F)

ANN (BROADWAY/PARK ROW - NASSAU)

North

No standing except trucks loading & unloading 7am-7pm (M-F)

South

No standing anytime

ANN (NASSAU - WILLIAM)

North

No standing except trucks loading & unloading 7am-7pm (M-F)

South

No standing anytime

ANN (WILLIAM - GOLD)

North

No standing anytime

South

No standing anytime

AVE OF FINEST (ST. JAMES - MADISON)

North

No parking anytime

South

No standing 7am - 7pm including Sun except authorized vehicles

BARCLAY (BROADWAY - CHURCH)

North

No standing 7am-10am & 4pm-7pm (except Sun)/No standing except trucks loading & unloading 10am-4pm (except Sun)/1 hr. metered parking (10am-4pm) including Sun

South

No standing 7am-10am & 4pm-7pm (except Sun)/No standing except trucks loading & unloading 10am-4pm (except Sun)

BARCLAY (CHURCH - W. BROADWAY)

North

1 hr. metered parking (8am-4pm) including Sun/No parking 7:30am-8am (except Sun)/No standing 4pm-7pm (M-F)

South

No standing 7am-7pm (M-F) except authorized vehicles

BARCLAY (W. BROADWAY - GREENWICH)

North

No standing anytime

South

No standing 7am-7pm (M-F) except authorized vehicles

BARCLAY (GREENWICH - WEST)

North

No standing anytime

South

No standing 7am-10am & 4pm-7pm (except Sun)/1 hr. metered parking 10am-4pm (including Sun)

BATTERY PL (W. THAMES - 3RD PL)

East

No parking 9am-10:30am (Tu & F)

West

No parking 9am-10:30am (M & Th)

BATTERY PL (3RD PL - 2ND PL)

East

No parking 9am-10:30am (Tu & F)

West

No parking 9am-10:30am (M & Th)

BATTERY PL (2ND PL - 1ST PL)

East

No parking 9am-10:30am (Tu & F)

West

No parking 9am-10:30am (M & Th)

BATTERY PL (1ST PL - WEST)

East

No standing anytime

West

No standing anytime

BATTERY PL (STATE-GREENWICH ST)

North

No standing anytime

South

No standing anytime

BATTERY PL (GREENWICH ST-WASHINGTON ST)

North

No standing anytime

South

1 hr. metered parking (9am-4pm) including Sun/No parking 2am-6am (Tu, F)/No standing 4pm-7pm (M-F)

BATTERY PL (WASHINGTON - WEST)

North

No standing anytime

South

No parking 2am-6am (Tu, F)

BATTERY PLACE PLAZA (WASHINGTON - WEST)

North

3 hour metered parking 9am-7pm (Including Sun)/No parking 2am-6am (M, Th)

South

3 hour metered parking 9am-7pm (Including Sun)/No parking 2am-6am (Tu, F)

BAXTER (WHITE - BAYARD)

East

No standing except trucks loading & unloading 7am-7pm (M-F)

West

No standing anytime except authorized vehicles

BAXTER (BAYARD - HOGAN)

East

No standing 7am-7pm (M-F) except authorized vehicles

West

No standing anytime except authorized vehicles

White Street | Battery Park

BAXTER (HOGAN - WORTH)

East

No standing 7am-7pm (M-F) except authorized vehicles

West

No standing 7am-7pm (M-F) except authorized vehicles

BAYARD (BAXTER - MULBERRY)

North

No standing 7am-7pm (M-F) except authorized vehicles

South

No standing anytime

BEACH (HUDSON - GREENWICH)

North

No parking anytime

South

No parking anytime

BEAVER (PEARL - HANOVER)

East

No standing 7am-1pm (M-F)/No standing except trucks loading & unloading 1pm-7pm (M-F)

West

No standing except trucks loading & unloading 7am-1pm (M-F)/No standing 1pm-7pm (M-F)

BEAVER (HANOVER - WILLIAM)

East

No standing except trucks loading & unloading 7am-7pm (M-F)

West

No standing except trucks loading & unloading 7am-7pm (M-F)

BEAVER (WILLIAM - NASSAU/BROAD)

East

No standing 7am-7pm (M-F) except authorized vehicles

West

No standing anytime

BEAVER (BROAD - NEW)

East

No standing except trucks loading & unloading 7am-7pm (M-F)

West

No standing 7am-7pm (M-F) except authorized vehicles

BEAVER (NEW - BROADWAY)

East

No standing except trucks loading & unloading 7am-7pm (M-F)

West

No standing 8am-6pm (M-F) except authorized vehicles

BEEKMAN (SOUTH - PECK SLIP)

North

No standing except trucks loading & unloading (M-F)/No parking Midnite - 11am (M-F)

South

No standing except trucks loading & unloading 7am-7pm (M-F)/No parking Midnite - 11am (M-F)

BEEKMAN (PECK SLIP - WATER)

North

No standing except trucks loading & unloading (M-F)/No parking Midnite - 11am (M-F)

South

No standing except trucks loading & unloading 7am-7pm (M-F)/No parking Midnite - 11am (M-F)

BEEKMAN (WATER - PEARL)

North

No standing 7am-7pm (M-F)/No parking Midnite - 11am (M-F)

South

No standing anytime

BEEKMAN (GOLD - WILLIAM)

North

No standing anytime

South

No standing 7am-7pm (M-F) except authorized vehicles

BEEKMAN (WILLIAM - NASSAU)

North

No standing anytime

South

No standing 7am-7pm (M-F) except authorized vehicles/No standing except trucks loading & unloading 7am-7pm (M-F)

BENSON (LEONARD - DEAD END)

East

No standing anytime

West

No standing except trucks loading & unloading 7am-7pm (M-F)

BRIDGE (STATE - WHITEHALL)

North

No standing anytime

South

No parking 7am-7pm (M-F)/No standing except trucks loading & unloading 7am-7pm (M-F)

BRIDGE (WHITEHALL - BROAD)

North

No standing anytime

South

No standing except trucks loading & unloading 7am-7pm (except Sun)

BROAD (SOUTH - WATER)

East

1 hr. metered parking (10am-7pm) including Sun/No standing 7am-10am (M-F)

West

1 hr. metered parking (8:30am-7pm) including Sun/No parking 8am-8:30am (except Sun)

BROAD (WATER - PEARL/BRIDGE)

East

No standing except trucks loading & unloading 7am-7pm (M-F)

West

No standing 7am-7pm (M-F)

BROAD (PEARL/BRIDGE - STONE)

East

No parking anytime

West

No standing anytime

BROAD (STONE - S. WILLIAM)

East

No parking anytime

West

No standing anytime

BROAD (S. WILLIAM - BEAVER)

East

No standing except trucks loading & unloading 7am-7pm (M-F)

West

No standing anytime

BROAD (BEAVER - EXCHANGE)

East

No standing except trucks loading & unloading 7am-7pm (M-F)

West

No standing except trucks loading & unloading 7am-7pm (M-F)

BROAD (EXCHANGE - WALL) ☹

East

No standing anytime

West

No standing anytime

BROADWAY (WHITE - FRANKLIN)

East

No standing except trucks loading & unloading 7am-7pm (M-F)/No parking 2am-6am (Tu & F)

West

No standing except trucks loading & unloading 7am-4pm (M-F)/No standing 4pm - 7pm (M-F)

BROADWAY (FRANKLIN - LEONARD)

East

No standing except trucks loading & unloading 7am-7pm (M-F)/No parking 2am-6am (Tu & F)

West

No standing except trucks loading & unloading 7am-4pm (M-F)/No standing 4pm - 7pm (M-F)

BROADWAY (LEONARD - WORTH)

East

No standing except trucks loading & unloading 7am-7pm (M-F)/No parking 2am-6am (Tu & F)

West

No standing except trucks loading & unloading 7am-4pm (M-F)/No standing 4pm - 7pm (M-F)

BROADWAY (WORTH - THOMAS) ☹

East

No standing anytime

West

No standing anytime

BROADWAY (THOMAS - DUANE)

East

No standing anytime

West

No standing 7am-7pm (except Sun)/No parking 2am-6am (M & Th)

BROADWAY (DUANE - READE)

East

No standing anytime

West

No standing 7am-7pm (except Sun)/No parking 2am-6am (M & Th)

BROADWAY (READE - CHAMBERS)

East

No standing except trucks loading & unloading 7am-4pm (M-F)/No standing 4pm - 7pm (M-F)/No parking 2am-6am (Tu & F)

West

No standing anytime

BROADWAY (CHAMBERS - WARREN)

East

No standing anytime

West

No standing 7am-7pm (except Sun)/No parking 2am-6am (M & Th)

BROADWAY (WARREN - MURRAY) ☹

East

No standing anytime

West

No standing anytime

BROADWAY (MURRAY- PARK PL.) ☹

East

No standing anytime

West

No standing anytime

BROADWAY (PARK PL - BARCLAY) ☹

East

No standing anytime

West

No standing anytime

BROADWAY (BARCLAY - VESEY) ☹

East

No standing anytime

West

No standing anytime

BROADWAY (VESEY - FULTON)

East

No standing 7am-10am & 4pm-7pm (except Sun)/No standing except trucks loading & unloading 10am-4pm (except Sun)/No parking 2am-6am (Tu & F)

West

No standing anytime

BROADWAY (FULTON - DEY (JOHN))

East

No standing 7am-10am & 4pm-7pm (except Sun)/No standing except trucks loading & unloading 10am-4pm (except Sun)/No parking 2am-6am (Tu & F)

West

No standing anytime

BROADWAY (DEY (JOHN) - CORTLAND (MAIDEN))

East

No standing 7am-10am & 4pm-7pm (except Sun)/No standing except trucks loading & unloading 10am-4pm (except Sun)/No parking 2am-6am (Tu & F)

West

No standing anytime

BROADWAY (CORTLAND (MAIDEN)) - LIBERTY)

East

No standing 7am-10am & 4pm-7pm (except Sun)/No standing except trucks loading & unloading 10am-4pm (except Sun)/No parking 2am-6am (Tu & F)

West

No standing anytime

BROADWAY (LIBERTY - CEDAR)

East

No standing 7am-10am & 4pm-7pm (except Sun)/No standing except trucks loading & unloading 10am-4pm (except Sun)/No parking 2am-6am (Tu & F)

West

No standing anytime

BROADWAY (CEDAR - PINE (THAMES))

East

No standing anytime

West

No standing 7am-7pm (except Sun)/No parking 2am-6am (M & Th)

BROADWAY (PINE (THAMES)- WALL ST.)

East

No standing 7am-7pm (M-F)/No parking 2am-6am (Tu & F)

West

No standing 7am-7pm (except Sun)/No parking 2am-6am (M & Th)

BROADWAY (WALL ST. - RECTOR)

East

No standing 7am-10am & 4pm-7pm (except Sun)/No standing except trucks loading & unloading 10am-4pm (except Sun)/No parking 2am-6am (Tu & F)

West

No standing anytime

BROADWAY (RECTOR - EXCHANGE PL)

East

No standing 7am-10am & 4pm-7pm (except Sun)/No standing except trucks loading & unloading 10am-4pm (except Sun)/No parking 2am-6am (Tu & F)

West

No standing anytime

BROADWAY (EXCHANGE PL - MORRIS)

East

No standing 7am-10am & 4pm-7pm (except Sun)/No standing except trucks loading & unloading 10am-4pm (except Sun)/No parking 2am-6am (Tu & F)

West

No standing anytime

BROADWAY (MORRIS - BOWLING GREEN)

East

No standing anytime

West

No standing anytime

CARDINAL HAYES (PEARL - DEAD END)

East

No parking anytime

West

No parking anytime

CARLISLE (GREENWICH - WASHINGTON)

North

No standing anytime

South

No standing anytime

CARLISLE (WASHINGTON - WEST)

North

No standing anytime

South

No standing anytime

CATHERINE LANE (BROADWAY - LAFAYETTE)

North

No standing anytime

South

No standing anytime

CATHERINE SLIP (DIVISION - E. BROADWAY)

North

No parking anytime

South

No parking anytime

CATHERINE SLIP (E. BROADWAY - HENRY)

North

No parking anytime

South

No parking anytime

CATHERINE SLIP (HENRY - MADISON)

North

No parking anytime

South

No parking anytime

CATHERINE SLIP (MADISON - MONROE)

North

No parking 11am-12:30pm (M & F)

South

No parking 11am-12:30pm (Tu & F)/No standing 7am-4pm (school days) except MIU vehicles

CATHERINE SLIP (MONROE - CHERRY)

North

No parking 11am-12:30pm (M & F)

South

No parking 11am-12:30pm (Tu & F)/No standing 7am-4pm (school days) except MIU vehicles

CATHERINE SLIP (CHERRY - WATER)

North

No parking 11am-12:30pm (M & F)

South

No parking 11am-12:30pm (Tu & F)

CATHERINE SLIP (WATER - SOUTH)

North

No parking anytime

South

No parking 11am-12:30pm (M & F)/No parking 11am-12:30pm (Tu & F)

CEDAR (PEARL - WILLIAM)

North

No standing anytime

South

No standing except trucks loading & unloading 7am-7pm (M-F)

CEDAR (NASSAU - BROADWAY)

North

No standing anytime

South

No standing except trucks loading & unloading 7am-7pm (M-F)

CEDAR (BROADWAY - TRINITY)

North

No standing anytime

South

No standing except trucks loading & unloading 7am-7pm (except Sun)

CEDAR (TRINITY - GREENWICH)

North

No standing anytime

South

No standing anytime

CEDAR (WASHINGTON - WEST)

North

No standing anytime

South

No standing except trucks loading & unloading 7am-7pm (M-F)/No standing 7am-7pm (except Sun)

CENTRE/PARK ROW (FULTON - VESEY)

East

No standing anytime

West

No standing anytime

CENTRE/PARK ROW (VESEY - CHAMBERS)

East

No standing anytime

West

No standing anytime

CENTRE (CHAMBERS - READE)

East

No standing anytime

West

No standing anytime

CENTRE (READE - PARK)

East

No standing anytime

West

No standing anytime

CENTRE (PARK - DUANE)

East

No standing anytime

West

No standing anytime

CENTRE (DUANE- PEARL)

East

No standing anytime

West

No standing anytime

CENTRE (PEARL - WORTH)

East

No standing anytime

West

No standing anytime

CENTRE (WORTH - LEONARD/HOGAN)

East

No standing 7am-7pm (M-F) except authorized vehicles

West

No standing 7am-7pm (M-F) except authorized vehicles

CENTRE (LEONARD/HOGAN - WHITE)

East

No standing 7am-7pm (M-F) except authorized vehicles/No standing 7am-7pm (M-F)

West

No standing 8am-6pm (M-F) except authorized vehicles

CHAMBERS (CENTRE - BROADWAY)

North

No standing except trucks loading & unloading 10am-7pm (M-F)/No standing 7am - 10am (M-F)

South

No standing except trucks loading & unloading

CHAMBERS (BROADWAY - CHURCH)

North

No standing except trucks loading & unloading 9am-7pm (M-F)/ No standing 7am-9am (M-F)

South

No standing except trucks loading & unloading 7am-4pm (M-F)/No standing 4pm - 7pm (M-F)

CHAMBERS (CHURCH - W. BROADWAY)

North

No standing except trucks loading & unloading 9am-7pm (M-F)/ No standing 7am-9am (M-F)

South

No standing except trucks loading & unloading 7am-4pm (M-F)/No standing 4pm - 7pm (M-F)

CHAMBERS (W. BROADWAY - HUDSON)

North

No standing except trucks loading & unloading 9am-7pm (M-F)/ No standing 7am-9am (M-F)

South

No standing except trucks loading & unloading 7am-4pm (M-F)/No standing 4pm - 7pm (M-F)

CHAMBERS (HUDSON - GREENWICH)

North

No standing except trucks loading & unloading 9am-7pm (M-F)/ No standing 7am-9am (M-F)

South

No standing except trucks loading & unloading 7am-4pm (M-F)/No standing 4pm - 7pm (M-F)

CHAMBERS (GREENWICH - WEST)

North

No standing anytime

South

No standing 7am-7pm (M-F)

CHAMBERS (WEST - NORTH END) ☺

North

No parking 9am-10:30am (M & Th)/No parking 7am-4pm (school days)

South

No parking 9am-10:30am (Tu & F)

CHAMBERS (NORTH END - RIVER TERR) ☺

North

No parking 9am-10:30am (M & Th)/No parking 7am-4pm (school days)

South

No parking 9am-10:30am (Tu & F)

CHATHAM SQ. (PARK ROW/ST. JAMES - BOWERY)

East

No standing anytime

West

No parking 7am-7pm (except Sun)

CHERRY (CLINTON - RUTGERS) ☺

East

No parking 11am-12:30pm (M & F)

West

No parking 11am-12:30pm (M & Th)

CHERRY (RUTGERS - PIKE) ☺

East

No parking 11am-12:30pm (M & F)

West

No parking 11am-12:30pm (M & Th)

CHERRY (PIKE - MARKET) ☺

East

No parking 11am-12:30pm (M & F)

West

No parking 11am-12:30pm (M & Th)

CHERRY (MARKET - CATHERINE) ☺

East

No parking 11am-12:30pm (M & F)

West

No parking 11am-12:30pm (M & Th)

CHURCH (CORTLANDT - DEY) ☹

East

No standing anytime

West

No standing anytime

CHURCH (DEY - FULTON)

East

No standing 7am-10am & 4pm-7pm (except Sun)/No standing except trucks loading & unloading 10am-4pm (except Sun)

West

No standing anytime

CHURCH (FULTON - VESEY)

East

No standing 7am-7pm (M-F)/No parking 2am-6am (Tu, F)

West

No standing anytime

CHURCH (VESEY - BARCLAY)

East

No standing except trucks loading & unloading 10am-4pm (M-F)/No parking 2am-6am (Tu, F)

West

No standing 7am-7pm (M-F) except authorized vehicles

CHURCH (BARCLAY - PARK PL)

East

No standing anytime

West

No standing 7am-10am & 4pm-7pm (except Sun)/1 hr. metered parking 10am-4pm (including Sun)/No parking 2am-6am (M, Th)

CHURCH (PARK PL - MURRAY)

East

No standing 7am-10am & 4pm-7pm (M-F)/No parking 2am-6am (Tu, F)

West

No standing 7am-10am & 4pm-7pm (except Sun)/1 hr. metered parking 10am-4pm (including Sun)/No standing except trucks loading & unloading/No parking 2am-6am (M, Th)

CHURCH (MURRAY - WARREN)

East

No standing 7am-10am & 4pm-7pm (M-F)/No parking 2am-6am (Tu, F)

West

No standing 7am-10am & 4pm-7pm (except Sun)/1 hr. metered parking 10am-4pm (including Sun)/No standing except trucks loading & unloading/No parking 2am-6am (M, Th)

CHURCH (WARREN - CHAMBERS)

East

No standing 7am-10am & 4pm-7pm (except Sun)/No standing except trucks loading & unloading 10am-4pm (except Sun)/No parking 2am-6am (Tu, F)

West

No standing 7am-10am & 4pm-7pm (except Sun)/1 hr. metered parking 10am-4pm (including Sun)/No standing except trucks loading & unloading/No parking 2am-6am (M, Th)

CHURCH (CHAMBERS -READE)

East

No standing except trucks loading & unloading 7am-7pm (M-F)/No parking 2am-6am (Tu, F)

West

No standing 7am-10am & 4pm-7pm (except Sun)/1 hr. metered parking 10am-4pm (including Sun)/No standing except trucks loading & unloading/No parking 2am-6am (M, Th)

CHURCH (READE - DUANE)

East

No standing except trucks loading & unloading 7am-7pm (M-F)/No parking 2am-6am (Tu, F)

West

No standing 7am-10am & 4pm-7pm (except Sun)/1 hr. metered parking 10am-4pm (including Sun)/No standing except trucks loading & unloading/No parking 2am-6am (M, Th)

CHURCH (DUANE - THOMAS)

East

No standing anytime

West

No standing 7am-10am & 4pm-7pm (except Sun)/1 hr. metered parking 10am-4pm (including Sun)/No standing except trucks loading & unloading/No parking 2am-6am (M, Th)

CHURCH (THOMAS - WORTH)

East

No standing 7am-10am & 4pm-7pm (M-F)/No parking 2am-6am (Tu, F)

West

No standing 7am-10am & 4pm-7pm (M-F)/No parking 2am-6am (M, Th)

CHURCH (WORTH - LEONARD)

East

No standing except trucks loading & unloading 7am-7pm (M-F)/No parking 2am-6am (Tu, F)

West

No standing 7am-10am & 4pm-7pm (M-F)/No parking 2am-6am (M, Th)/1 hr. metered parking (8am-7pm) including Sun

CHURCH (LEONARD- FRANKLIN)

East

No standing except trucks loading & unloading 7am-7pm (M-F)/No parking 2am-6am (Tu, F)

West

No standing anytime (except authorized vehicles)

CLIFF (FULTON - DEY)

East

No standing anytime

West

No standing anytime

COENTIES ALLEY (PEARL - STONE)

East

No standing anytime

West

No standing anytime

COENTIES SLIP (PEARL - WATER)

North

No standing except trucks loading & unloading 7am-7pm (M-F)

South

No standing anytime

CORTLANDT (BROADWAY - CHURCH)

North

No standing except trucks loading & unloading 8am-7pm (M-F)

South

No standing anytime

CORTLANDT ALLEY (FRANKLIN - WHITE)

East

No standing except trucks loading & unloading

West

No standing except trucks loading & unloading

DEY (BROADWAY - CHURCH)

North

No standing 7am-7pm (M-F)

South

No standing anytime

DOVER (PEARL - WATER) ☺

North

No parking 8am-6pm (M-F)

South

No parking 11:30am-1pm (Tu & F)

DOVER (WATER - FRONT) ☺

North

No standing anytime

South

No parking 11:30am-1pm (Tu & F)

DOVER (FRONT - SOUTH) ☺

North

No standing anytime

South

No parking 11:30am-1pm (Tu & F)

DOYERS (PELL - BOWERY) ☹

East

No standing anytime

West

No standing except trucks loading & unloading

DUANE (GREENWICH - STAPLE)

North

No standing except trucks loading & unloading 7am-7pm (except Sun)

South

No standing except trucks loading & unloading 7am-7pm (except Sun)

DUANE (STAPLE - HUDSON)

North

No parking 8am-6pm (M-F)

South

No parking 8am-6pm (M-F)/No standing 7am-7pm (M-F) except authorized vehicles

DUANE (HUDSON - W. BROADWAY)

North

1 hour metered parking 9am-7pm (including Sun)/No parking 2am-6am (W, Sat)

South

No parking 8am-6pm (M-F)

DUANE (W. BROADWAY - CHURCH)

North

No parking 8am-6pm (M-F)

South

1 hour metered parking 9am-7pm (including Sun)/No parking 2am-6am (Tu, F)

DUANE (CHURCH - TRIMBLE)

North

No standing except trucks loading & unloading 8am-6pm (M-F)

South

No standing except trucks loading & unloading 8am-6pm (M-F)

DUANE (TRIMBLE - BROADWAY)

North

No standing anytime

South

No standing except trucks loading & unloading 8am-6pm (M-F)

DUANE (BROADWAY - ELK) ☹

North

No standing anytime

South

No standing anytime

DUANE (ELK - LAFAYETTE/CENTRE) ☹

North

No standing anytime

South

No standing anytime

DUTCH (FULTON - JOHN) ☹

North

No standing anytime

South

No standing anytime

EDGAR (GREENWICH - TRINITY) ☹

North

No standing anytime

South

No standing anytime

ELK (CHAMBERS - READE)

East

No standing 7am-7pm (M-F) except authorized vehicles

West

No standing anytime

ELK (READE - DUANE)

East

No standing 7am-7pm (M-F) except authorized vehicles

West

No standing anytime

EXCHANGE (TRINITY - BROADWAY) ☹

North

No standing anytime

South

No standing anytime

EXCHANGE (BROADWAY - NEW) ☹

North

No standing anytime

South

No standing anytime

EXCHANGE (NEW - NASSAU) ☹

North

No standing anytime

South

No standing anytime

EXCHANGE (NASSAU - WILLIAM)

North

No standing except trucks loading & unloading 7am-7pm (M-F)

South

No standing anytime

EXCHANGE (WILLIAM - HANOVER)

North

No standing except trucks loading & unloading 7am-7pm (M-F)

South

No standing anytime

FLETCHER (SOUTH - FRONT)

North

No standing anytime

South

No standing anytime

FLETCHER (FRONT - WATER)

North

No standing anytime

South

No standing anytime

FLETCHER (WATER - PEARL)

North

No standing anytime

South

No standing anytime

FORSYTH (HENRY - E. BROADWAY)

North

No parking anytime

South

No parking anytime

FRANKFORT (WATER - GOLD)

North

No standing anytime

South

No standing anytime

FRANKFORT (GOLD - PARK ROW)

North

No standing anytime

South

No standing 7am-7pm (M-F) except authorized vehicles

FRANKLIN (GREENWICH - HUDSON)

North

No parking 7am-7pm (M-F)

South

No parking 7am-7pm (M-F)

FRANKLIN (W. BROADWAY - CHURCH)

North

No standing except trucks loading & unloading 7am-7pm (except Sun)

South

No parking 8am-6pm (M-F)

FRANKLIN (CHURCH - BROADWAY)

North

No standing except trucks loading & unloading 7am-7pm (M-F)

South

No standing except trucks loading & unloading 7am-7pm (M-F)

FRANKLIN (BROADWAY - CORTLANDT ALLEY)

North

No standing except trucks loading & unloading 7am-7pm (M-F)

South

No standing except trucks loading & unloading 7am-7pm (M-F)

FRANKLIN (CORTLANDT ALLEY - LAFAYETTE)

North

No standing 8am-6pm (M-F) except authorized vehicles

South

No standing 8am-6pm (M-F) except authorized vehicles

FRANKLIN PL (OFF FRANKLIN) ☹

East

No standing anytime

West

No standing anytime

FRONT (JOHN - FLETCHER)

East

No standing except trucks loading & unloading 8am-6pm (M-F)/3 hour metered parking 6pm-10pm (M-F) & 10am-10pm (Sat & Sun)

West

No standing except trucks loading & unloading 7am-6pm (M-F)/3 hour metered parking 6pm-10pm (M-F) & 10am-10pm (Sat & Sun)

FRONT (FLETCHER - MAIDEN)

East

No standing anytime

West

No standing except trucks loading & unloading 7am-6pm (M-F)/3 hour metered parking 6pm-10pm (M-F) & 10am-10pm (Sat & Sun)

FRONT (MAIDEN - WALL)

East

No standing except trucks loading & unloading 8am-6pm (M-F)/3 hour metered parking 6pm-10pm (M-F) & 10am-10pm (Sat & Sun)

West

2 hr. metered parking (9am-midnite) including Sun/No parking 8:30am-9am (M-F)

FRONT (WALL - GOVENEUR)

East

No standing except trucks loading & unloading 8am-6pm (M-F)/3 hour metered parking 6pm-10pm (M-F) & 10am-10pm (Sat & Sun)

West

2 hr. metered parking (9am-midnite) including Sun/No parking 8:30am-9am (M-F)

FRONT (GOVENEUR - OLD SLIP)

East

No standing except trucks loading & unloading 8am-6pm (M-F)/3 hour metered parking 6pm-10pm (M-F) & 10am-10pm (Sat & Sun)

West

No standing anytime

FRONT (DOVER - PECK SLIP)

North

No parking 11:30am-1pm (M & Th)

South

No parking 11:30am-1pm (Tu & F)

FRONT (PECK SLIP - BEEKMAN)

North

No parking 11:30am-1pm (M & Th)

South

No parking 11:30am-1pm (Tu & F)

FULTON (WATER - PEARL)

North

No standing anytime

South

No standing except trucks loading & unloading

FULTON (PEARL - CLIFF)

North

No standing 7am-7pm (M-F) except authorized vehicles/No standing except trucks loading & unloading 7am-7pm (M-F)

South

No standing 7am-7pm (M-F) except authorized vehicles/No standing except trucks loading & unloading 7am-7pm (M-F)

FULTON (CLIFF - GOLD)

North

No standing 7am-7pm (M-F) except authorized vehicles/No standing except trucks loading & unloading 7am-7pm (M-F)

South

No standing 7am-7pm (M-F) except authorized vehicles/No standing except trucks loading & unloading 7am-7pm (M-F)

FULTON (GOLD - WILLIAM)

North

No standing 7am-7pm (M-F)

South

No standing 11am - 2pm (M-F)/No standing except trucks loading & unloading 7am-11am & 2pm-7pm (M-F)

FULTON (WILLIAM - DUTCH)

North

No standing 7am-7pm (M-F)

South

No standing 11am - 2pm (M-F)/No standing except trucks loading & unloading 7am-11am & 2pm-7pm (M-F)

FULTON (DUTCH - NASSAU)

North

No standing 7am-7pm (M-F)

South

No standing 11am - 2pm (M-F)/No standing except trucks loading & unloading 7am-11am & 2pm-7pm (M-F)

FULTON (NASSAU - BROADWAY)

North

No standing 11am - 2pm (M-F)/No standing except trucks loading & unloading 7am-11am & 2pm-7pm (M-F)

South

No standing 7am-7pm (M-F)

FULTON (BROADWAY - CHURCH)

North

No standing anytime

South

No standing except trucks loading & unloading 7am-7pm (M-F)

GOLD (FRANKFORT -SPRUCE)

East

1 hr. metered parking (8:30am-7pm) including Sun/No parking 8am-8:30am (except Sun)

West

1 hr. metered parking (8am-7pm) including Sun/No parking 7:30am-8am (except Sun)

GOLD (SPRUCE - BEEKMAN)

East

1 hr. metered parking (8:30am-7pm) including Sun/No parking 8am-8:30am (except Sun)

West

No standing anytime except ambulances

GOLD (BEEKMAN -ANN)

East

1 hr. metered parking (8:30am-7pm) including Sun/No parking 8am-8:30am (except Sun)

West

1 hr. metered parking (8am-7pm) including Sun/No parking 7:30am-8am (except Sun)

GOLD (ANN - FULTON)

East

No standing anytime

West

No standing 8am-6pm (M-F)

GOLD (MAIDEN - PLATT) ☹

East

No standing anytime

West

No standing anytime

GOLD (PLATT - JOHN/DEY) ☹

East

No standing anytime

West

No standing anytime

GOLD (JOHN/DEY - FULTON)

East

No standing anytime

West

No standing anytime

GOVENEUR LANE (WATER - FRONT)

North

No standing anytime

South

No standing anytime

GOVENEUR LANE (FRONT - SOUTH)

North

No standing anytime

South

No standing anytime

GREENWICH (HUBERT - BEACH)

East

No standing except trucks loading & unloading 7am-7pm (except Sun)

West

No standing anytime

GREENWICH (BEACH - N. MOORE)

East

No parking 9am-10:30am (M & Th)

West

No standing anytime

GREENWICH (N. MOORE - FRANKLIN)

East

No parking 8am-6pm (M-F)

West

No standing anytime

GREENWICH (FRANKLIN - HARRISON)

East

No parking 7am-7pm (M-F)

West

No standing anytime

GREENWICH (HARRISON - JAY) ☺

East

No standing except trucks loading & unloading 7am-7pm (except Sun)

West

No parking 7am-7pm (M, W, F)

GREENWICH (JAY - DUANE) ☺

East

2 hour metered parking 9am-7pm (including Sun)/No parking 8am-9am (except Sun)

West

No standing 7am-7pm (M-F) except school buses/No standing except trucks loading & unloading 7am-7pm (except Sun)

GREENWICH (DUANE - READE) ☺

East

2 hour metered parking 9am-7pm (including Sun)/No parking 8am-9am (except Sun)

West

No standing except trucks loading & unloading 7am-7pm (except Sun)/No standing anytime

GREENWICH (READE - CHAMBERS) ☺

East

No standing 7am-7pm (except Sun)

West

No standing anytime

GREENWICH (CHAMBERS - WARREN)

East

No standing 7am-7pm (M-F) except authorized vehicles/No standing except trucks loading & unloading 8am-6pm (M-F)

West

No standing 7am-7pm (M-F) except authorized vehicles/No standing 7am-6pm (school days)

GREENWICH (WARREN - MURRAY)

East

No standing except trucks loading & unloading 8am-6pm (M-F)

West

No standing 7am-7pm (M-F) except authorized vehicles

GREENWICH (MURRAY- PARK PL.)

East

No standing 7am-7pm (M-F) except authorized vehicles

West

No standing 7am-7pm (M-F) except authorized vehicles

GREENWICH (PARK PL. - BARCLAY)

East

No standing 7am-7pm (M-F) except authorized vehicles

West

No standing except trucks loading & unloading 7am-7pm (M-F)

GREENWICH (LIBERTY - CEDAR) ☹

East

No standing anytime

West

No standing anytime

GREENWICH (CEDAR - ALBANY)

East

No parking 8am-6pm (M-F)

West

No standing except trucks loading & unloading 8am-7pm (M-F)

GREENWICH (ALBANY - CARLISLE)

East

No standing anytime

West

No standing except trucks loading & unloading 7am-7pm (except Sun)

GREENWICH (CARLISLE - RECTOR)

East

No standing except trucks loading & unloading 7am-7pm (M-F)

West

1 hr. metered parking (9am-7pm) including Sun/No parking 2am-6am (Wed & Sat)

GREENWICH (RECTOR - EDGAR)

East

No standing 7am-7pm (M-F) except authorized vehicles

West

1 hr. metered parking (9am-7pm) including Sun/No parking 2am-6am (Wed & Sat)

GREENWICH (RECTOR - BATTERY PL.) ☹

East

No parking anytime

West

No parking anytime

HANOVER (WALL ST - EXCHANGE)

East

No standing anytime

West

No standing except trucks loading & unloading 7am-7pm (M-F)

HANOVER (EXCHANGE - BEAVER)

East

No standing anytime

West

No standing anytime

HANOVER (BEAVER - PEARL)

East

No standing anytime

West

No standing anytime

HANOVER SQ/WILLIAM (STONE - PEARL)

North

No standing anytime

South

No standing anytime

HANOVER SQ (PEARL - WATER)

North

No standing anytime

South

No standing except trucks loading & unloading 8am-6pm (M-F)/3 hour metered parking 6pm-10pm (M-F) & 10am-10pm (Sat & Sun)

HARRISON (WEST - GREENWICH)

North

No parking 7am - 7pm (M, W, F)

South

No parking 7am - 7pm (Tu, Th)

HARRISON (GREENWICH - HUDSON)

North

No parking 7am-7pm (M-F)

South

No parking 7am-7pm (M-F)

HENRY (OLIVER - CATHERINE)

East

No parking 11am-12:30pm (M & F)/No parking 7am-4pm (school days)

West

No parking 11am-12:30pm (M & Th)/No parking 7am-4pm (school days)

HENRY (CATHERINE - MARKET)

East

No parking 11am-12:30pm (M & F)/No standing except trucks loading & unloading 7am-7pm (except Sun)

West

No parking 11am-12:30pm (M & Th)/No standing except trucks loading & unloading 7am-7pm (except Sun)

HENRY (MARKET - FORSYTH)

East

No parking 8am-6pm (M-F)

West

No parking 11am-12:30pm (M & Th)

HENRY (FORSYTH - PIKE)

East

No standing anytime

West

No parking 11am-12:30pm (M & Th)

HOGAN (CENTRE - BAXTER)

North

No standing 7am-7pm (M-F) except authorized vehicles

South

No standing 7am-7pm (M-F) except authorized vehicles

HUDSON (CHAMBERS -READE)

East

No standing anytime

West

No parking 8am-6pm (M-F)

HUDSON (READE - DUANE ST. S)

East

No standing except trucks loading & unloading 8am-6pm (M-F)

West

No parking 8am-6pm (M-F)

HUDSON (DUANE ST. S - DUANE ST. N)

East

No standing except trucks loading & unloading 8am-6pm (M-F)

West

1 hr. metered parking (9am-7pm) including Sun/No parking 2am-6am (Tu & F)

HUDSON (DUANE ST. N - JAY)

East

No standing 7am-7pm (M-F) except authorized vehicles

West

1 hr. metered parking (9am-7pm) including Sun/No parking 2am-6am (Tu & F)

HUDSON (JAY - WORTH)

East

1 hr. metered parking (9am-7pm) including Sun/No parking 2am-6am (Tu & F)

West

No standing except trucks loading & unloading 7am-7pm (M-F)

HUDSON (WORTH - HARRISON)

East

No parking 8am-6pm (M-F)

West

No standing 7am-7pm (M-F) except authorized vehicles

JAMES (JAMES - MADISON) ☹

East

No standing anytime

West

No standing anytime

JAY (GREENWICH - STAPLE)

North

No standing except trucks loading & unloading 7am-7pm (M-F)

South

No standing except trucks loading & unloading 7am-7pm (M-F)

JAY (STAPLE - HUDSON)

North

No standing 7am-7pm (M-F) except authorized vehicles

South

No standing except trucks loading & unloading 7am-7pm (M-F)

JOHN (BROADWAY - NASSAU)

North

No standing 11am - 2pm (M-F)/No standing except trucks loading & unloading 7am-11am & 2pm-7pm (M-F)

South

No standing 7am-7pm (M-F)

JOHN (NASSAU - DUTCH)

North

No standing 11am - 2pm (M-F)/No standing except trucks loading & unloading 7am-11am & 2pm-7pm (M-F)

South

No standing 7am-7pm (M-F)

JOHN (DUTCH - WILLIAM)

North

No standing 11am - 2pm (M-F)/No standing except trucks loading & unloading 7am-11am & 2pm-7pm (M-F)

South

No standing 7am-7pm (M-F)

JOHN (WILLIAM - GOLD)

North

No standing anytime

South

No standing 7am-7pm (M-F) except authorized vehicles/No standing except trucks loading & unloading 7am-7pm (M-F)

JOHN (GOLD - CLIFF)

North

No standing anytime

South

No standing 7am-7pm (M-F) except authorized vehicles/No standing except trucks loading & unloading 7am-7pm (M-F)

JOHN (CLIFF - PEARL)

North

No standing anytime

South

No standing 7am-7pm (M-F) except authorized vehicles/No standing except trucks loading & unloading 7am-7pm (M-F)

JOHN (PEARL - WATER)

North

No standing except trucks loading & unloading 7am-6pm (M-F) except authorized vehicles

South

No standing except trucks loading & unloading 7am-6pm (M-F) except authorized vehicles/3 hour metered parking 6pm-10pm (M-F) & 10am-10pm (Sat & Sun)

JOHN (WATER - FRONT)

North

No standing anytime

South

No standing anytime

JOHN (FRONT - SOUTH)

North

No standing except trucks loading & unloading 5pm-midnite (M-F) (except TLC lis-censed vehicles)/No parking Midnite-11am (M-F)

South

No standing anytime

JP WARD (WEST - WASHINGTON)

North

No standing except trucks loading & unloading 7am-7pm (M-F)

South

No standing anytime

LAFAYETTE (WHITE - FRANKLIN)

East

No standing 7am-7pm (M-F) except authorized vehicles

West

No standing 7am-7pm (M-F) except authorized vehicles

LAFAYETTE (FRANKLIN - LEONARD)

East

No standing 7am-7pm (M-F) except authorized vehicles

West

No standing 8am-6pm (M-F) except authorized vehicles

LAFAYETTE (LEONARD - WORTH)

East

No standing 7am-7pm (M-F) except authorized vehicles

West

No standing anytime

LAFAYETTE (WORTH - DUANE)

East

No standing 7am-7pm (M-F) except authorized vehicles

West

No standing 7am-7pm (M-F) except authorized vehicles

LAFAYETTE (DUANE - READE)

East

No standing anytime

West

No standing except trucks loading & unloading 7am-7pm (M-F)

LEONARD (CENTRE - LAFAYETTE) - ("MUNICIPAL PARKING PLAZA")

North

2 hour metered parking 6am-10pm (including Sun) minimum 3 quarters/tokens

South

No standing 7am-7pm (M-F) except authorized vehicles/No standing 7am-7pm (M-F)

LEONARD (LAFAYETTE - BENSON)

North

No standing 7am-7pm (M-F) except authorized vehicles

South

No standing 7am-7pm (M-F) except authorized vehicles

LEONARD (BENSON - BROADWAY)

North

No standing 7am-7pm (M-F) except authorized vehicles

South

No standing except trucks loading & unloading 8am-6pm (M-F)

LEONARD (BROADWAY - CHURCH)

North

No standing except trucks loading & unloading 7am-7pm (M-F)

South

No standing except trucks loading & unloading 7am-7pm (M-F)

LEONARD (CHURCH - W. BROADWAY)

North

No standing except trucks loading & unloading 7am-7pm (M-F)

South

No standing except trucks loading & unloading 7am-7pm (M-F)

LIBERTY (SOUTH END - WEST) ☹

North

No standing anytime

South

No standing anytime

LIBERTY (WEST - WASHINGTON) ☹

North

No standing anytime

South

No standing anytime

LIBERTY (WASHINGTON - GREENWICH)

North

No standing anytime

South

No standing 7am-10am & 4pm-7pm (except Sun)/No standing except trucks loading & unloading 10am-4pm (except Sun)

LIBERTY (GREENWICH - TRINITY)

North

No standing anytime

South

No standing 7am-10am & 4pm-7pm (except Sun)/No standing except trucks loading & unloading 10am-4pm (except Sun)

LIBERTY (TRINITY - BROADWAY)

North

No parking 8am-6pm (M-F)

South

No standing 7am-10am & 4pm-7pm (M-F)/No parking 10am-4pm (M-F)

LIBERTY (BROADWAY - LIBERTY PL)

North

No standing except trucks loading & unloading 10am-7pm (M-F)/No standing 7am - 10am (M-F)

South

No standing 7am-7pm (M-F)

LIBERTY (LIBERTY PL - NASSAU)

North

No standing except trucks loading & unloading 7am-7pm (M-F)

South

No standing 7am-7pm (M-F)

LIBERTY (NASSAU - WILLIAM)

North

No stopping any time

South

No standing except trucks loading & unloading 7am-7pm (M-F)

LIBERTY PL (MAIDEN - LIBERTY ST)

East

No standing anytime

West

No standing anytime

LITTLE WEST (W. THAMES - 3RD PL)

North

No parking anytime

South

No parking anytime

LITTLE WEST (3RD PL - 2ND PL)

North

No parking anytime

South

No parking anytime

LITTLE WEST (2ND PL - 1ST PL)

North

No parking anytime

South

No parking anytime

LITTLE WEST (1ST PL - DEAD END)

North

No parking anytime

South

No parking anytime

MADISON (PEARL - ST. JAMES)

East

No standing anytime

West

No standing except trucks loading & unloading 8am-6pm (except Sun)

MADISON (ST. JAMES - JAMES)

East

No parking 11am-12:30pm (M & F)

West

No standing except trucks loading & unloading 8am-6pm (except Sun)

MADISON (JAMES - OLIVER)

East

No parking 11am-12:30pm (M & F)

West

No parking 11am-12:30pm (M & Th)

MADISON (OLIVER - CATHERINE)

East

No parking 11am-12:30pm (M & F)

West

No parking 11am-12:30pm (M & Th)

MADISON (CATHERINE - MARKET)

East

No standing 4pm-7pm (except Sun)/No standing except trucks loading & unloading 7am-4pm (except Sun)

West

No standing 7am-10am (except Sun)/No standing except trucks loading & unloading 10am-7pm (except Sun)

MADISON (MARKET - PIKE)

East

No parking anytime

West

No parking anytime

MADISON (PIKE - RUTGERS)

East

No parking 11am-12:30pm (M & F)/No parking 8am-6pm (M-F)

West

No parking anytime

MAIDEN (BROADWAY - LIBERTY PL)

North

No standing anytime

South

No standing except trucks loading & unloading 7am-7pm (M-F)

MAIDEN (LIBERTY PL - NASSAU)

North

No standing anytime

South

No standing except trucks loading & unloading 7am-7pm (M-F)

MAIDEN (NASSAU - WILLIAM) ☹

North

No standing anytime

South

No standing anytime

MAIDEN (WILLIAM - GOLD) ☹

North

No standing anytime

South

No standing anytime

MAIDEN (GOLD - PEARL) ☹

North

No standing anytime

South

No standing anytime

MAIDEN (PEARL - WATER)

North

No standing 7am-1pm (M-F)/No standing except trucks loading & unloading 1pm-7pm (M-F)

South

No standing 7am-10am & 4pm-6pm (except Sun)/No standing except trucks loading & unloading 10am-4pm (except Sun)/3 hr metered parking 6pm-10pm (M-F) & 10am-10pm (Sa & Sun)

MAIDEN (WATER - FRONT)

North

No standing anytime (except authorized vehicles) 7am-6pm (M-F)/3 hr parking (no meters!) 6pm-10pm (M-F) & 10am-10pm (Sa & Sun)

South

2 hr. metered parking (9am-10pm) including Sun/No parking 8:30am-9am (M-F)

MAIDEN (FRONT - SOUTH)

North

No standing except trucks loading & unloading 7am-7pm (M-F)

South

2 hr. metered parking (9am-10pm) including Sun/No parking 8:30am-9am (M-F)

MARKET (SOUTH - WATER) ☺

North

No parking 11am-12:30pm (M & F)

South

No standing except trucks loading & unloading

MARKET (WATER - CHERRY) ☺

North

No parking 11am-12:30pm (M & F)

South

No parking 11am-12:30pm (Tu & F)

MARKET (CHERRY - MONROE) ☺

North

No parking 11am-12:30pm (M & F)

South

No parking 11am-12:30pm (Tu & F)

MARKET (MONROE - MADISON)

North

No parking 8am-6pm (M-F)

South

No standing except trucks loading & unloading 7am-6pm (M-F)

MARKET (MADISON - HENRY) ☺

North

No parking 11am-12:30pm (M & F)

South

No parking 11am-12:30pm (Tu & F)

MARKET (HENRY - E. BROADWAY) ☺

North

No parking 11am-12:30pm (M & F)

South

2 hr. metered parking (8am-7pm) including Sun/No parking 7:30am-8am (except Sun)

MARKET (E. BROADWAY - DIVISION)

North

1 hour metered parking 9am - 4pm (including Sun)/No parking 3am-6am (M,W,F)/No standing 4pm-7pm (except Sun)/No standing except trucks loading & unloading 8am-4pm (M-F)

South

1 hour metered parking 9am - 4pm (including Sun)/No parking 3am-6am (Tu,Th,Sat)/No standing 4pm-7pm (except Sun)

MARKETFIELD (NEW - BROAD)

East

No standing anytime

West

No standing anytime

MILL LANE (S. WILLIAM - STONE)

North

No standing anytime

South

No standing anytime

MONROE (CATHERINE - MARKET)

East

No parking 11am-12:30pm (M & F)

West

No parking 11am-12:30pm (M & Th)/No parking 7am-4pm (school days)

MONROE (MARKET - PIKE)

East

No parking 11am-12:30pm (M & F)/No parking 7am-7pm (M-F)

West

No parking 11am-12:30pm (M & Th)

MOORE (PEARL - WATER)

North

No standing except trucks loading & unloading

South

No standing anytime

MORRIS (TRINITY - BROADWAY)

North

No standing anytime

South

No standing 7am-7pm (M-F) except authorized vehicles

MORRIS (WEST - WASHINGTON)

North

No standing anytime

South

No standing except trucks loading & unloading

MOTT (CANAL - PELL)

East

1 hour metered parking 7:30 am - Midnite (including Sun)/No Parking 7am - 7:30am (except Sun)

West

No standing except trucks loading & unloading

MOTT (PELL - MOSCO)

East

1 hour metered parking 7:30 am - Midnite (including Sun)/No Parking 7am - 7:30am (except Sun)

West

No standing 7am-4pm (school days) except authorized vehicles

MOTT (MOSCO - WORTH)

East

1 hour metered parking 7:30 am - Midnite (including Sun)/No Parking 7am - 7:30am (except Sun)

West

No standing except trucks loading & unloading

MULBERRY (WORTH - MOSCO)

East

No parking anytime

West

No parking anytime

MURRAY (BROADWAY - CHURCH)

North

No standing except trucks loading & unloading 7am-7pm (M-F)

South

No standing 7am-7pm (M-F) except authorized vehicles/No standing except trucks loading & unloading 7am-7pm (M-F)

MURRAY (CHURCH - W. BROADWAY)

North

No standing except trucks loading & unloading 7am-7pm (M-F)

South

No standing 7am-7pm (M-F) except authorized vehicles/No standing except trucks loading & unloading 7am-10am & 4pm-7pm (except Sun)/1 hour metered parking 10am-4pm (including Sun)

MURRAY (W. BROADWAY - GREENWICH)

North

No standing 7am-7pm (M-F) except authorized vehicles/No standing except trucks loading & unloading 7am-7pm (M-F)

South

No standing 7am-7pm (M-F) except authorized vehicles/No standing except trucks loading & unloading 7am-7pm (M-F)

MURRAY (GREENWICH - WEST)

North

No standing 7am-7pm (M-F) except authorized vehicles

South

1 hr. metered parking (8am-7pm) including Sun/No parking 7:30am-8am (except Sun)

MURRAY (WEST - NORTH END)

North

No standing 7am-7pm (M-F) except authorized vehicles

South

No standing anytime

N. MOORE (VARICK - HUDSON)

North

No parking 8am-6pm (M-F)

South

No parking 8am-6pm (M-F)

N. MOORE (HUDSON - GREENWICH)

North

No parking 8am-6pm (M-F)

South

No parking 8am-6pm (M-F)

N. MOORE (GREENWICH - WEST) ☺

North

No parking 9am-10:30am (M & Th)

South

No parking 9am-10:30am (Tu & F)

NASSAU (WALL - PINE)

East

No standing anytime

West

No standing except trucks loading & unloading 7am-7pm (M-F)

NASSAU (PINE- CEDAR)

East

No standing anytime

West

No standing except trucks loading & unloading 7am-7pm (M-F)

NASSAU (CEDAR - LIBERTY) ☹

East

No standing anytime

West

No parking (taxi stand)

NASSAU (LIBERTY - MAIDEN)

East

No standing anytime

West

No standing except trucks loading & unloading 7am-7pm (M-F)

NASSAU (MAIDEN - JOHN)

East

No standing anytime

West

No standing except trucks loading & unloading 7am-7pm (M-F)

NASSAU (JOHN - FULTON) ☹

East

No standing anytime

West

No standing 10pm - 6am including Sun/No standing except trucks loading & unloading other times

NASSAU (FULTON - ANN) ☹

East

No standing anytime

West

No standing 10pm - 6am including Sun/No standing except trucks loading & unloading other times

NASSAU (ANN - BEEKMAN) ☹

East

No standing anytime

West

No standing 10pm - 6am including Sun/No standing except trucks loading & unloading other times

NASSAU (BEEKMAN - SPRUCE)

East

No standing anytime

West

No standing 10pm-6am including Sun/No standing except trucks loading & unloading (other times)

NEW (WALL - EXCHANGE)

East

No standing except trucks loading & unloading 7am-7pm (M-F)

West

No standing anytime

NEW (EXCHANGE - BEAVER)

East

No standing except trucks loading & unloading 7am-7pm (M-F)

West

No standing anytime

NEW (BEAVER - MARKETFIELD)

East

No standing anytime

West

No standing anytime

NORTH END (VESEY - DEAD END)

East

No standing anytime

West

No standing anytime

NORTH END (VESEY - MURRAY)

East

No standing anytime

West

No standing anytime

NORTH END (MURRAY - PARK PL)

East

No standing anytime

West

No standing anytime

NORTH END (PARK PL -WARREN)

East

No standing anytime

West

No standing anytime

NORTH END (WARREN - CHAMBERS)

East

No parking 9am-10:30am (Tu & F)

West

No standing anytime

OLD SLIP (SOUTH - FRONT)

North

2 hr. metered parking (9am-midnite) including Sun/No parking 8:30am-9am (M-F)

South

No standing except trucks loading & unloading 7am-6pm (M-F)/3 hour metered parking 6pm-10pm (M-F) & 10am-10pm (Sat & Sun)

OLD SLIP (FRONT - WATER)

North

2 hr. metered parking (9am-midnite) including Sun/No parking 8:30am-9am (M-F)

South

No standing except trucks loading & unloading 7am-6pm (M-F)/3 hour metered parking 6pm-10pm (M-F) & 10am-10pm (Sat & Sun)

OLIVER (MADISON - HENRY)

North

No parking 11am-12:30pm (M & F)/No parking 7am-4pm (school days)

South

No parking 11am-12:30pm (Tu & F)

OLIVER (HENRY - E. BROADWAY)

North

No parking 11am-12:30pm (M & F)

South

No parking 11am-12:30pm (Tu & F)

PARK (PEARL - CENTRE)

East

No parking anytime

West

No parking anytime

PARK PL. WEST (NORTH END - WEST) ☹

North

No standing anytime

South

No standing anytime

PARK PL. (GREENWICH - W. BROADWAY)

North

No standing 7am-7pm (M-F) except authorized vehicles

South

No standing 7am-7pm (M-F) except authorized vehicles

PARK PL. (W. BROADWAY - CHURCH)

North

No standing except trucks loading & unloading 7am-6pm (M-F)

South

No standing except trucks loading & unloading 7am-6pm (M-F)/No standing 7am-7pm (M-F) except authorized vehicles

PARK PL. (CHURCH - BROADWAY)

North

No standing 7am-7pm (M-F) except authorized vehicles/No standing except trucks loading & unloading 7am-7pm (M-F)

South

No standing 7am-10am & 4pm-7pm (except Sun)/No standing except trucks loading & unloading 10am-4pm (except Sun)

PARK ROW (FRANKFORT - PEARL) ☹

East

No standing anytime

West

No standing anytime

PARK ROW (PEARL - WORTH)

East

No parking 7am-7pm (M-F)

West

1 hour metered parking 7:30am - 7pm (including Sun)/No parking 7am-7:30am (except Sun)

PARK ROW (WORTH - MOTT)

East

No parking 7am-7pm (M-F)

West

1 hour metered parking 7:30am - 7pm (including Sun)/No parking 7am-7:30am (except Sun)

PARK ROW (MOTT -ST. JAMES)

East

No parking 7am-7pm (M-F)

West

1 hour metered parking 7:30am - 7pm (including Sun)/No parking 7am-7:30am (except Sun)

PEARL/WATER (FULTON - BEEKMAN)

East

No standing 7am-7pm (M-F)

West

No standing anytime

PEARL (BEEKMAN - PECK SLIP)

East

2 hr. metered parking (9am-10pm) including Sun/No parking 8:30am-9am (except Sun)

West

2 hour metered parking 8:30am-7pm (including Sun)/No parking 8am - 8:30am (M-F)

PEARL (PECK SLIP - DOVER)

East

2 hr. metered parking (9am-10pm) including Sun/No parking 8:30am-9am (except Sun)

West

2 hour metered parking 8:30am-7pm (including Sun)/No parking 8am - 8:30am (M-F)

PEARL (FULTON - JOHN)

East

No standing except trucks loading & unloading 7am-7pm (M-F)

West

No standing except trucks loading & unloading 7am-7pm (M-F)

PEARL (JOHN - PLATT)

East

No standing except trucks loading & unloading 7am-6pm (M-F) except authorized vehicles/3 hour metered parking 6pm-10pm (M-F) & 10am-10pm (Sat & Sun)

West

No standing anytime

PEARL (PLATT - FLETCHER)

East

No standing except trucks loading & unloading 7am-6pm (M-F) except authorized vehicles/3 hour metered parking 6pm-10pm (M-F) & 10am-10pm (Sat & Sun)

West

No standing except trucks loading & unloading 7am-7pm (M-F)

PEARL (FLETCHER - MAIDEN)

East

No standing anytime

West

No standing except trucks loading & unloading 7am-7pm (M-F)

PEARL (MAIDEN - CEDAR)

East

No standing except trucks loading & unloading 7am-6pm (M-F) except authorized vehicles/3 hour metered parking 6pm-10pm (M-F) & 10am-10pm (Sat & Sun)

West

No standing anytime

PEARL (CEDAR - PINE)

East

No standing except trucks loading & unloading 8am-6pm (M-F) except authorized vehicles/3 hour metered parking 6pm-10pm (M-F) & 10am-10pm (Sat & Sun)

West

No standing anytime

PEARL (PINE - WALL)

East

No standing except trucks loading & unloading 8am-6pm (M-F) except authorized vehicles/3 hour metered parking 6pm-10pm (M-F) & 10am-10pm (Sat & Sun)

West

No standing anytime

PEARL (WALL - BEAVER)

East

No standing except trucks loading & unloading 8am-6pm (M-F)/3 hour metered parking 6pm-10pm (M-F) & 10am-10pm (Sat & Sun)

West

No standing anytime

PEARL (BEAVER - HANOVER)

East

No standing except trucks loading & unloading 8am-6pm (M-F)/3 hour metered parking 6pm-10pm (M-F) & 10am-10pm (Sat & Sun)

West

No standing anytime

PEARL (HANOVER - COENTIES)

East

No standing except trucks loading & unloading 7am-7pm (M-F)

West

No standing anytime

PEARL (COENTIES - BROAD)

East

No standing except trucks loading & unloading 7am-5pm (M-F)

West

No standing anytime

PEARL (BROAD - MOORE)

East

No standing except trucks loading & unloading 7am-7pm (M-F)

West

No standing anytime

PEARL (MOORE - WHITEHALL)

East

No standing except trucks loading & unloading 7am-7pm (M-F)

West

No standing anytime

PEARL (WHITEHALL - STATE)

North

No standing except trucks loading & unloading 7am-7pm (M-F)

South

No standing anytime

PEARL (ST. JAMES - MADISON)

North

No standing anytime

South

No parking 7am-7pm except authorized vehicles All days!

PEARL (MADISON - PARK ROW) ☹

North

No standing anytime

South

No standing anytime

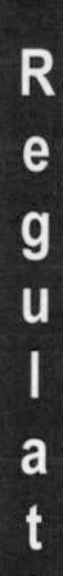

PEARL (PARK ROW - CARDINAL HAYES)

North

No parking anytime

South

No parking anytime

PEARL (CARDINAL HAYES - PARK)

North

No parking anytime

South

No parking anytime

PEARL (PARK - CENTRE)

North

No parking anytime

South

No parking anytime

PECK SLIP (PEARL - WATER)

North

No standing anytime

South

No parking anytime

PECK SLIP (WATER - FRONT)

North

No standing except trucks loading & unloading 7am-7pm (M-F)/No parking Midnite - 11am (M-F)

South

No parking Midnite - 11am (M-F)

PECK SLIP (FRONT - SOUTH)

North

No parking Midnite - 11am (M-F)

South

No parking Midnite - 11am (M-F)

PIKE (CHERRY - MONROE)

North

No parking 11am-12:30pm (M & F)

South

No parking anytime

PIKE (MONROE - MADISON)

North

No parking 11am-12:30pm (M & F)

South

No parking 11am-12:30pm (Tu & F)

PIKE (MADISON - HENRY)

North

No parking 11am-12:30pm (M & F)/No parking 7am-4pm (school days)

South

No parking 11am-12:30pm (Tu & F)

PIKE (HENRY - E. BROADWAY)

North

2 hr. metered parking (8am-7pm) including Sun/No parking 7:30am-8am (except Sun)

South

2 hr. metered parking (8am-7pm) including Sun/No parking 7:30am-8am (except Sun)

PIKE SLIP (SOUTH-WATER)

North

No parking 8am-6pm (M-F)

South

No parking 10am-6pm (including Sun) except tour buses

PINE (WATER - PEARL)

North

No standing anytime

South

No standing anytime

PINE (PEARL - WILLIAM)

North

No standing anytime

South

No standing anytime

PINE (WILLIAM - NASSAU)

North

No standing except trucks loading & unloading 7am-7pm (M-F)

South

No standing except trucks loading & unloading 7am-7pm (M-F)

PINE (NASSAU - BROADWAY)

North

No standing anytime

South

No standing except trucks loading & unloading 7am-7pm (M-F)

PLATT (WILLIAM - GOLD) ☹

North

No standing anytime

South

No standing anytime

PLATT (GOLD - PEARL)

North

No standing 7am-7pm (M-F) except authorized vehicles

South

No standing anytime

READE (LAFAYETTE - ELK)

North

No standing except trucks loading & unloading 7am-7pm (M-F)/No standing 7am-7pm (M-F)

South

No standing 7am-7pm (M-F)

READE (ELK - BROADWAY)

North

No standing 7am-7pm (M-F)

South

No standing except trucks loading & unloading 7am-7pm (M-F)/No standing 7am-7pm (M-F)

READE (BROADWAY - CHURCH)

North

No standing 7am-7pm (M-F) except authorized vehicles/No standing except trucks loading & unloading 7am-7pm (M-F)

South

No standing 7am-7pm (M-F) except authorized vehicles/No standing except trucks loading & unloading 7am-7pm (M-F)

READE (CHURCH - W. BROADWAY)

North

No standing except trucks loading & unloading 7am-7pm (M-F)

South

No standing except trucks loading & unloading 7am-7pm (M-F)

READE (W. BROADWAY - HUDSON)

North

No standing anytime

South

No standing anytime

READE (HUDSON - GREENWICH)

North

No standing except trucks loading & unloading 8am-7pm (M-F)

South

No standing except trucks loading & unloading 7am-7pm (M-F)

RECTOR (SOUTH END - MAKES A CIRCLE!)

North

No parking 9am-10:30am (M & Th)

South

No parking 9am-10:30am (Tu & F)

RECTOR (WEST - WASHINGTON)

North

No standing anytime

South

No standing anytime

RECTOR (WASHINGTON - GREENWICH)

North

No standing anytime

South

No standing anytime

RECTOR (GREENWICH - TRINITY/CHURCH)

North

No standing anytime

South

No standing anytime

RECTOR (TRINITY/CHURCH - BROADWAY)

North

No standing anytime

South

No standing except trucks loading & unloading 7am-7pm (M-F)

RF WAGNER (SOUTH - PEARL) ☺

North

No parking 11am-12:30pm (M & F)

South

No standing 7am - 7pm including Sun except authorized vehicles

RIVER TERR (CHAMBERS - WARREN) ☺

East

No parking 9am-10:30am (Tu & F)

West

No standing anytime

RIVER TERR (WARREN - PARK PL W.) ☹

East

No standing anytime

West

No standing anytime

RIVER TERR (PARK PL W. - MURRAY) ☹

East

No standing anytime

West

No standing anytime

RIVER TERR (MURRAY- VESEY/NORTH END) ☹

East

No standing anytime

West

No standing anytime

ROSE ST (FRANKFORT - MADISON) ☹

East

No standing anytime

West

No standing anytime

RUTGERS SLIP (CHERRY - SOUTH)

North

No parking 8am-6pm (M-F)

South

No standing anytime

RUTGERS SLIP (SOUTH-WATER)

North

No parking 8am-6pm (M-F)

South

No parking anytime

S. WILLIAM (BROAD - MILL LANE)

East

No standing anytime

West

No standing except trucks loading & unloading 7am-7pm (M-F)

S. WILLIAM (MILL LANE - WILLIAM)

East

No standing anytime

West

No standing except trucks loading & unloading 7am-7pm (M-F)

SOUTH (RUTGERS SLIP - PIKE SLIP)

East

No parking anytime

West

No parking 8am-6pm (M-F)

SOUTH (PIKE SLIP - MARKET SLIP)

East

No parking anytime

West

No parking 10am-6pm (including Sun) except tour buses

SOUTH (MARKET SLIP - CATHERINE SLIP)

East

No parking anytime

West

No standing except trucks loading & unloading 7am-7pm (except Sun)

SOUTH (CATHERINE SLIP - R.F. WAGNER)

East

No parking anytime

West

No parking 11am-12:30pm (M & Th)

SOUTH (R.F. WAGNER - DOVER)

East

No standing anytime

West

No standing anytime

SOUTH (DOVER - PECK SLIP)

East

No standing anytime

West

No standing anytime

SOUTH (PECK SLIP -BEEKMAN)

East

No parking anytime

West

No standing 11am-11pm (no days listed)

SOUTH (BEEKMAN - FULTON)

East

No parking anytime

West

No standing anytime

SOUTH (FULTON - JOHN)

East

No parking anytime

West

No standing anytime

SOUTH (JOHN - FLETCHER)

East

No standing anytime

West

No parking 8am-7pm (M-F)/No parking Midnite-11am (M-F)

SOUTH (FLETCHER - MAIDEN)

East

No standing anytime

West

No parking 8am-7pm (M-F)

SOUTH (MAIDEN - PINE) ☹

East

No standing anytime

West

No standing anytime except authorized vehicles (Department of Transportation)

SOUTH (PINE - WALL ST)

East

No standing anytime

West

No standing anytime except authorized vehicles/No parking 8am-7pm (M-F)

SOUTH (WALL ST - GOUVENOUR) ☹

East

No standing anytime

West

No standing anytime

SOUTH (GOUVENOUR - OLD SLIP) ☹

East

No standing anytime

West

No standing anytime

SOUTH (OLD SLIP - BROADWAY)

East

No standing anytime

West

No standing except trucks loading & unloading 12 noon-7pm (M-F)/No standing 7pm-noon (M-Sun!!) except authorized vehicles (DBS)/1 hr. metered parking (8am-7pm) including Sun/No parking 2am-6am (M, Th)

SOUTH (BROADWAY - WHITEHALL) ☹

East

No standing anytime

West

No standing anytime

SOUTH END (LIBERTY - ALBANY)

East

No standing anytime

West

No standing except trucks loading & unloading 8am-6pm (M-F)

SOUTH END (ALBANY - RECTOR)

East

No parking 9am-10:30am (Tu & F)

West

No parking 9am-10:30am (M & Th)

SOUTH END (RECTOR - WEST THAMES)

East

No parking 9am-10:30am (Tu & F)

West

No parking 9am-10:30am (M & Th)

SOUTH END (WEST THAMES - DEAD END)

East

No parking 9am-10:30am (Tu & F)

West

No parking 9am-10:30am (M & Th)

SPRUCE (NASSAU - GOLD)

North

2 hour metered parking 8am - 6pm (including Sun)/No parking 7:30am-8am (except Sun)/No standing 7am-7pm (M-F) except authorized vehicles

South

2 hour metered parking 8am - 6pm (including Sun)/No parking 7:30am-8am (except Sun)/No standing 7am-7pm (M-F) except authorized vehicles

ST. JAMES (PARK ROW - JAMES)

East

No standing except trucks loading & unloading 8am-6pm (except Sun)

West

1 hour metered parking 7:30am - 7pm (including Sun)/No parking 7am-7:30am (except Sun)

ST. JAMES (JAMES - MADISON)

East

No standing 7am-6pm (M-F) except authorized vehicles/No standing 7am-4pm (school days)

West

No parking 11am-12:30pm (M & Th)

ST. JAMES (MADISON - PEARL)

East

No standing except trucks loading & unloading 8am-6pm (M-F)

West

No parking 7am -7pm all days! except police vehicles

ST. JAMES (PEARL - AVE OF FINEST)

East

No standing except trucks loading & unloading 8am-6pm (M-F)/No parking 11am-12:30pm (M & F)

West

No parking 7am -7pm all days! except police vehicles

ST. JAMES (AVE OF FINEST - DOVER)

East

No standing anytime

West

No standing anytime

STAPLE (DUANE - JAY)

East

No standing anytime

West

No standing anytime

STAPLE (JAY - HARRISON)

East

No standing anytime

West

No standing anytime

STATE (BATTERY PL - BRIDGE)

East

No standing anytime

West

No standing anytime

STATE (BRIDGE - WATER)

East

No standing 7am-10am & 4pm-7pm (except Sun)/No standing except trucks loading & unloading 10am-4pm (except Sun)

West

No standing anytime

STATE (WATER-PEARL)

East

No standing anytime

West

No standing anytime

STATE (PEARL - WHITEHALL)

East

No standing anytime

West

No standing anytime

STATE (WHITEHALL - MOORE)

East

No standing anytime (taxi stand)

West

No standing anytime

STONE (COENTIES - MILL LANE)

East

No standing anytime

West

No standing anytime

STONE (MILL LANE - WILLIAM)

East

No standing anytime

West

No standing except trucks loading & unloading 2am-10am (including Sun)

STONE (WHITEHALL - BROAD)

East

No standing except trucks loading & unloading 7am-7pm (M-F)

West

No standing anytime

THAMES (BROADWAY - CHURCH/TRINITY)

North

No standing anytime

South

No standing anytime

THAMES (CHURCH/TRINITY - GREENWICH)

North

No parking anytime

South

No parking anytime

THOMAS (BROADWAY - CHURCH)

North

No standing 7am-7pm (M-F) except authorized vehicles

South

No standing anytime

THOMAS (CHURCH - W. BROADWAY)

North

No standing anytime

South

No standing except trucks loading & unloading 8am-6pm (M-F)

THOMAS (W. BROADWAY - HUDSON)

North

No standing 7am-7pm (M-F) except authorized vehicles

South

No parking anytime

TRIMBLE (THOMAS - DUANE)

East

No parking 8am-6pm (M-F)

West

No standing anytime

TRINITY (RECTOR - THAMES)

East

No standing anytime

West

No standing except trucks loading & unloading 10am-7pm (M-F)/No standing 7am - 10am (M-F)/No parking 2am-6am (M, Th)

TRINITY (THAMES - CEDAR)

East

No standing anytime

West

No standing 7am-7pm (M-F)/No parking 2am-6am (M, Th)

TRINITY (CEDAR - LIBERTY)

East

No standing anytime

West

No standing 7am-7pm (M-F)/No parking 2am-6am (M, Th)

TRINITY (LIBERTY - CORTLANDT)

East

No standing 7am-10am & 4pm-7pm (except Sun)/No standing except trucks loading & unloading 10am-4pm (except Sun)/No parking 2am-6am (Tu, F)

West

No standing anytime

TRINITY PL (BATTERY PL - MORRIS)

East

No standing anytime

West

No standing except trucks loading & unloading 7am-3pm (except Sun)/No standing 3pm-6pm (except Sun) except authorized buses

TRINITY PL (MORRIS - EDGAR) ☹

East

No standing anytime

West

No standing anytime

TRINITY PL (EDGAR - EXCHANGE)

East

No standing 7am-10am & 4pm-7pm (except Sun)/No standing except trucks loading & unloading 10am-4pm (except Sun)/No parking 2am-6am (Tu, F)

West

No standing 7am-10am & 4pm-7pm (except Sun)/No standing except trucks loading & unloading 10am-4pm (except Sun)/No parking 2am-6am (M, Th)

TRINITY PL (EXCHANGE - RECTOR)

East

No standing anytime

West

No standing 7am-10am & 4pm-7pm (except Sun)/No standing except trucks loading & unloading 10am-4pm (except Sun)/No parking 2am-6am (M, Th)

VARICK (FRANKLIN - W. BROADWAY)

East

No parking 8am-6pm (M-F)

West

No parking 8am-6pm (M-F)

VESEY (BROADWAY - CHURCH)

North

No standing 7am-10am & 4pm-7pm (except Sun)/No standing except trucks loading & unloading 10am-4pm (except Sun)

South

No standing anytime

VESEY (CHURCH - W. BROADWAY)

North

No standing anytime

South

No standing anytime

VESEY (W. BROADWAY - WASHINGTON)

North

No standing anytime

South

No standing anytime

VESEY (WASHINGTON - WEST)

North

No standing 7am-7pm (M-F) except authorized vehicles

South

No standing anytime

VESEY (WEST - NORTH END)

North

No parking anytime

South

No standing anytime

W. BROADWAY (FRANKLIN - LEONARD)

East

No standing anytime

West

No standing except trucks loading & unloading 7am-7pm (M-F)

W. BROADWAY (LEONARD - WORTH)

East

No standing 7am-7pm (M-F) except authorized vehicles

West

No standing except trucks loading & unloading 7am-7pm (M-F)/No standing 7am-7pm (M-F) except authorized vehicles

W. BROADWAY (WORTH - THOMAS)

East

No standing except trucks loading & unloading 7am-7pm (M-F)/No standing 7am-7pm (M-F) except authorized vehicles

West

No standing except trucks loading & unloading 7am-7pm (M-F)/No standing 7am-7pm (M-F) except authorized vehicles

W. BROADWAY (THOMAS - DUANE)

East

1 hr. metered parking (8am-7pm) including Sun/No Parking 7:30 am-8am (Tu, F)

West

1 hr. metered parking (8am-7pm) including Sun/No Parking 7:30 am-8am (M, Th)

W. BROADWAY (DUANE - READE)

East

1 hr. metered parking (8am-7pm) including Sun/No Parking 7:30 am-8am (Tu, F)

West

1 hr. metered parking (8am-7pm) including Sun/No Parking 7:30 am-8am (M, Th)

W. BROADWAY (READE - CHAMBERS)

East

1 hr. metered parking (8am-7pm) including Sun/No Parking 7:30 am-8am (Tu, F)

West

No standing anytime

W. BROADWAY (CHAMBERS - WARREN)

East

1 hr. metered parking (8am-7pm) including Sun/No Parking 7:30 am-8am (Tu, F)

West

1 hr. metered parking (8am-7pm) including Sun/No Parking 7:30 am-8am (M, Th)

W. BROADWAY (WARREN - MURRAY)

East

1 hr. metered parking (8am-7pm) including Sun/No Parking 7:30 am-8am (Tu, F)

West

1 hr. metered parking (8am-7pm) including Sun/No Parking 7:30 am-8am (M, Th)

W. BROADWAY (MURRAY- PARK PL.)

East

No standing anytime (except authorized vehicles)

West

No standing except trucks loading & unloading 7am-7pm (M-F)

W. BROADWAY (PARK PL - BARCLAY)

East

No standing except trucks loading & unloading 7am-7pm (M-F)

West

No standing 7am-7pm (M-F) except authorized vehicles

W. BROADWAY (BARCLAY - VESEY)

East

No standing 7am-7pm (M-F) except authorized vehicles

West

No standing anytime (except authorized vehicles)

W. THAMES (WEST - SOUTH END)

North

No standing anytime

South

No parking 9am-10:30am (Tu & F)

W. THAMES (SOUTH END - DEAD END)

North

No parking 9am-10:30am (M & Th)

South

No parking 9am-10:30am (Tu & F)

WALL ST (SOUTH - FRONT)

North

No standing except trucks loading & unloading 7am-6pm (M-F)/3 hour metered parking 6pm-10pm (M-F) & 10am-10pm (Sat & Sun) ***center plaza*** 2 hr. metered parking (9am-midnite) including Sun/No parking 8:30am-9am (M-F)

South

No standing except trucks loading & unloading 7am-6pm (M-F)/3 hour metered parking 6pm-10pm (M-F) & 10am-10pm (Sat & Sun)

WALL ST (FRONT - WATER)

North

No standing except trucks loading & unloading 7am-7pm (M-F)

South

No standing anytime

WALL ST (WATER - PEARL)

North

No standing except trucks loading & unloading 8am-6pm (M-F)/3 hour metered parking 6pm-10pm (M-F) & 10am-10pm (Sat & Sun)

South

No standing except trucks loading & unloading 7am-7pm (M-F)

WALL ST (PEARL - HANOVER)

North

No standing except trucks loading & unloading 7am-7pm (M-F)

South

No standing anytime

WALL ST (HANOVER - WILLIAM)

North

No standing except trucks loading & unloading 7am-7pm (M-F)

South

No standing anytime

WALL ST (WILLIAM - NASSAU)

North

No standing except trucks loading & unloading 7am-7pm (M-F)

South

No standing anytime

WALL ST (NASSAU -NEW)

North

No standing anytime

South

No standing anytime

WALL ST (NEW - BROADWAY)

North

No standing anytime

South

No standing anytime

WARREN (RIVER TERR - NORTH END)

North

No parking 9am-10:30am (M & Th)

South

No parking 9am-10:30am (Tu & F)

WARREN (NORTH END - WEST)

North

No parking 9am-10:30am (M & Th)

South

No standing anytime/No parking 7am-4pm (school days)

WARREN (WEST - WASHINGTON)

North

No parking 8am-4pm (M-F)/No standing 4pm - 7pm (M-F) except buses

South

No standing except trucks loading & unloading 7am-4pm (M-F)/No standing 4pm - 7pm (M-F) except buses

WARREN (WASHINGTON - GREENWICH)

North

No parking 8am-4pm (M-F)/No standing 7am-4pm (M-F)

South

No standing except trucks loading & unloading 7am-6pm (M-F)

WARREN (GREENWICH - W. BROADWAY)

North

No standing except trucks loading & unloading 7am-6pm (M-F)

South

No standing except trucks loading & unloading 7am-6pm (M-F)

WARREN (W. BROADWAY - CHURCH)

North

No standing except trucks loading & unloading 7am-6pm (M-F)

South

No standing except trucks loading & unloading 7am-6pm (M-F)

WARREN (CHURCH - BROADWAY)

North

No standing except trucks loading & unloading 7am-6pm (M-F)

South

No standing except trucks loading & unloading 7am-6pm (M-F)

WASHINGTON (JP WARD - RECTOR) ☹

East

No standing anytime

West

No standing anytime

WASHINGTON (RECTOR - CARLISLE)

East

No standing 7am-7pm (M-F) except authorized vehicles

West

No standing anytime police vehicles only

WASHINGTON (CARLISLE - ALBANY)

East

No standing 7am-7pm (M-F) except authorized vehicles

West

No standing anytime police vehicles only

WASHINGTON (ALBANY - CEDAR)

East

No standing 7am-7pm (M-F)

West

No standing 7am-7pm (M-F) except authorized vehicles/No parking 8am-6pm (except Sun)

WASHINGTON (CEDAR - LIBERTY)

East

No standing 7am-7pm (M-F)

West

No parking 8am-6pm (M-F)

WASHINGTON/WILL PLAZA (MORRIS-BATT. PL)

East

No standing anytime

West

No standing except trucks loading & unloading

WATER (WHITEHALL - MOORE)

East

1 hr. metered parking (8:30am-7pm) including Sun/No parking 8am-8:30am (except Sun)

West

No standing except trucks loading & unloading 7am-7pm (M-F)

WATER (MOORE - BROAD)

East

No standing anytime

West

No standing except trucks loading & unloading 7am-7pm (M-F)

WATER (BROAD - COENTIES)

East

No standing except trucks loading & unloading 7am-7pm (M-F)

West

No standing except trucks loading & unloading 7am-7pm (M-F)

WATER (COENTIES - OLD SLIP)

East

No standing except trucks loading & unloading 7am-7pm (M-F)

West

No standing except trucks loading & unloading 7am-5pm (M-F)

WATER (OLD SLIP - GOVENEUR)

East

No standing except trucks loading & unloading 8am-6pm (M-F)/3 hour metered parking 6pm-10pm (M-F) & 10am-10pm (Sat & Sun)

West

No standing 8am-6pm (M-F)/No standing 6pm - Midnite except authorized vehicles

WATER (GOVENEUR - WALL)

East

2 hr. metered parking (9am-10pm) including Sun/No parking 8am-8:30am (except Sun)

West

No standing except trucks loading & unloading 8am-6pm (M-F)/3 hour metered parking 6pm-10pm (M-F) & 10am-10pm (Sat & Sun)

WATER (WALL - PINE)

East

2 hr. metered parking (9am-10pm) including Sun/No parking 8:30am-9am (except Sun)

West

2 hr. metered parking (8:30am-10pm) including Sun/No parking 8am-8:30am (except Sun)

WATER (PINE - MAIDEN)

East

2 hr. metered parking (9am-10pm) including Sun/No parking 8:30am-9am (except Sun)

West

No standing except trucks loading & unloading 7am-7pm (M-F)

WATER (MAIDEN - FLETCHER)

East

No standing anytime

West

No standing except trucks loading & unloading 7am-6pm (M-F)/3 hour metered parking 6pm-10pm (M-F) & 10am-10pm (Sat & Sun)

WATER (FLETCHER - JOHN)

East

2 hr. metered parking (9am-10pm) including Sun/No parking 8:30am-9am (except Sun)

West

No standing except trucks loading & unloading 7am-6pm (M-F)/3 hour metered parking 6pm-10pm (M-F) & 10am-10pm (Sat & Sun)

WATER (JOHN - FULTON)

East

1 hr. metered parking (9am-7pm) including Sun/No parking 8:30am - 9am (M-F)

West

2 hr. metered parking (8:30am-10pm) including Sun/No parking 8am - 8:30am (M-F)

WATER/PEARL (FULTON - BEEKMAN)

East

No standing 7am-7pm (M-F)

West

No standing anytime

WATER (BEEKMAN - PECK SLIP)

East

No parking 11:30am-1pm (Tu & F)

West

No standing anytime

WATER (PECK SLIP - DOVER)

East

No parking 11:30am-1pm (Tu & F)

West

No standing anytime

WATER (CATHERINE - MARKET)

East

No parking 11am-12:30pm (M & F)

West

No parking 11am-12:30pm (M & Th)

WEST (BATTERY PL - J P WARD)

East

No standing anytime

West

No standing anytime

WEST (J P WARD-RECTOR)

East

No standing 7am-10am & 4pm-7pm (except Sun)/1 hr. metered parking 10am-4pm (including Sun)

West

No standing anytime

WEST (RECTOR - CARLISLE)

East

No standing anytime

West

No standing anytime

WEST (CARLISLE - ALBANY)

East

No standing anytime

West

No standing anytime

WEST (ALBANY- CEDAR)

East

No standing anytime

West

No standing anytime

WEST (CEDAR- LIBERTY)

East

No standing anytime

West

No standing anytime

WEST (LIBERTY- VESEY)

East

No standing 7am-7pm (M-F) except authorized vehicles (FLEO)

West

No standing anytime

WEST (VESEY - BARCLAY)

East

No standing anytime

West

No standing anytime

WEST (BARCLAY-MURRAY)

East

2 hour parking (no meters!) 10am-4pm (except Sun)

West

2 hour parking (no meters!) 10am-4pm (except Sun)

WEST (MURRAY - PARK PL WEST)

East

No standing anytime

West

No standing anytime

WEST (PARK PL WEST - WARREN)

East

No standing anytime

West

No standing anytime

WEST (WARREN - CHAMBERS)

East

No standing anytime

West

No standing anytime

WEST (CHAMBERS - HARRISON)

East

4 hour parking (no meters) 8am-7pm (except Sun)

West

No standing anytime

WEST (HARRISON-NORTH MOORE)

East

No standing anytime

West

No standing anytime

WEST (NORTH MOORE - HUBERT)

East

No standing anytime

West

No standing anytime

WHITEHALL (SOUTH - STATE/WATER)

East

No standing anytime

West

No standing anytime

WHITEHALL (STATE/WATER - PEARL)

East

No standing except trucks loading & unloading 8am-7pm (M-F)

West

No standing except trucks loading & unloading 7am-7pm (M-F)

WHITEHALL (PEARL - BRIDGE)

North

No standing except trucks loading & unloading 7am-7pm (M-F)

South

No standing except trucks loading & unloading 7am-7pm (M-F)

WHITEHALL (BRIDGE - STONE)

North

No standing except trucks loading & unloading 7am-7pm (M-F)

South

No standing except trucks loading & unloading 7am-7pm (M-F)

WHITEHALL (STONE - BEAVER/BROADWAY(ALT))

North

No standing 7am-7pm (M-F) except authorized vehicles

South

No standing anytime

WHITEHALL (BEAVER/BROADWAY (ALT) - BROADWAY)

North

No standing 7am-10am & 4pm-7pm (except Sun)/No standing except trucks loading & unloading 10am-4pm (except Sun)/No parking 2am-6am (M, Th)

South

No standing anytime

WILLIAM (STONE - BEAVER)

North

No standing except trucks loading & unloading 7am-7pm (M-F)

South

No standing anytime

WILLIAM (BEAVER - EXCHANGE)

North

No standing anytime

South

No standing 7am-7pm (M-F) except authorized vehicles

WILLIAM (EXCHANGE - WALL ST)

North

No standing anytime

South

No standing except trucks loading & unloading 7am-7pm (M-F)

WILLIAM (WALL ST - PINE) ☹

North

No standing anytime

South

No standing anytime

WILLIAM (PINE - CEDAR) ☹

North

No standing anytime

South

No standing anytime

WILLIAM (CEDAR - LIBERTY)

East

No standing except trucks loading & unloading 7am-7pm (M-F)

West

No standing anytime

WILLIAM (LIBERTY - MAIDEN)

East

No standing except trucks loading & unloading 7am-7pm (M-F)

West

No standing anytime

WILLIAM (MAIDEN -PLATT)

East

No standing anytime

West

No standing except trucks loading & unloading 7am-7pm (M-F)

WILLIAM (PLATT - JOHN/DEY)

East

No standing anytime

West

No standing except trucks loading & unloading 7am-7pm (M-F)

WILLIAM (JOHN/DEY - FULTON)

East

No standing except trucks loading & unloading 7am-7pm (M-F)

West

No standing anytime

WILLIAM (FULTON - ANN)

East

No standing 7am-7pm (M-F) except authorized vehicles/No standing except trucks loading & unloading 7am-7pm (M-F)

West

No standing anytime

WILLIAM (ANN - BEEKMAN)

East

No standing 7am-7pm (M-F) except authorized vehicles

West

No standing anytime

WORTH (HUDSON - W. BROADWAY)

North

No standing except trucks loading & unloading 7am-7pm (M-F)

South

No standing 9am - 7pm (M-F) except authorized vehicles

WORTH (W. BROADWAY - CHURCH)

North

No standing except trucks loading & unloading 7am-7pm (M-F)

South

No standing 7am-7pm (except Sun) except authorized vehicles

WORTH (CHURCH - BROADWAY)

North

No standing except trucks loading & unloading 7am-7pm (M-F)/No standing 7am-7pm (M-F) except authorized vehicles

South

No standing anytime

WORTH (BROADWAY - LAFAYETTE) ☹

North

No standing anytime except authorized vehicles

South

No standing anytime except authorized vehicles

WORTH (LAFAYETTE - CENTRE)

North

No standing 7am-7pm (except Sun)

South

No standing anytime

WORTH (CENTRE - BAXTER)

North

No standing 7am-7pm (except Sun)

South

No standing anytime

WORTH (BAXTER - MULBERRY)

North

No standing except trucks loading & unloading 7am-7pm (except Sun)

South

No standing anytime

WORTH (MULBERRY - PARK ROW/ST. JAMES)

North

No standing except trucks loading & unloading 7am-7pm (except Sun)

South

No standing anytime

Chapter 7 -

DOWNTOWN WEST:

Parking Garage Locations

(West 30TH Street - White Street)

☺363 W. 30th St. (8th & 9th Ave)

SECURE PARKING LLC (ICON)

Hours of Operation

24 HOURS

Contact information

1-877-PARKING (1-877-727-5464)

Please call for rates

Please see our ad on page 411

32-34 W. 29th St. (Broadway & 6th Ave)

32-34 W. 29TH ST. (CENTRAL PARKING SYSTEM)

Hours of Operation

Please call for hours of operation

Contact information

212-252-5993

Please call for rates

245-251 W. 28th St. (7th & 8th Ave.)

EDISON PARKFAST

Hours of Operation

24 HOURS

Contact information

1-888-PARKFAST (1-888-727-5987)

Please call for rates

☺241 W. 28th St. (7th & 8th Ave)

W 28TH STREET PARKING LLC (ICON)

Hours of Operation

24 HRS

Contact information

1-877-PARKING (1-877-727-5464)

Please call for rates

Please see our ad on page 411

29 W. 28th St. (B/way & 6th Ave.)

29 W. 28TH ST. (CENTRAL PARKING SYSTEM)

Hours of Operation

Please call for hours of operation

Contact information

212-532-3370

Please call for rates

7-11 W. 28th St. & 6-10 W. 29th St.

DRUCKER LOT (CENTRAL PARKING SYSTEM)

Hours of Operation

Please call for hours of operation

Contact information

212-889-1020

Please call for rates

☺254 W. 26th St. (corner of 26th and 8th)

HAG OPERATING CORP.

Hours of Operation

24 hours

Contact information

212-807-8207

Please call for rates

Please see our ad on page 376

☺241 W. 26th St. (btwn 7th and 8th)

TORI PARKING CORP.

Hours of Operation

24 hours

Contact information

212-242-9559

Please call for rates

Please see our ad on page 376

220 W. 26th St. (Bet. 7th & 8th Ave.)

220 WEST 26TH GAR CORP (IMPERIAL)

Hours of Operation

M-TH 6AM-1AM * FRI 6AM-2AM, SAT 7AM-2AM * SUN 7AM-1AM

Contact information

646-336-6574, 646-486-2148

Rates

$13.50 (EARLY BIRD (Mon-Fri) + tax), $350 (24Hr Monthly + tax)

50 W. 26th St. (6th-Broadway)

ELDORADO

Hours of Operation

7am-7pm

Contact information

212-604-9044

Please call for rates

☺161 W. 24th St. (6th & 7th Ave)

TACT PARKING LLC (ICON)

Hours of Operation

24 HOURS

Contact information

1-877-PARKING (1-877-727-5464)

Please call for rates

Please see our ad on page 411

☺510 W. 23rd St. (10th and 11th Ave)

514 WEST CORP.

Hours of Operation

24 hours

Contact information

212-807-8207

Please call for rates

Please see our ad on page 376

☺170 W. 23rd St. (6th & 7th Ave)

EFFICIENT PARKING LLC. (ICON)

Hours of Operation

24 HOURS

Contact information

1-877-PARKING (1-877-727-5464)

Please call for rates

Please see our ad on page 411

☺39 W. 23rd St. (5th and 6th Ave)

23-24 ASSOC. LLC

Hours of Operation

7 am – 11 pm 7 days a week

Contact information

212-272-0141

Please call for rates

Please see our ad on page 376

235 W. 22nd St. (7th & 8th Ave.)

235 W. 22ND ST. (CENTRAL PARKING SYSTEM)

Hours of Operation

Please call for hours of operation

Contact information

646-638-4213

Please call for rates

☺51 W. 22nd St. (5th & 6th Ave)

22ND & SIXTH PARKING LLC (ICON)

Hours of Operation
24 HOURS
Contact information
1-877-PARKING (1-877-727-5464)
Please call for rates
Please see our ad on page 411

507-509 W. 21st St. (10th & 11th Ave.)

EDISON PARKFAST

Hours of Operation
24 HOURS
Contact information
1-888-PARKFAST (1-888-727-5987)
Please call for rates

☺121-129 W. 21st St. (6 & 7th Ave)

121-129 WEST 21ST ST PARK LLC (LOT) (ICON)

Hours of Operation
24 HOURS
Contact information
1-877-PARKING (1-877-727-5464)
Please call for rates
Please see our ad on page 411

120 W. 21st St. (6th & 7th Ave.)

21ST STREET (CENTRAL PARKING SYSTEM)

Hours of Operation
Please call for hours of operation
Contact information
212-633-6488
Please call for rates

☺35 W. 21st St. (5th & 6th Ave)

35-39 WEST 21ST ST PARK LLC(LOT) (ICON)

Hours of Operation
24 HOURS
Contact information
1-877-PARKING (1-877-727-5464)
Please call for rates
Please see our ad on page 411

10 W. 21st St. (5th & 6th Ave)

LADIES LANE (GMC)

Hours of Operation

6am-2am

Contact information

917-305-0212

Please call for rates

7 W. 21st St. (enter 21st or 22nd St. btwn 5th & 6th Ave)

WEST 21ST ST. (GMC)

Hours of Operation

6am-2am

Contact information

212-243-6540

Please call for rates

180 W. 20th St. (6th & 7th Ave.)

THE WESTMINSTER (CENTRAL PARKING SYSTEM)

Hours of Operation

Please call for hours of operation

Contact information

646-638-0695

Please call for rates

☺21-25 W. 20th St. (5th & 6th Ave)

BANNER ASSOCIATES LLC (ICON)

Hours of Operation

24 HOURS

Contact information

1-877-PARKING (1-877-727-5464)

Please call for rates

Please see our ad on page 411

250 W. 19th St. (Bet. 7th & 8th Ave.)

250 WEST PARKING CORP (IMPERIAL)

Hours of Operation

24 HRS

Contact information

646-638-3558, 212-627-1704

Rates

$10.13 (EARLY BIRD (Mon-Fri) + tax), $325 (24Hr Monthly + tax)

27 W. 19th St. (5th & 6th Ave.)

27 W. 19TH ST. (CENTRAL PARKING SYSTEM)

Hours of Operation

Please call for hours of operation

Contact information

212-352-8647

Please call for rates

149-151 W. 17th St. (6th & 7th Ave.)

W. 17TH ST PKG. CORP (IMPERIAL)

Hours of Operation

7AM-1AM SUN-TH * 7AM-2AM FRI * 7AM-3AM SAT *

Contact information

212-647-8893, 212-807-1737

Rates

$400 (24Hr Monthly + tax)

☺111 (8th Ave) at W. 16th St. (8th & 9th)

111 EIGHTH AVE PARKING (ICON)

Hours of Operation

24 HOURS

Contact information

1-877-PARKING (1-877-727-5464)

Please call for rates

Please see our ad on page 411

☺16 W. 16th St. (5th & 6th Ave)

CREATIVE PARKING LLC (ICON)

Hours of Operation

24 HOURS

Contact information

1-877-PARKING (1-877-727-5464)

Please call for rates

Please see our ad on page 411

☺44-50 W. 15th St. (5th & 6th Ave)

44-50 WEST 15TH ST PARK LLC (LOT) (ICON)

Hours of Operation

24 HOURS

Contact information

1-877-PARKING (1-877-727-5464)

Please call for rates

Please see our ad on page 411

☺85 (8th Ave) at W. 14th St. (8th & 9th Ave)

14TH AND 8TH AVE. LLC (ICON)

Hours of Operation
24 HOURS
Contact information
1-877-PARKING (1-877-727-5464)
Please call for rates
Please see our ad on page 411

☺55 W. 14th St. (5th & 6th Ave)

UNIVERSAL PARKING LLC (ICON)

Hours of Operation
24 HOURS
Contact information
1-877-PARKING (1-877-727-5464)
Please call for rates
Please see our ad on page 411

107 W. 13th St. (Bet. 6th & 7th Ave.)

107 GARAGE CORP (IMPERIAL)

Hours of Operation
24 HOURS
Contact information
212-741-9016, 212-243-3943
Rates
$10.97 (EARLY BIRD (Mon-Fri) + tax) * $380 (24Hr Monthly + tax)

☺25 W. 13th St. (btwn 5th and 6th Ave.)

RONEL PARKING CORP.

Hours of Operation
7am-12am (midnite) Mon-Fri
Contact information
212-229-0548
Please call for rates
Please see our ad on page 376

20 W. 13th St. (5th & 6th Ave.)

20 W. 13TH ST. (CENTRAL PARKING SYSTEM)

Hours of Operation
Please call for hours of operation
Contact information
212-352-8628
Please call for rates

160 W. 10th St. (Corner 7th Ave S)

TRAVELERS (GMC)

Hours of Operation

6am-2am

Contact information

212-929-3041

Please call for rates

122 W. 3rd St. (Macdougal & 6th Ave)

MINETTA (GMC)

Hours of Operation

24 HRS

Contact information

212-777-3530

Please call for rates

2 5th Ave. (enter 8th St. or Wash Sq N. btwn 5th & Macdougal)

WASHINGTON SQUARE (GMC)

Hours of Operation

24 HRS

Contact information

212-833-8312

Please call for rates

69 5th Ave. (14th & 15th St.)

69 5TH AVE. (CENTRAL PARKING SYSTEM)

Hours of Operation

Please call for hours of operation

Contact information

212-727-9063

Please call for rates

776-792 6th Ave. (a/k/a 55 West 26th)

776 6TH AVE. (CENTRAL PARKING SYSTEM)

Hours of Operation

Please call for hours of operation

Contact information

212-252-1673

Please call for rates

800 6th Ave. (28th St. @ 6th Ave.)

ASTON GARAGE (CENTRAL PARKING SYSTEM)

Hours of Operation

Please call for hours of operation

Contact information

212-779-2272

Please call for rates

839 6th Ave. (29th & 30th)

TRADE CENTER (CENTRAL PARKING SYSTEM)

Hours of Operation

Please call for hours of operation

Contact information

212-695-3896

Please call for rates

252 7th Ave. (25th St. Bet. 7th & 8th Ave.)

CHELSEA 7TH GAR CORP (IMPERIAL)

Hours of Operation

24 HRS

Contact information

212-627-1681, 212-807-1819

Rates

$13.50 (EARLY BIRD (Mon-Fri) + tax), $400 (24Hr Monthly + tax)

☺70 8th Ave. (corner of 13th St)

JESSI PARKING CORP.

Hours of Operation

24 hours

Contact information

646-638-1746

Please call for rates

Please see our ad on page 376

161-165 10th Ave. @20th St.

EDISON PARKFAST

Hours of Operation

24 HOURS

Contact information

1-888-PARKFAST (1-888-727-5987)

Please call for rates

☺249 10th Ave. (btwn 24th and 25th)

249 PARKING CORP.

Hours of Operation

24 hours

Contact information

212-645-7548

Please call for rates

Please see our ad on page 376

☺279 10th Ave. (corner of 26th and 10th)

WEST 26TH PARKING CORP.

Hours of Operation
24 hours
Contact information
212-967-2705
Please call for rates
Please see our ad on page 376

☺520 Broome St. (Broome & Thompson)

BROOME-THOMPSON PARKING LLC (ICON)

Hours of Operation
24 HRS
Contact information
1-877-PARKING (1-877-727-5464)
Please call for rates
Please see our ad on page 411

370 Canal St. (Canal & Lispenard)

370 CANAL ST. (CENTRAL PARKING SYSTEM)

Hours of Operation
Please call for hours of operation
Contact information
212-966-7043
Please call for rates

174 Centre St. (Hester & Canal)

EDISON PARKFAST

Hours of Operation
24 HOURS
Contact information
1-888-PARKFAST (1-888-727-5987)
Please call for rates

☺22 Ericsson Place (Tribeca - btwn Hudson and Varick)

ICE HOUSE PARKING CORP.

Hours of Operation
24 hours
Contact information
212-966-1984
Please call for rates
Please see our ad on page 376

142 Grand St. (Grand & Lafayette)

EDISON PARKFAST

Hours of Operation

Please call for hours of operation

Contact information

1-888-PARKFAST (1-888-727-5987)

Please call for rates

☺375 Hudson St. (Hudson & Greenwich)

375 HUD PARKING LLC (ICON)

Hours of Operation

24 HRS

Contact information

1-877-PARKING (1-877-727-5464)

Please call for rates

Please see our ad on page 411

☺396 Hudson St. (Carmine & W. Houston)

396 HUDSON STREET PARK LLC (LOT) (ICON)

Hours of Operation

24 HRS

Contact information

1-877-PARKING (1-877-727-5464)

Please call for rates

Please see our ad on page 411

☺11 Jane St. (Greenwich Ave & W. 4th St.)

VALUE MGMT. CORP.

Hours of Operation

24 hours

Contact information

212-462-4585

Please call for rates

Please see our ad on page 376

61 Jane St. (Bet. Hudson & Greenwich)

61 JANE PKG CORP (IMPERIAL)

Hours of Operation

24 HRS

Contact information

212-213-6303, 212-212-0163

Rates

$12.66 (EARLY BIRD (Mon-Fri) + tax), $400 (24Hr Monthly + tax)

☺99 Jane St. (West & Washington)

99 JANE STEET PARKING LLC (ICON)

Hours of Operation
24 HRS
Contact information
1-877-PARKING (1-877-727-5464)
Please call for rates
Please see our ad on page 411

☺134-136 Jane St. (West & Washington)

SALEM PARKING LLC (LOT) (ICON)

Hours of Operation
24 HRS
Contact information
1-877-PARKING (1-877-727-5464)
Please call for rates
Please see our ad on page 411

☺561-565 (Greenwich St.) at King St. (Greenwich & Hudson St.)

GREENWICH STREET PARKING LLC (ICON)

Hours of Operation
24 HRS
Contact information
1-877-PARKING (1-877-727-5464)
Please call for rates
Please see our ad on page 411

☺410 Lafayette St. (Astor Pl. & E. 4th St.)

LAFAYETTE PARKING

Hours of Operation
24 hours
Contact information
212-260-9122
Please call for rates
Please see our ad on page 376

☺403 Lafayette St. (Astor Pl. & E. 4th St.)

403 LAFAYETTE LLC

Hours of Operation
24 hours
Contact information
212-254-1263
Please call for rates
Please see our ad on page 376

375-379 Lafayette St. @ Great Jones St.

EDISON PARKFAST

Hours of Operation

24 HOURS

Contact information

1-888-PARKFAST (1-888-727-5987)

Please call for rates

18-20 Morton St. (Bleecker & 7th Ave)

18-20 MORTON ST. (CENTRAL PARKING SYSTEM)

Hours of Operation

Please call for hours of operation

Contact information

212-242-8451

Please call for rates

166 Perry St. (West & Washington)

PERRY ST. (GMC)

Hours of Operation

24 HRS

Contact information

212-741-9773

Please call for rates

246 Spring St. (Varick & Spring)

VARICK ST. LOT (CENTRAL PARKING SYSTEM)

Hours of Operation

Please call for hours of operation

Contact information

212-929-9891

Please call for rates

272-276 Spring St. (Hudson & Varick)

EDISON PARKFAST

Hours of Operation

24 HOURS

Contact information

1-888-PARKFAST (1-888-727-5987)

Please call for rates

☺221 Thompson St. (Bleecker St. & W. 3rd)

THOMPSON PARKING CORP.

Hours of Operation

24 hours

Contact information

212-677-8741

Please call for rates

Please see our ad on page 376

Van Dam St. @ Charlton St. (enter Van Dam)

14-18 CHARLTON ST. (CENTRAL PARKING SYSTEM)

Hours of Operation

Please call for hours of operation

Contact information

212-691-3109

Please call for rates

20-24 Varick St. (N.Moore & Beech St.)

20-24 VARICK ST. (CENTRAL PARKING SYSTEM)

Hours of Operation

Please call for hours of operation

Contact information

212-625-0323

Please call for rates

☺114-122 Varick St. (Dominick & Broome)

VARICK STREET PARKING LLC (ICON)

Hours of Operation

24 HRS

Contact information

1-877-PARKING (1-877-727-5464)

Please call for rates

Please see our ad on page 411

☺575 Washington St. (W. Houston & Clarkson)

ELBA OPERATING CORP.

Hours of Operation

24 hours

Contact information

212-645-1132

Please call for rates

Please see our ad on page 376

84-86 White St. (Lafayette & W Bway)

84-86 WHITE ST. (CENTRAL PARKING SYSTEM)

Hours of Operation

Please call for hours of operation

Contact information

212-925-2782

Please call for rates

☺6-10 Wooster St. (Canal St. & Grand St.)

WOOSTER PARKING CORP.

Hours of Operation

24 hours

Contact information

212-925-4850

Please call for rates

Please see our ad on page 376

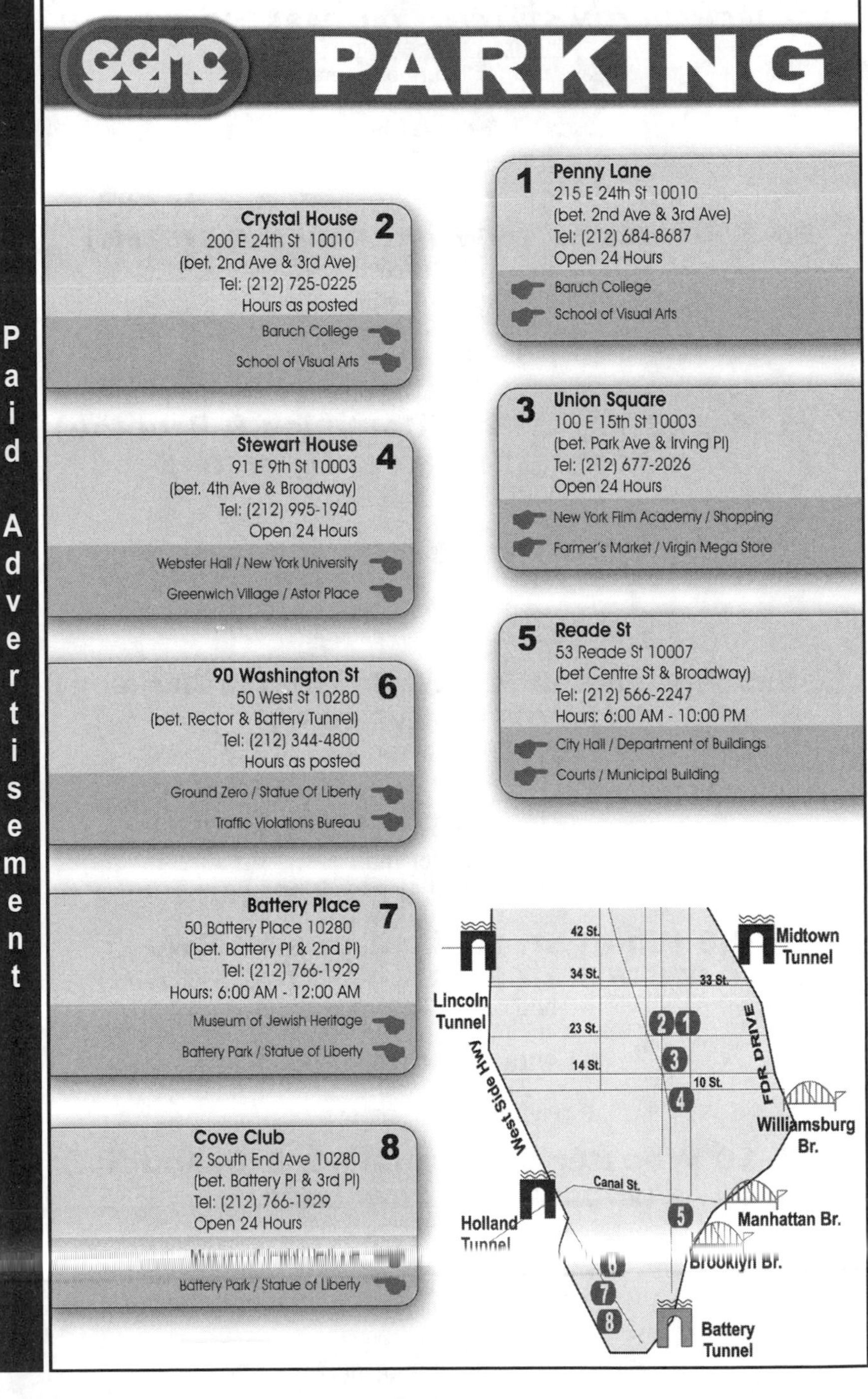
GGMC PARKING
1 Penny Lane
215 E 24th St 10010
(bet. 2nd Ave & 3rd Ave)
Tel: (212) 684-8687
Open 24 Hours
Baruch College
School of Visual Arts
Crystal House 2
200 E 24th St 10010
(bet. 2nd Ave & 3rd Ave)
Tel: (212) 725-0225
Hours as posted
Baruch College
School of Visual Arts
3 Union Square
100 E 15th St 10003
(bet. Park Ave & Irving Pl)
Tel: (212) 677-2026
Open 24 Hours
New York Film Academy / Shopping
Farmer's Market / Virgin Mega Store
Stewart House 4
91 E 9th St 10003
(bet. 4th Ave & Broadway)
Tel: (212) 995-1940
Open 24 Hours
Webster Hall / New York University
Greenwich Village / Astor Place
5 Reade St
53 Reade St 10007
(bet Centre St & Broadway)
Tel: (212) 566-2247
Hours: 6:00 AM - 10:00 PM
City Hall / Department of Buildings
Courts / Municipal Building
90 Washington St 6
50 West St 10280
(bet. Rector & Battery Tunnel)
Tel: (212) 344-4800
Hours as posted
Ground Zero / Statue Of Liberty
Traffic Violations Bureau
Battery Place 7
50 Battery Place 10280
(bet. Battery Pl & 2nd Pl)
Tel: (212) 766-1929
Hours: 6:00 AM - 12:00 AM
Museum of Jewish Heritage
Battery Park / Statue of Liberty
Cove Club 8
2 South End Ave 10280
(bet. Battery Pl & 3rd Pl)
Tel: (212) 766-1929
Open 24 Hours
Battery Park / Statue of Liberty
42 St.
34 St.
33 St.
23 St.
14 St.
10 St.
Canal St.
Lincoln Tunnel
Midtown Tunnel
West Side Hwy
FDR DRIVE
Williamsburg Br.
Holland Tunnel
Manhattan Br.
Brooklyn Br.
Battery Tunnel

Chapter 8 -

DOWNTOWN EAST: Parking Garage Locations

(East 30TH Street - White Street)

350 E. 30th St. (1st & 2nd Ave.)

350 E 30TH ST. (CENTRAL PARKING SYSTEM)

Hours of Operation

Please call for hours of operation

Contact information

212-779-8311

Please call for rates

☺500-520 (2nd Ave) @ E. 29th St. (1st & 2nd)

WEST PLAZA GARAGE LLC-29 (ICON)

Hours of Operation

24 HOURS

Contact information

1-877-PARKING (1-877-727-5464)

Please call for rates

Please see our ad on page 411

☺155 E. 29th St. (3rd & Lexington)

EXCELLENT PARKING LLC (ICON)

Hours of Operation

24 HOURS

Contact information

1-877-PARKING (1-877-727-5464)

Please call for rates

Please see our ad on page 411

☺479-493 (1st Ave) @ E. 28th St. (1st & 2nd)

EAST PLAZA GARAGE LLC (ICON)

Hours of Operation

24 HOURS

Contact information

1-877-PARKING (1-877-727-5464)

Please call for rates

Please see our ad on page 411

E. 28th St. (Btwn 2nd & 3rd Ave.)

E. 28TH ST GAR CORP (IMPERIAL)

Hours of Operation

6AM 1AM M-TH * 6AM-3AM FRI * 7AM-3AM SAT * 7AM-1AM SUN

Contact information

212-889-3330, 212-686-4910

Rates

$11.81 (EARLY BIRD (Mon-Fri) + tax), $325 (24Hr Monthly + tax)

240 E. 27th St. (2nd & 3rd Ave)

PARC EAST (CENTRAL PARKING SYSTEM)

Hours of Operation

Please call for hours of operation

Contact information

212-684-8934

Please call for rates

☺460-490 (2nd Ave) @ E. 26th St. (1st & 2nd)

WEST PLAZA GARAGE LLC-26 (ICON)

Hours of Operation

24 HOURS

Contact information

1-877-PARKING (1-877-727-5464)

Please call for rates

Please see our ad on page 411

☺442-458 (2nd Ave) @ E. 26th St. (1st & 2nd)

SOUTH PLAZA GARAGE LLC-A (ICON)

Hours of Operation

24 HOURS

Contact information

1-877-PARKING (1-877-727-5464)

Please call for rates

Please see our ad on page 411

☺215 E. 24th St. (bet. 2nd & 3rd Ave)

PENNY LANE (GGMC)

Hours of Operation

24 HOURS

Contact information

(212) 684-8687

Please call for rates

Please see our ad on page 392

☺200 E. 24th St. (bet. 2nd & 3rd Ave)

CRYSTAL HOUSE (GGMC)

Hours of Operation

Please call for hours of operation

Contact information

(212) 725-0225

Please call for rates

Please see our ad on page 392

☺318-322 E. 23rd St. (1st & 2nd Ave)

23RD STREET PARKING LLC (ICON)

Hours of Operation

24 HOURS

Contact information

1-877-PARKING (1-877-727-5464)

Please call for rates

Please see our ad on page 411

301 E. 22nd St. (1st & 2nd Ave.)

301 E. 22ND ST. (CENTRAL PARKING SYSTEM)

Hours of Operation

Please call for hours of operation

Contact information

212-475-1701

Please call for rates

☺5 E. 22nd St. (Broadway & Park Ave S.)

PROUD PARKING LLC (ICON)

Hours of Operation

24 HOURS

Contact information

1-877-PARKING (1-877-727-5464)

Please call for rates

Please see our ad on page 411

329 E. 21st St. (1st & 2nd Ave)

GRAMERCY (CENTRAL PARKING SYSTEM)

Hours of Operation

Please call for hours of operation

Contact information

212-473-0400

Please call for rates

☺41-47 E. 21st St. (Park & Broadway)

UNIQUE PARKING LLC (ICON)

Hours of Operation

24 HOURS

Contact information

1-877-PARKING (1-877-727-5464)

Please call for rates

Please see our ad on page 411

☺245 E. 19th St. (2nd & 3rd Ave)

245 E 19TH ST PARKING LLC (ICON)

Hours of Operation

24 HOURS

Contact information

1-877-PARKING (1-877-727-5464)

Please call for rates

Please see our ad on page 411

☺205 (3rd Ave) @ E. 19th St. (2nd & 3rd)

205 THIRD PARKING LLC (ICON)

Hours of Operation

24 HOURS

Contact information

1-877-PARKING (1-877-727-5464)

Please call for rates

Please see our ad on page 411

E. 18th St. (Bet. Irvin Pl. & 3rd Ave.)

130 E. 18TH GAR CORP (IMPERIAL)

Hours of Operation

7AM-MID M-F * 24 HOURS KEY

Contact information

212-475-8091, 212-674-4230

Rates

$13.50 (EARLY BIRD (Mon-Fri) + tax), $375 (24Hr Monthly + tax)

☺211 E. 18th St. (2nd and 3rd Ave)

211 PARKING CORP.

Hours of Operation

24 HOURS

Contact information

212-473-9345

Please call for rates

Please see our ad on page 376

☺202 E. 18th St. (2nd & 3rd Ave)

18TH AND THIRD PARKING LLC (ICON)

Hours of Operation

24 HOURS

Contact information

1-877-PARKING (1-877-727-5464)

Please call for rates

Please see our ad on page 411

144 E. 17th St. (Irving & 3rd Ave.)

SLEEPY HOLLOW (GMC)

Hours of Operation

6am-2am

Contact information

212-533-7362

Please call for rates

☺110 E. 16th St. (Park Ave S. & Irving)

110 E. 16TH ST ASSOCIATES LLC (ICON)

Hours of Operation

24 HOURS

Contact information

1-877-PARKING (1-877-727-5464)

Please call for rates

Please see our ad on page 411

☺100 E. 15th St. (Park Ave & Irving Pl)

UNION SQUARE (GGMC)

Hours of Operation

24 HOURS

Contact information

(212) 677-2026

Please call for rates

Please see our ad on page 392

20 E. 15th St. (Union Sq & 5th)

UNION SQ. WEST (CENTRAL PARKING SYSTEM)

Hours of Operation

Please call for hours of operation

Contact information

212-741-5163

Please call for rates

333 E. 14th St. (between 1st & 2nd Ave)

GEMA PARKING CORP.

Hours of Operation

6am to 1am

Contact information

212-477-4043

Rates

$23.63 + tax (Up to 12 hours), $390.00 (Monthly - regular vehicles)

E. 14th St. (5th Ave. & Union S. West)

EAST 14TH GAR CORP (IMPERIAL)

Hours of Operation
24 HOURS
Contact information
212-929-8529, 212-691-5786
Rates
$14.35 (EARLY BIRD (Mon-Fri) + tax), $400 (24Hr Monthly + tax)

☺101 E. 13th St. (3rd & 4th Ave)

AMBER PARK, LLC (ICON)

Hours of Operation
24 HOURS
Contact information
1-877-PARKING (1-877-727-5464)
Please call for rates
Please see our ad on page 411

21 E. 12th St. (enter 12th St. or University)

BREVOORT (GMC)

Hours of Operation
24 HOURS
Contact information
212-924-1604
Please call for rates

☺311 E. 11th St. (1st and 2nd Ave)

NITE PARKING CORP.

Hours of Operation
24 HOURS
Contact information
212-929-9404
Please call for rates
Please see our ad on page 376

64 E. 11th St. (University & B'way)

64 E. 11TH ST. (CENTRAL PARKING SYSTEM)

Hours of Operation
Please call for hours of operation
Contact information
212-475-5425
Please call for rates

60-62 E. 10th St. (B'way & University)

EDISON PARKFAST

Hours of Operation

Please call for hours of operation

Contact information

1-888-PARKFAST (1-888-727-5987)

Please call for rates

220 E. 9th St. (2nd & 3rd Ave)

220 E. 9TH ST. (CENTRAL PARKING SYSTEM)

Hours of Operation

Please call for hours of operation

Contact information

212-979-5708

Please call for rates

☺115 E. 9th St. (3rd & 4th Ave)

KEY PARKING LLC (ICON)

Hours of Operation

24 HOURS

Contact information

1-877-PARKING (1-877-727-5464)

Please call for rates

Please see our ad on page 411

☺91 E. 9th St. (bet. 4th Ave & Broadway)

STEWART HOUSE (GGMC)

Hours of Operation

24 HOURS

Contact information

(212) 995-1940

Please call for rates

Please see our ad on page 392

☺40 E. 9th St. (University Ave & B'way)

30-40-60 EAST 9TH ST. PARK LLC (ICON)

Hours of Operation

24 HOURS

Contact information

1-877-PARKING (1-877-727-5464)

Please call for rates

Please see our ad on page 411

☺12-20 E. 9th St. (University & 5th)

BREVOORT PARKING LLC (ICON)

Hours of Operation

24 HOURS

Contact information

1-877-PARKING (1-877-727-5464)

Please call for rates

Please see our ad on page 411

☺11 (5th ave) at E. 8th St. (University & 5th)

8TH ST. PARKING LLC (ICON)

Hours of Operation
24 HOURS
Contact information
1-877-PARKING (1-877-727-5464)
Please call for rates
Please see our ad on page 411

5th Ave. At 15th St.

5TH AVE GAR CORP. (IMPERIAL)

Hours of Operation
7AM-11PM M-F * 24 HOURS KEY
Contact information
212-691-3070, 212-675-0335
Rates
$13.50 (EARLY BIRD (Mon-Fri) + tax), $325 (24Hr Monthly + tax)

☺146-154 3rd Ave. (15 & 16th St.)

CONSOLIDATED PARKING LLC (ICON)

Hours of Operation
24 HOURS
Contact information
1-877-PARKING (1-877-727-5464)
Please call for rates
Please see our ad on page 411

☺395 Broome St. (corner of Mulberry St.)

395 PARKING CORP.

Hours of Operation
7 am – 12 am (midnite) 7 days a week
Contact information
212-226-9797
Please call for rates
Please see our ad on page 376

227 Cherry St. (Cherry & South St)

PATHMARK (CENTRAL PARKING SYSTEM)

Hours of Operation
Please call for hours of operation
Contact information
212-619-4749
Please call for rates

☺2-12 Cooper Square (4th St. & Cooper Sq.)

COOPER PARKING LLC (LOT) (ICON)

Hours of Operation

24 HOURS

Contact information

1-877-PARKING (1-877-727-5464)

Please call for rates

Please see our ad on page 411

☺275 Delancey St. (corner of Columbia St. next to Williamsburg Bridge)

AREA GARAGE CORP.

Hours of Operation

24 HOURS

Contact information

212-228-9200

Please call for rates

Please see our ad on page 376

☺303 Elizabeth St. (Bleecker & E. Houston)

COMFORT PARKING LLC (ICON)

Hours of Operation

24 HOURS

Contact information

1-877-PARKING (1-877-727-5464)

Please call for rates

Please see our ad on page 411

207-215 E. Houston St. (Essex & Ludlow)

EDISON PARKFAST

Hours of Operation

24 HOURS

Contact information

1-888-PARKFAST (1-888-727-5987)

Please call for rates

224 Mulberry St. (Spring & Prince St.)

224 MULBERRY ST. (CENTRAL PARKING SYSTEM)

Hours of Operation

Please call for hours of operation

Contact information

212-343-8401

Please call for rates

Chapter 9 -

DOWNTOWN SOUTH: Parking Garage Locations

(White Street - Battery Park)

350 Albany St. (Battery Park City)

HUDSON TOWER (GMC)

Hours of Operation
24 Hrs
Contact information
212-945-3646
Please call for rates

☺50 Battery Place (Battery Pl & 2nd Pl)

BATTERY PLACE (GGMC)

Hours of Operation
6:00 AM - 12:00 AM
Contact information
(212) 766-1929
Please call for rates
Please see our ad on page 392

☺233 (B'way) at Barclay St. (B'way & Church)

BARCLAY STREET PARKING LLC (ICON)

Hours of Operation
24 Hrs
Contact information
1-877-PARKING (1-877-727-5464)
Please call for rates
Please see our ad on page 411

☺75 (West St.) at Carlisle St. (West St. & Washington St.)

CARLISLE PARKING LLC

Hours of Operation
24 Hrs
Contact information
1-877-PARKING (1-877-727-5464)
Please call for rates
Please see our ad on page 411

☺110-118 Church St. (W. Bway & Church)

CHURCH STREET PARKING LLC (ICON)

Hours of Operation
24 Hrs
Contact information
1-877-PARKING (1-877-727-5464)
Please call for rates
Please see our ad on page 411

167-175 Front St. (Front & South)

EDISON PARKFAST

Hours of Operation

Please call for hours of operation

Contact information

1-888-PARKFAST (1-888-727-5987)

Please call for rates

☺308 Greenwich St. (Duane & Jay St.)

PATRIOT PARKING LLC - A (ICON)

Hours of Operation

24 Hrs

Contact information

1-877-PARKING (1-877-727-5464)

Please call for rates

Please see our ad on page 411

☺350 Greenwich St. (Franklin & N. Moore)

PATRIOT PARKING LLC - E (ICON)

Hours of Operation

24 Hrs

Contact information

1-877-PARKING (1-877-727-5464)

Please call for rates

Please see our ad on page 411

☺374 Greenwich St. (Franklin & N. Moore)

PATRIOT PARKING LLC - D (ICON)

Hours of Operation

24 Hrs

Contact information

1-877-PARKING (1-877-727-5464)

Please call for rates

Please see our ad on page 411

☺35 Harrison St. (Greenwich & West)

PATRIOT PARKING LLC - B (ICON)

Hours of Operation

24 Hrs

Contact information

1-877-PARKING (1-877-727-5464)

Please call for rates

Please see our ad on page 411

☺74 Hudson St. (corner of Worth)

HUDSON PARKING CORP.

Hours of Operation

7am-7pm Mon- Sat.

Contact information

212-966-9837

Please call for rates

Please see our ad on page 376

85 John St. (enter Gold St. btwn John & Fulton)

JOHN STREET (GMC)

Hours of Operation

24 Hrs

Contact information

212-385-9182

Please call for rates

90 John St. (Gold & Pearl)

90 JOHN STREET (CENTRAL PARKING SYSTEM)

Hours of Operation

Please call for hours of operation

Contact information

212-732-2844

Please call for rates

☺99 John St. at Cliff St.

CLIFF ST PARKING LLC-GARAGE (ICON)

Hours of Operation

24 Hrs

Contact information

1-877-PARKING (1-877-727-5464)

Please call for rates

Please see our ad on page 411

151-159 Maiden Lane (Front & South)

EDISON PARKFAST

Hours of Operation

Please call for hours of operation

Contact information

1-888-PARKFAST (1-888-727-5987)

Please call for rates

56 N. Moore St. (Hudson & Greenwich)

NORTH MOORE PK. (CENTRAL PARKING SYSTEM)

Hours of Operation

Please call for hours of operation

Contact information

212-941-7633

Please call for rates

75 Park Place (W. Bway & Murray)

75 PARK PLACE (CENTRAL PARKING SYSTEM)

Hours of Operation

Please call for hours of operation

Contact information

212-732-6637

Please call for rates

☺243 Pearl St. (Fulton & John St.)

PEARL PARKING LLC (ICON)

Hours of Operation

24 Hrs

Contact information

1-877-PARKING (1-877-727-5464)

Please call for rates

Please see our ad on page 411

251 Pearl St. (John St. & Fulton St.)

PEARL STREET (GMC)

Hours of Operation

24 Hrs

Contact information

212-406-1938

Please call for rates

☺53 Reade St. (Centre St & Broadway)

READE ST (GGMC)

Hours of Operation

6:00 AM - 10:00 PM

Contact information

(212) 566-2247

Please call for rates

Please see our ad on page 392

333 Rector Pl. (Battery Park City)

RIVER ROSE (GMC)

Hours of Operation

6am-2am

Contact information

212-945-0028

Please call for rates

River Terrace (West St. & Chambers)

400 CHAMBERS ST. (CENTRAL PARKING SYSTEM)

Hours of Operation

Please call for hours of operation

Contact information

212-566-9783

Please call for rates

☺2 South End Ave. (Battery Pl & 3rd Pl)

COVE CLUB (GGMC)

Hours of Operation

24 Hrs

Contact information

(212) 766-1929

Please call for rates

Please see our ad on page 392

220 South St. @Market Slip

EDISON PARKFAST

Hours of Operation

24 Hrs

Contact information

1-888-PARKFAST (1-888-727-5987)

Please call for rates

South St. @ Old Slip Under FDR Dr.

EDISON PARKFAST

Hours of Operation

Please call for hours of operation

Contact information

1-888-PARKFAST (1-888-727-5987)

Please call for rates

99 Washington St. (Washington & Rector)

RECTOR (CENTRAL PARKING SYSTEM)

Hours of Operation

Please call for hours of operation

Contact information

212-843-2367

Please call for rates

☺111 Washington St. (Carlisle Street & Rector St)

111 WASHINGTON STREET PARKING LLC (ICON)

Hours of Operation

24 Hrs

Contact information

1-877-PARKING (1-877-727-5464)

Please call for rates

Please see our ad on page 411

199 Water St. (Water & South St.)

SEAPORT PLAZA (CENTRAL PARKING SYSTEM)

Hours of Operation

Please call for hours of operation

Contact information

212-785-4552

Please call for rates

☺50 West St. (Rector & Battery Tunnel)

90 WASHINGTON ST (GGMC)

Hours of Operation

Please call for hours of operation

Contact information

(212) 344-4800

Please call for rates

Please see our ad on page 392

☺14-26 S. William St. (Broad & Hanover)

SOUTH WILLIAM STREET PARKING LLC (ICON)

Hours of Operation

24 Hrs

Contact information

1-877-PARKING (1-877-727-5464)

Please call for rates

Please see our ad on page 411

169 William St. (Corner of Beekman)

169 WILLIAM ST. (CENTRAL PARKING SYSTEM)

Hours of Operation

Please call for hours of operation

Contact information

212-962-0979

Please call for rates

15-21 Worth St. @ Worth & West Broadway

EDISON PARKFAST

Hours of Operation

24 Hrs

Contact information

1-888-PARKFAST (1-888-727-5987)

Please call for rates

40 Worth St. (Church St. & W. Broadway)

WORTH ST PKG (IMPERIAL)

Hours of Operation

7AM-11PM M-F

Contact information

212-219-2304, 212-925-8357

Rates

$16.88 (EARLY BIRD (Mon-Fri) + tax), $340 (24Hr Monthly + tax)

☺95 Worth St. (Worth & Catherine Lane)

95 WORTH LLC (ICON)

Hours of Operation

24 Hrs

Contact information

1-877-PARKING (1-877-727-5464)

Please call for rates

Please see our ad on page 411

INDEX - Downtown West Street Parking Regulations

INDEX - Downtown East Street Parking Regulations

INDEX - Downtown South Street Parking Regulations

INDEX - Parking Garage Locations:

Downtown West

Downtown East

Downtown South

Quick Order Form

☎ **Telephone Orders:** Call toll free 877-412-PARK (877-412-7275). Please have your credit card ready.

☎ **Fax Orders:** Call 516-897-2797. Fax this form.

🖱 **Internet Orders:** Visit www.federguide.com (major credit cards accepted)

📫 **Postal Orders** (send this form):
Rhythmo Productions
525 East Olive Street
Long Beach, NY 11561 USA

Please send me _______ copy(ies) of:
The *Feder* Guide to
Where to Park Your Car in Manhattan
(and Where Not to Park It!) Downtown Edition

Name:____

Address:____

City:_________________________ State:_____Zip:__________

E-mail:______________________ Phone:__________________

Please include $17.95 per book + $3.50 shipping & handling (per book) (NY residents add 8.25% sales tax) (International orders please add $7 shipping per book)

Methods of payment: ☐ Check ☐ Credit card

Card type:___________ Name on card:___________________

Card number:____________________________ Exp. date:_____

This book makes a great gift - any time of year!